CHOPIN

SERIES EDITED BY

SIR JACK WESTRUP
M.A., Hon.D.Mus.(Oxon.), F.R.C.O.

CHOPIN
by T. Kwiatkowski
(Alfred Cortot Collection)

THE MASTER MUSICIANS SERIES

CHOPIN

by

ARTHUR HEDLEY

*With eight pages of plates
and music examples in the text*

LONDON
J. M. DENT AND SONS LTD

FARRAR, STRAUS AND GIROUX INC.
NEW YORK

Made in Great Britain
at the
Aldine Press · Letchworth · Herts
for
J. M. DENT & SONS LTD
Aldine House · Bedford Street · London
First published 1947
Reprinted 1949, 1953, 1957
2nd ~~Revised~~ edition 1963
Reprinted 1966, 1971

for my friend
ENA MAKIN

ISBN: 0 460 03107 4

FOREWORD

THE present account of Chopin's life and work has not had as its basis Professor Niecks's *Chopin as a Man and Musician*, a work still regarded, in English-speaking countries at least, as the standard and final authority on everything relating to the composer.

For many years it has been evident that Niecks's book, however great its original value, is no longer entitled to be looked upon with unquestioning piety. As long ago as 1904 Ferdynand Hoesick, in his monumental *Chopin: his Life and Work* (not yet translated from the Polish) showed that Niecks had no knowledge of even the existence of the large amount of material that was available to Polish investigators, which could have enlightened the author on many points. During the past forty years still more material has come to light, so that no modern writer on Chopin is justified in offering to his readers a mere *résumé* of what Niecks said in 1888.

For the purposes of this volume I have, wherever possible (especially in Warsaw before the war), gone back to the original sources. I have not taken another writer's word whenever I could consult an original document or manuscript. Regarding the collected edition of Chopin's letters, published in English in 1931, I have made no use of this, for two reasons: (1) it is incomplete, and practically all the letters given were already available to students of Chopin; (2) from a biographer's point of view the collection is of little assistance—editorial guess-work has played havoc with the true chronology of the letters.

To quote references for every statement would be to encumber the book with footnotes. In addition to my own investigations I have, in fact, placed most reliance on the following authors: F. Hoesick, Leopold Binental, Édouard Ganche, 'Wladimir Karénine' and Ludwik Bronarski. No writer on Chopin can afford to overlook Hugo Leichtentritt's *Analysis of Chopin's Piano*

v

Works, and I have frequently had recourse to it as well as to works by Paul Egert and Helena Windakiewiczowa. The chronolog-ical list of Chopin's works has been drawn up after consideration of all the widely dispersed evidence, not on the basis of 'style-criticism,' which is dangerous and unnecessary in Chopin's case.

My thanks are due to M. Alfred Cortot for permission to re-produce a portrait of Chopin which belongs to him, and to Miss S. Brookshaw for a hitherto unknown letter from Chopin to Camille Pleyel.

A. H.

LONDON, 1946.

NOTE TO NEW EDITION

SINCE 1946 two visits to Poland and further collaboration with Polish researchers have enabled me to amend the text of this book in a number of details. The Catalogue of Works in Appendix B has been revised in the light of Maurice Brown's excellent *Index of Chopin's Works* (1960) and of my own continued studies in this field.

A. H.

LONDON, JUNE 1963.

CONTENTS

ILLUSTRATIONS

CHAPTER I

EARLY YEARS

'THIS exquisite, lofty and eminently aristocratic celebrity has remained unattacked. A complete silence of criticism already reigns around it as if posterity had already come.'

Such were the words used by Liszt in 1841 to assess the reputation of Frederick Chopin as a pianist and composer, and now that over a century separates us from Chopin's death one may glance back over the years and mark what upheavals and revolutions in the world of music that reputation has survived. Alone among his contemporaries Chopin has not suffered even a temporary eclipse. While Mendelssohn has fallen from a dizzy height to a respectable but undistinguished place and Schumann has been the victim of the caprices of fashion, it can be said of Chopin that his fame has not diminished but rather increased, as his finest works have become more widely known and his less worthy compositions have been laid aside. His place in musical history is in many ways an enviable one. It may not be situated on the highest level of all—no one would claim that—but to him has been granted what has been given to few: to be unique and unapproachable within his own, limited domain; to become almost at once a classic and a model of perfection; to speak his own native tongue and yet be universally understood; to be played wherever a piano is to be found and yet to keep intact his familiar but subtle power of touching the imagination and speaking to the hearts of men of every nation. The extraordinary popularity of Chopin has few parallels in the annals of music: from the beginning his appeal was immediate and almost universal. And yet of the man himself how little is generally known. The very nature of his genius and personality has perhaps made it inevitable that his life-story should become entangled in a web of legend and invention. The 'romantic' elements in his history have seemed to accord so well with the mysterious and suggestive elements in his music that they have been eagerly seized upon, first by his biographers, then by the novelists and finally by the scenario writers, so that when each of these has made his contri/bution to the accepted Chopin portrait, the ordinary music/lover is left with a picture which is far from bearing a perfect resemblance to the original it is supposed to represent.

There are several reasons why, for lack of solid facts, writers on Chopin have had to draw on their imaginations, the most important being that Chopin was a Pole who revealed himself, as a man, to few save his compatriots; and until the Poles them/selves began to take pride and interest in the achievements of their great countryman a considerable amount of information relating to his career (particularly his early days) remained hidden away in his native land to be brought to light only in recent years. Chopin's first serious English biographer, Frederick Niecks, had no access to this material, and since most subsequent writers have followed him closely, his account of Chopin's life has come to be accepted as the standard version. To/day, thanks to the researches of musicologists like F. Hoesick and Leopold Binental in Poland, and Édouard Ganche in France, a clearer view of Chopin emerges from the mists of fiction and legend. The main lines of his relatively uneventful career remain, of course, unaltered; but many important details can now be added to the picture we have of the man and the musician, and proven facts can replace the ingenious guesses of the older writers. There still remain enough problems in Chopin's life and work to occupy the attention of musical historians; in a work of this size we can only hope to make the reader aware of their existence and to show what bearing they have on the understanding and interpretation of his music.

At the very outset we are confronted with a puzzle—the true date of Chopin's birth. Since the discovery of a baptismal certifi/cate in the register of Brochów church, near Zelazowa Wola, where he was born, it has been taken as proven that Chopin first saw the light of day on 22nd February 1810, but unquestion/ing acceptance of that date is made difficult by so many other circumstances that it will be as well to set the full facts before the reader.

The date '22nd February 1810' was established on the declaration of Nicholas Chopin, the father. The parish register states that on 23rd April 1810—that is, after two months' unaccountable delay

Nicholas Chopin, the father, aged 40, dwelling in the village of Zelazowa Wola, showed to Us a child of the male sex which was born in his house on the 22nd day of the month of February in this present year [1810] . . . and that it is his wish to give the child the two names Fryderyk Franciszek.[1]

From that moment there seems to have been a general conspiracy to alter the date! (It may be mentioned that Nicholas Chopin did not know his own age: when he had to apply for his pension he made himself out to be a year older than he really was.)

The composer himself believed that he had been born on 1st March 1810. This is the date which he gave in a letter written on 16th January 1833 to the Polish Literary Society in Paris and supplied to Fétis, the musicographer, on 28th March 1836, for use in the first edition of his *Biographie universelle des musiciens*. Chopin's mother and sisters, his school friends and his pupils agreed in naming 1st March as his birthday. In 1837 his mother writes: 'I have been thinking much of you, my dear child, on the anniversary days of your birth and your name-day, 1st and 5th March.' Now the author of the first 'official' biography, M. Karasowski, obtained from Chopin's sister Isabella '1st March 1809,' and Liszt, who, incidentally, had no first-hand knowledge, confirmed this for Frederick Niecks in 1878. Is it not strange that the parents of a wonder-child, the talk of the town, such as little Frederick soon became, should forget the correct date, especially as questions such as: 'How old do you say he is? Really!' must have been asked over and over again?

It is to be noted that Chopin's first published composition, the

---

[1] There is also an entry in Latin.

Polonaise in G minor, dedicated to Countess Victoire Skarbek, appeared in 1817 and was described as being by 'Frédéric Chopin, a musician aged 8 years.' A review of the piece in a Warsaw newspaper speaks of young Chopin as 'a lad who has completed his eighth year,' and it is hard to believe that the fond parents would claim that their prodigy was *older* than he really was. (Infant prodigies can never be too young!) Moreover we learn that when the Empress Maria Teodorowna visited the Warsaw University and Lyceum on 26th September 1818 'Mr. Chopin, a nine-year-old boy, presented to her Imperial Highness two Polish dances of his composition,' while on 3rd January 1820 Angelica Catalani, the famous singer, presented a gold watch 'to Frédéric Chopin, aged 10 years.' And finally (to show how surprising it is that any one should have forgotten the boy's real birthday), a one-act sketch written early in 1818 actually introduces the question of Chopin's age in the form of a comic incident. Madame Zamoyska begins with a monologue in her drawing-room:

> Young Chopin is to play at the concert; his tender age is bound to attract people. I've got a splendid idea! Young Chopin is already nine years old, but to arouse public interest we'll print in the announcements that he's only three. That will startle them . . . seeing the little hands of a three-year-old running up and down the piano!

an indication, by the way, of the boy's amazing execution.

Such are the arguments against 22nd February 1810.[1] It has been suggested that Nicholas Chopin, to escape the penalties for not registering the birth within the period laid down by the law, deliberately stated that his son, born on 1st March 1809, had been born in 1810, which would imply conspiracy between father and parish priest. There is also the possibility of confusion with his godfather's birthday—also the 22nd February. However, this is the official birthday in Poland.

Zelazowa Wola is a little village to the west of Warsaw. The house where Chopin was born, a sort of spacious bungalow surrounded by a large garden, is situated on what was formerly

[1] The difference between the Russian and western calendars does not suffice to explain these discrepancies.

the estate of the Skarbek family. The house is now a museum
and the property has been considerably renovated. All around
stretch the endless Polish fields, away to the horizon with scarcely
a tree to limit the vision. Here and there a farm-house such as
one finds in the Fen district of England. Storks are a common
sight here, and the peasant folk welcome their arrival and treat
them with loving respect. You may still see a merry wedding
party, with the girls in all their finery, troop out of the nearby
church, and it is not hard to imagine Frederick Chopin, on
holiday from Warsaw, drinking in those melodies and rhythms
which, sublimated by his art, have been carried to the four
corners of the earth in his polonaises and mazurkas.

In 1810 Nicholas Chopin was thirty-nine years old. He had
been born in France, on 15th April 1771,[1] at Marainville in the
Vosges and came of purely French stock, being the son of
François Chopin, a wheelwright and vine-grower, himself the
son of one Nicholas Chopin, also a vine-grower, born in 1738.
Nothing is known of the younger Nicholas's early years, but he
must have been a lad of enterprise, for at the age of sixteen he left
his native Lorraine and made his way to Poland in 1787, banishing
from his mind the memory of the father and mother and two
sisters whom he had left behind.[2] For some strange, unknown
reason he never spoke of his family in France and kept his
children so completely in the dark regarding them that Frederick
Chopin lived for nearly twenty years in Paris without knowing
that in a French village, not so very far away, lived his two
aunts, simple peasant folk, all unaware that their nephew was one
of the most famous musicians of the day and the *enfant gâté* of
the highest aristocratic circles. Once in Poland, Nicholas
Chopin lost no time in becoming willingly and wholeheartedly
a Polish citizen, to the point, indeed, of speaking of France later
as a 'foreign country.' At first he worked as a clerk in a tobacco
factory owned by a Frenchman. He soon mastered the Polish
language and was settling down in his new life when, as a result

[1] Not 17th April 1770 as formerly thought.
[2] A single letter to them has survived (15th September 1790).

of the growing political uncertainty (the second and third parti, tions of Poland being at hand), his firm and many others went bankrupt. With all his prospects gone he thought of returning to France, but on the eve of his departure he fell ill, and by the time he was convalescent the revolt of 1794 had broken out. Young Chopin at once joined the Polish National Guard and fought against the Russians in the defence of Warsaw, thus identifying himself completely with his new country. When the revolt was crushed and the partition of the country completed, Warsaw became a mere provincial town, and Nicholas Chopin thought once more of returning to Lorraine. A second time, however, he fell ill, this time seriously, and when he recovered he believed that providence had meant him to stay in Poland. 'Twice,' he said, 'I have tried to leave, and twice I have nearly died. I must bow before the will of providence and I will stay.'

From this time he obtained employment as a tutor and served in various noble Polish families, being eventually engaged by the Laczyńskis, in whose house he taught the little girl who later became the celebrated and unhappy Maria Walewska, the heroine of one of Napoleon's romances. It was while he was with this family that Nicholas Chopin was brought to the notice of the Skarbeks of Zelazowa Wola, near Warsaw, and in 1802 he became the tutor of their children. The family was not par, ticularly well-to-do (Count Skarbek lived abroad to avoid his creditors), and at one time Nicholas Chopin lent a fairly con, siderable sum to one of the sons, Nicholas, who, when he died in 1834, left all his estate to a complete stranger, without any provision for the repayment of the debt. But life was pleasant at Zelazowa Wola. Living on the Skarbek estate was a well, born but poor relation of the family, Tekla-Justyna Krzyzanowska, at whose baptism, on 14th September 1782, we are told 'illus, trissimae' and 'magnificae' persons were present. She was a pretty girl, educated and capable, and just the wife for the ambitious young tutor who married her on 2nd June 1806.

It was in every respect a happy marriage, for the pair were admirably suited to each other. From the portraits painted by

CHOPIN'S BIRTHPLACE AT ZELAZOWA WOLA
Photo: Instytut Fryderyka Chopina, Warsaw 1946

the Polish artist Miroszewski and from the letters which they
wrote to Frederick after he had left home, we may obtain a lively
picture of Nicholas and Justyna, and one which confirms the
accounts of those who knew them. He was a dark, distin-
guished-looking man with bright, intelligent eyes and a firm
mouth. His early struggles had left their mark on his character
and made him careful and cautious. Although he was generous
and indulgent towards his children, his constant refrain was
'Save up for a rainy day!' 'Save as much as you can—my
heart bleeds that I can't send you more,' he writes to Frederick
in June 1831; or again: 'It's always as well to have a couple of
thousand francs by you in case of need.' He played the flute
and violin, and even when an old man he enjoyed scraping his
way through quartets and sonatas with his Warsaw friends. Of
his wife Justyna less is known. She was a quiet, pious woman,
devoted to her family, and we get a fleeting glimpse of her nature
in the one or two rather pathetic letters of hers to Frederick which
have survived and in which she gently reproaches him with
not writing:

We saw from the papers that you had given a concert and were
grieved that we did not hear about it from you. You forgot, my
dearest child, that your old father and mother live only for you and
pray God every day to bless and keep you.

Four children were born to Nicholas and Justyna Chopin:
Ludwika (Louise) (1807–55), who married Dr. Josef Kalasanty
Jedrzejewicz; Fryderyk Franciszek; Isabella (1811–81), who
married the mathematician and school inspector Anton Barciński;
and Emilia, who was born in 1812 and died of consumption
in 1827.

All the children were unusually gifted. Louise, the eldest,
bore (as an old daguerreotype shows) an extraordinary resemblance
to her brother, and this resemblance was not merely physical.
There was a close temperamental affinity between her and
Frederick, and this was shared by Isabella who, although not
so musical as Louise (the composer of some excellent mazurkas),

was nevertheless among the first to realize the significance and beauty of her brother's music. In the letters which the two sisters wrote from Warsaw to Chopin in Germany and France the bond of sympathy which united the three is fully revealed.

Isabella writes that she is overwhelmed by the thought that the beautiful music she has received was composed by *her* brother, and Louise in her letters stands out clearly as Chopin's only really intimate friend and confidante. Emilia, the youngest child, was in some respects the most precocious of them all, and before her death at the age of fourteen she had already written poems and short pieces which justify the belief that, had she lived, she might have achieved something considerable.

It was fortunate for Frederick Chopin that he was brought up in such a household. As the only boy in the family he naturally received his full share of attention, and when, to his parents' delight, he began to show signs of possessing musical talent, they did not hesitate to deprive themselves in order that he might have every encouragement and opportunity to develop his gifts. Shortly after Frederick was born his father obtained the post of professor of French in the newly founded Lyceum (High School) at Warsaw, and the family moved from Zelazowa Wola to the capital, where they occupied an apartment in the very centre of the town. Nicholas Chopin added to his income by taking in boarders from the school where he taught, and later (in 1812) accepted another post as teacher of French at the School of Artillery and Military Engineering, in order to be able to meet the expense of maintaining a refined and comfortable home in the most fashionable part of the city. Thanks to their central situation the Chopins were in immediate contact with all the social and artistic life of Warsaw, and to this circumstance Frederick Chopin owed his superior manners and that air of breeding which so greatly impressed his contemporaries, who were unaccustomed to find such distinction in a 'piano-player.'

It has been too readily assumed that because he became a chronic invalid in later life Chopin must have been a frail and ailing boy, without interest in the normal activities of young children. He was certainly not a big, strong lad, but he was quite well able to take part in the games and amusements of his companions. What he lacked in strength he made up by nimbleness and quick-wittedness. We hear of his going skating and cracking his head on the ice; and when he was a schoolboy he was as keen as any of the others to stay out late in the park, flirting with the girls, while his anxious father looked high and low for him. On one such occasion a confederate of his, G. Wielislaw, was rewarded with a large bag of sweets for having adroitly misdirected Mr. Nicholas Chopin in his search for Frederick, who was hiding with a young lady in the botanical gardens. There is nothing to justify the legend of a Chopin morbid and unhealthy from childhood. He was doubtless mollycoddled by his mother and sisters, but it is well to remember that he was never really ill until he was over twenty. His little ailments did not prevent him from making, without any ill effects, long uncomfortable stage-coach journeys which might have tried far tougher constitutions than his. In those happy years of boyhood there was no fore-boding of the tragedy that was ultimately to overtake him and reduce him to a living shadow before he was thirty-five. True, Emilia Chopin had died of consumption, but there was no indication that either Frederick or his other sisters were likely to be struck down by the same disease. We shall see later in what circumstances the fatal tendency within him at length claimed its victim; but for the moment we may return to consider the development of Chopin's personality and genius in the unclouded atmosphere of a sheltered and cultivated home.

From his earliest days the child showed an extraordinary sensi-tiveness to music. The simple airs and dances which his mother and sister Louise played on the piano (a real *grand* piano, by the way, *not* a spinet, clavichord or square piano) had an overwhelming effect on him. His first reaction was to give vent to his emotion in tears, but soon curiosity gained the upper hand, and he was irresistibly attracted to the magic keyboard that produced the sounds which disturbed and delighted him. By the time he was six, his natural gifts (shown mainly in improvisation) were so evident that his parents realized it was their duty to provide him with a teacher who would set him on the right road. Their choice fell upon a competent and unpretentious musician, Adal-bert Zywny, who, although he was primarily a violinist, was enough of a pianist to see to it that the boy should receive a thorough grounding in the rudiments of music and piano-playing. To Zywny Chopin owed his early introduction to the keyboard works of Bach; for this he never ceased to be grateful, and for the rest of his life Bach came second only to Mozart in his affections. As for the virtuosity which he soon acquired, that can be set down only to his amazing natural predisposition, not to Zywny's modest example and instruction. In the young Chopin were combined those rare physical and mental gifts which absolve their lucky possessor from the drudgery to which ordinary mortals are condemned. His mental alertness and sen-sitiveness were accompanied by perfect muscular control and co-ordination, extending not merely to the use of arms and fingers in piano-playing. While still a boy he showed remarkable powers of mimicry; he could distort his features into any shape he pleased, surprising and sometimes frightening the spectators. And when he learned to set down his musical ideas on paper the actual writing was of a microscopic neatness and delicacy, obviously traceable to the same perfection of muscular control. His father is the best witness to the readiness with which the boy took to the piano. Writing to Frederick in November 1831 he says: 'The mechanism of playing took you little time, and your mind rather than your fingers were busy. If others have spent whole days struggling with the keyboard you rarely spent a whole hour at it. . . .' Since his progress on the mechanical side was so rapid and his sight-reading excellent, he was able, under old Zywny's guidance, to work his way through the Viennese classics, Haydn, Mozart, Beethoven, and on to later German composers like Hummel and Ries. Bach he never ceased to study. A great deal of his time was given, of course, to improvising, and we see him gradually feeling his way towards that profound and original understanding of the nature of the piano which, when fully matured, was to assure his place in musical history.

By the end of 1817 the boy already enjoyed a certain local celebrity. Alexandra Tańska records in her diary:

Mme Grabowska invited me to her soirée—a large gathering. In the course of the evening young Chopin played the piano—a child in his eighth year whom connoisseurs declare to be Mozart's successor.

When his first little Polonaise appeared it was welcomed as the work of

a real musical genius. Not only does he play with complete facility and wonderful taste the most difficult compositions, but is already the composer of dances and variations which amaze the connoisseurs.

Almost at the same time there appeared (without the boy composer's name) a Military March. Chopin played it so brilliantly before the Grand Duke Constantine that the latter caused it to be scored and had it played by his band on parade in front of the Saxon Palace. All these pieces were written out by Żywny (Chopin was not quite the equal of Mozart in these matters). At length, on 24th February 1818, Mr. *Schoppin*, as he was described in the announcements, made his first public appearance at a charity concert, playing a concerto by Gyrowetz. An innocent legend has it that after the concert, when his mother asked him what the audience had admired most, the boy promptly answered: 'My collar, mamma,' for he was dressed up in what was quaintly conceived to be the 'English manner,' with a velvet jacket and an immense collar. The immediate result of this début was to bring Chopin to the notice of some of the most aristocratic families in Warsaw, the Radziwills, Potockis and Czartoryskis, names which embody the greatest Polish traditions and which occur again and again in the course of Chopin's life- story. In November 1819 the 'impatiently awaited' prima donna, Angelica Catalani, arrived in Warsaw to give a series of con- certs; young Chopin was among the first to be presented to her, and his playing made such an impression on her that she rewarded

him with a gold watch, inscribed: 'Mme Catalani à Frédéric
Chopin, âgé de 10 ans.'

In the midst of these excitements, however, his parents were
not neglecting his education. Nicholas Chopin had very definite
ideas on the subject and was resolved on not sending his son to
school until his lessons at home should have enabled him to go
at once into the fourth class, i.e. at the age of thirteen or fourteen.
This time was now approaching. The piano lessons with Zywny,
having long been superfluous, ceased at the end of 1822. Frederick
honoured the old man's birthday on 23rd April 1821 with a
Polonaise in A♭ major (published in a barbarous transcription
in 1902) and remained affectionately attached to him. In the
autumn of 1823 Chopin entered the fourth class at the Warsaw
High School where his father was French master, and for the
next three years his music studies had to take second place. Not
that he did not give every spare moment to them, struggling to
master harmony with the aid of Karol Anton Simon's newly
published *Short Guide to the Rules of Harmony in a Manner Easy
to Learn* and with a few lessons from Joseph Elsner, head of the
Warsaw Conservatoire, who was taking an interest in the gifted
lad; but his father was determined that his general education
should come first. Although his real interests lay elsewhere,
Chopin was a quick and industrious pupil. At the end of his
first year he received a book prize (very handsome but very dull!),
and was glad to escape for a holiday to the village of Szafarnia,
where he was free to amuse himself and give his mind to his
beloved music. At this time he wrote his *Swiss Boy* Variations,
which show a great advance, and Emilia and he enjoyed sending
home letters in the form of a newspaper. It was called the
Szafarnia Courier and is of interest in that it shows how boyish
and unspoilt young Frederick was, in spite of his flattering
experiences in Warsaw society. Out in the country villages he
was able to make first-hand acquaintance with the unspoilt
Polish folk music. Mazurkas and other folk dances were to be
heard in plenty at Warsaw, but refined and shorn of their primitive
characteristics. During his holidays Chopin steeped himself in

the real thing, and the influence of this music came to penetrate every fibre of his musical being. We have only to look at the Mazurka in A minor, Op. 17, No. 4, sketched about this time but not published till later, when the composer was surer of himself, to see the results of his contact with peasant music heard at country fairs and weddings.

But for the time being Frederick had to keep his experiments to himself. He was developing rapidly, and his reputation now began to travel beyond the bounds of Warsaw. On 27th April 1825 Tsar Alexander I arrived in Warsaw for the opening of the Polish Diet. All Poland flocked to the capital for the celebrations; the town was in an uproar with an unceasing round of fêtes, gala performances and concerts. Seizing his opportunity, an instrument-maker named Brunner, who had constructed a kind of organ-piano, the Aeolomelodikon, arranged that Chopin should display its good points at a charity concert given in the Conservatoire hall on 27th May. Being the only one who could handle the instrument satisfactorily, he made a great impression with his improvised fantasia and his playing of a Moscheles piano concerto. In a day or two talk of the new instrument came to the ears of the tsar, and Chopin was commanded to put it through its paces. As a result

His Majesty was most graciously pleased to present with diamond rings Mr. Brunner, inventor of the Aeolomelodikon, and Mr. Fryderyk Chopin, a pupil of the High School, whose talent for piano-playing has been much admired at public concerts.

Striking while the iron was hot, Chopin now made his formal bow as a composer with his Op. 1, the Rondo in C minor dedicated to Madame Linde, the publication of which was announced on 2nd June. The concert was repeated on 10th June, and Chopin had the satisfaction of obtaining his first press notice from the outside world—a short appreciation in the July number of the Leipzig *Allgemeine musikalische Zeitung.*

These events were decisive for his future career. His parents could not be indifferent to such success, especially when it was accompanied by the flattering notice of Prince Antoine Radziwill (himself a composer), who was in Warsaw for the festivities. Acquaintances such as this were to prove very important to the rising musician. When he returned to school in the autumn, after an excursion to Danzig, he was asked to play the organ on Sundays in the school chapel. This he did, and enjoyed, but it had no noticeable influence on his playing or composition. During this last year at school he was not allowed to slacken. A high standard of Latin, Greek, mathematics, etc., had to be reached, and his father was determined that he should acquit himself well. The boy was quite exhausted by the end of the school year. He did well in the examinations, however, and on the evening of prize day, 27th July, free at last, off he went to hear Rossini's *Gazza ladra* at the Opera with his schoolmate William Kolberg. On returning home he dashed off a Polonaise in Bb minor (using a tune from the opera for the trio), to which he gave the title 'Farewell to William Kolberg.' It was farewell indeed, for the next day he set off with his mother and sisters Louise and Emilia for Reinertz, a watering-place in Silesia. Emilia was by this time desperately ill and this was a last effort to save her. She died in the following April.

At Reinertz, besides drinking the waters and submitting to the 'whey-cure,' the Chopins met a number of Polish acquaintances and took their share of the somewhat tedious pleasures of the place. There was little music—'not a single good piano in the town,' Chopin wrote to Elsner; but nevertheless the young virtuoso was easily persuaded to give a concert for the benefit of two orphans whose father had died suddenly and left them penniless. Chopin played at the Kurhaus on 16th August, and the concert was such a success that it had to be repeated.[1] The

[1] In 1897 a plaque to commemorate these concerts was placed in the Kurhaus and a memorial to Chopin's visit was set up in the park.

letter to Elsner, referred to just now, is interesting and significant. It is formal and in elegant French, as would become a young man writing to his future professor; for it was now decided that Frederick was to pursue his musical studies more seriously, under the best tuition that Warsaw could offer. Immediately on his return he was enrolled as a full-time student at the 'Principal Music School,' and in the autumn of 1826 he entered upon the course which was to last until July 1829.

The Music School was a department of the Conservatoire, which had been founded in 1821. Owing to disagreements between its two directors, Elsner and Soliva, which came to a head in 1826, the purely musical side of the teaching was separated from that of the Conservatoire proper (dramatic art, etc.), and Elsner and Soliva were left in sole charge of their respective sections. The full music course lasted three years and was intended to form 'complete professional artists.' Here are some details of the programme, which should dispose of the legend of a Chopin self-taught and ignorant of basic principles:

The theory of music, thorough-bass and composition, considered in their grammatical, rhetorical and aesthetic aspects, will be taught in one of the University halls; practical exercises on the same, and all instrumental teaching to be given in the Conservatoire buildings. The course of counterpoint and composition will last three years, the last year being devoted to practical exercises.

The actual time-table of the course has a solemn ring:

Josephus Elsner explicabit Theoriam compositionis musicae altera quaque hebdomade, die Jovis hora 12–1. Compositionem vero musico-practicam tradet in Conservatorio diebus Lunae, Mercurii et Veneris, hora 4–6.

Joseph Elsner (1769–1854), who was to be Chopin's mentor for the next three years, was a German who after many wanderings had finally established himself in Warsaw, becoming thoroughly Polish in spirit and outlook. He was a facile composer, having an impressive number of operas, masses, symphonies and quartets to his credit. Regarding the value of these different opinions have been held. Fétis, the learned compiler of the *Biographie universelle*, did not consider that Elsner paid enough respect to 'the rules,' and thought his works commonplace and uninspired, but in Poland his music was held in high esteem. His great Coronation Mass is said to be his masterpiece. Whether or not he observed the strict rules in his own work, there is no doubt that he was perfectly competent to teach them; but his greatest merit lies in the fact that he made no attempt to force Chopin to conform in these matters. He realized that genius will out and that superstitious pedantry might easily stifle his pupil's impulse towards achieving an original and personal expression of the music within him.

Chopin was by no means Elsner's 'favourite pupil.' He did not do so well as his classmates Nidecki and Dobrzyński in the routine practical exercises of the music course, which consisted of 'masses with Polish and Latin text, trios, quartets, septets, sonatas, fugues, vocal compositions for choir and orchestra,' and so forth. Thomas Nidecki, who left the Conservatoire in 1827, obtained a State grant for foreign travel on the strength of his 'Mass for four voices with orchestral accompaniment,' but later, as we shall see, Chopin failed to accomplish this, doubtless owing to his inability or unwillingness to turn out a formal composition of the kind required. By 1829 he was fully conscious of the nature of his own genius and nothing could force him from the path he had chosen for himself as a composer of piano music.

While zealously pursuing his regular studies with Elsner during this first year (1826–7) he devoted every spare moment to his 'own' piano compositions. Among these was the *Rondo à la Mazur*, published in February 1828. In this early piece appear for the first time those 'Chopinesque' qualities and that individuality which were to become more marked in each successive work by the young genius. The Rondo is full of elegance and verve while bearing the unmistakable stamp of the Polish folk music with which he was becoming more fully acquainted. Even greater is the advance shown in the *Variations on a Theme of Mozart* ('Là ci darem la mano') which he began to compose after the summer holidays spent at Strzyzewo, a country place near

16

Poznan, and Danzig. Characteristically, Chopin could not resist drawing on the last blank sheet of his manuscript several sketches —a monument, a general, etc.—and was still unsophisticated enough to write on the music itself comments like: 'This chord will sound well.'

He was very happy at this time. His school and university friends, Julius Fontana, Jan Matuszyński, Titus Woyciechowski and many others, were full of admiration and encouragement for him, and during his student days he formed friendships which lasted for as long as he lived.

(It is necessary at this point to warn the reader against a too literal interpretation of the extravagant expressions of affection to be found in Chopin's letters to his friends. The literal English translation is completely misleading and may lead to the wildest conjectures. It must be remembered that the highly coloured language used by the Slavonic peoples a hundred years ago did not correspond to realities which would in many cases scandalize and embarrass western Europeans. When Chopin writes to Titus 'My dearest life! My soul! . . . I love you to madness . . . give me your lips,' and so forth, we must beware of taking such effusiveness too seriously. An English translation of Chopin's letters should make the necessary allowances for these idiomatic differences between the Polish and English languages.)

The year 1828 brought a new pleasure to Frederick, who was beginning to exhaust the resources of Warsaw. The composer and pianist Hummel gave a series of concerts in the town, and Chopin was able to make his acquaintance. His brilliant playing, his poetic improvisations and the romantic elements in his style were to have a considerable influence on Chopin's own develop, ment. Into the classical forms Hummel, a pupil of Mozart, infused a romantic freshness and new colour, and it is not diffi, cult to trace his influence in Chopin's concertos and rondos. With the example of Hummel's achievement to inspire him Frederick was now working very hard and had to take his summer holiday early, thus missing the second,year examinations at the Music School. At Sanniki, a small country place, he rewrote his Rondo in C major, arranging it for two pianos. (It was not, however, published during his lifetime.)

On his return to Warsaw a great surprise awaited him. He was invited to accompany a colleague of his father's, Professor Jarocki, to Berlin. Frederick went nearly crazy with delight. Jarocki was to attend a scientific congress, but all this meant nothing to Chopin, whose only desire was to meet other musicians and hear some first-class opera performances, Spontini's *Cortez* being the great attraction.

The venerable professor and his enthusiastic young companion, a strangely matched pair, set off on 9th September and reached Berlin five days later. Chopin was not at all impressed by the town itself or its inhabitants. He was, of course, like a fish out of water at the scientists' meetings and the official receptions. He felt that he was wasting his time and would have preferred to spend every moment in Schlesinger's music shop, where all the latest musical novelties were to be found. He heard a fair amount of music, however—mainly operas—and Handel's *Ode on St. Cecilia's Day* made a profound impression on him. (Later, in Paris, he regretted that so little of Handel was to be heard.) On one occasion he found himself in the presence of Spontini and Mendelssohn, but he was too shy to introduce himself and left Berlin without having made any notable new acquaintance. Nevertheless, it had been an interesting experience for the young man who was now looking at the world through adult eyes and learning to rely upon himself. He had a quick eye for the ridiculous and brought back with him from Berlin many caricatures and sketches which he had been tempted to make of the eccentric old gentlemen assembled at the congress.

On the return journey to Warsaw occurred an incident for whose authenticity Chopin's mother and sisters always vouched, and which may be again related here, though without the embellishments so many writers have lavished upon it. The stagecoach in which Professor Jarocki and Chopin were travelling was held up at a small coaching station for a change of horses, and the travellers were faced with a long and tedious wait. In

the postmaster's house Chopin came across a piano, old and
worn (but in tune!), and he immediately sat down and began to
improvise in his best style, to the amazement and delight of the
postmaster and his household, who had never had such a treat.
They would not let him leave the piano, and when he did at
last tear himself away they carried him in triumph to the waiting
coach. This took place near Poznan, and on arriving there
Chopin spent two days visiting friends such as Archbishop
Wolicki and Prince Radziwill, who lived near by and who,
being himself a cellist, showed particular interest in the Trio in
G minor which was half finished.

Back in Warsaw on 6th October Chopin at once resumed
work with Elsner. He now concentrated on the 'practical
exercises' appropriate to the third and last year of the course, and
we find him applying himself to composition on a larger scale,
such as the *Fantasia on Polish Airs* and the *Rondo à la Krakowiak*,
both for piano and orchestra. At the same time he was busy
with a number of smaller piano pieces. He now had a small
'studio' of his own at the top of the house and was able to devote
himself uninterruptedly to his music. We must not imagine
him to have been something of a recluse, however. He took his
full share of the social life of Warsaw, soirées, balls, routs and so
forth, and this taste for life and society never left him. When
the spring of 1829 came, his family realized more than ever that
he had nothing to gain by remaining in Poland and that it was
indispensable for him to travel abroad in order to widen his
experience, to make his mark in the larger musical world and,
as his father used to put it succinctly, 'to smell new smells.'
But where were the funds to come from? Building his hopes on
his son's already considerable reputation, Nicholas Chopin, on
13th April 1829, addressed the following petition to the Minister
for Public Instruction, Grabowski:

I have a son whose innate musical gifts call out for him to be educated
in this art. His late Imperial Majesty Tsar Alexander, of blessed
memory, graciously deigned to present him with a precious ring as a
mark of His satisfaction when my son had the honour to be heard by

the Monarch, His Imperial Majesty. His Imperial Highness the Grand Duke, Supreme Commander of the Army, has often been most graciously pleased to allow him to give proofs of his growing talent in His Most Serene presence. And lastly, many of the highest personages and musical connoisseurs can support the view that my son could be a credit to his country in his chosen profession if he were given the opportunity to pursue the necessary studies to their conclusion. He has completed his preliminary studies; all that he now needs is to visit foreign countries, especially Germany, Italy and France, so as to form himself upon the best models. For the purposes of such a journey, which might last three years, funds are required which my modest resources, based exclusively upon my salary as a teacher, are insufficient to provide.

Minister Grabowski supported the application with a note to the treasury authorities asking for 'a yearly grant of 5,000 zlotys for the promising youth.'

The time for this appeal was well chosen, for on 17th May Nicholas I, accompanied by the royal family, came to Warsaw for his coronation as king of Poland. Once again there was tremendous excitement in the town, and it is stated that in a short time the population rose to 200,000. On the day before the coronation (24th May) the limelight was somewhat stolen from His Majesty by the arrival of no other than Paganini, who gave ten concerts between 23rd May and 19th July. This was vastly more interesting to Frederick than all the coronation ceremonies, for like the rest of his compatriots he could not but look sceptically on the whole proceedings. Polish national feeling was growing stronger every day and the storm which was to burst in 1831 was already brewing. The effect, one might say the shock, made on Chopin by Paganini's colossal virtuosity was similar to that experienced by Schumann and Liszt. A world of undreamt-of possibilities was revealed to him, and it is no mere coincidence that the first of his *Études* date from this time. After hearing Paganini's version of *Le Carnaval de Venise*, he wrote some piano variations which he called *Souvenir de Paganini* (published 1881). This work foreshadows the style of his *Berceuse*, Op. 57.

Paganini—The Petition Rejected

On 20th July, the day after Paganini's departure, Chopin sat for the final examination at the Music School and passed brilliantly. Alas! on 10th June his father had been informed that his petition had been coldly turned down: 'Public funds cannot be used [*wasted* was written in the first place] for the support of this class of artists.' Thus Frederick was to face the world without any outside help. But his family had full confidence in him and were prepared to scrape and save in order to assure his career. As for old Elsner, he could be justly proud of his pupil; it was not for nothing that his last report on him read:

Chopin, Fryderyk (third-year student): outstanding abilities, *musical genius, etc.*

CHAPTER II

Now that he had finished his formal musical education Chopin naturally turned his gaze towards Vienna, the city of Haydn, Mozart and Beethoven, which, although it had fallen low in its taste and standards, was still, after Paris, a centre of European artistic activity and the Mecca of ambitious composers. He had already sent off to the music publisher Haslinger his Variations on 'Là ci darem,' the Sonata in C minor (Op. 4) and his *Swiss Boy* Variations, but so far he had heard nothing of their fate. The business-like publisher was not inclined to take risks with unusually difficult works by an unknown composer, and it was necessary that Frederick should take the matter in hand personally. Before the end of July he set off with four Warsaw friends who happened to be travelling to Vienna, and made the journey in easy stages, spending an agreeable week at Cracow and its neighbourhood and arriving in the Austrian capital on 31st July. He brought with him a letter of introduction to Haslinger from Elsner, and after hearing him play the shrewd publisher quickly changed his mind and declared himself ready to publish the Variations, Op. 2, if the composer would play them in public. There was to be no fee, but the music would be handsomely produced. Chopin was hardly prepared for this; he was afraid that Elsner might be displeased by an untimely and ill-considered début, and he was out of practice. But soon a veritable clamour for a concert arose, for every one who heard him was fascinated by the perfection and originality of his playing. There was so much goodwill on all sides that difficulties melted away; a magnificent Graff piano was provided and Count Gallenberg graciously lent the Kärntnertor Theatre. (He could afford to do so as it was in the dead summer season; besides, he pocketed the receipts!)

22

And so, on 11th August 1829, Chopin made his bow before
the fastidious and capricious Viennese public. He had intended
to play both the Variations, Op. 2, and the *Krakowiak* Rondo,
but the latter could not be properly rehearsed owing to the badly
written orchestral parts, and it had to be omitted. Instead, he
improvised on melodies from Boïeldieu's *Dame blanche* and the
Polish wedding-song *Chmiel* (the hop-plant). His success was
instantaneous. The Variations were heartily applauded, the
members of the orchestra joining in, and the improvisation on
Chmiel, in which we may be sure Chopin did not fail to exploit
the irresistible rhythms of Polish folk music, 'electrified the public
which was unfamiliar with this type of song.' On the whole
the Viennese found his playing too delicate, although the papers
were full of praise for the originality of his style and 'the indescribable perfection of his technique.' They had become accustomed to hammer-and-tongs virtuosity, and the type of playing
which best pleased them was that provided by young Liszt when
roused: 'Terrified pianos flee into every corner . . . gutted instruments strew the stage, and the audience sits mute with fear and
amazement.' But the more discerning members of the public
realized that Chopin's chief desire was to make good music
rather than to impress by brilliance and noise, and in spite of his
modesty and willingness to learn he was not prepared to modify
his own natural style in order to please the Viennese. In many
things Chopin could easily be influenced by the opinions of
others, but where his art was concerned an instinctive obstinacy
protected him almost at the outset of his career from yielding,
where to yield would have meant surrendering his originality and
doing violence to his artistic conscience.

A second concert was loudly called for, and although Chopin
was not anxious to appear again, he did so in order to forestall
possible malicious comment in Warsaw ('What! He only gave
one concert and then vanished! Perhaps he made a poor
impression.') He would not hear of playing a third time, for
there was no question of a fee, and his eyes were being opened
to the methods of the concert-giving fraternity. 'I feel at least

four years wiser and more experienced,' he wrote to his parents. On 18th August his second concert took place, again at the Kärntnertor Theatre, and this time the *Krakowiak* Rondo was satisfactorily performed, the orchestral parts having been re-written with the help of Thomas Nidecki. Chopin felt that he had won the esteem of all the professional musicians with his Rondo, all, that is, except the 'petrified Germans,' who were suspicious of this brilliant meteor that had appeared on the musical horizon. He accepted with modesty the compliments that were showered on him, spoke of coming back to Vienna for lessons, and when his admirers expressed surprise at his having learnt 'all that' in Warsaw, he loyally spoke up for his old masters: 'With Messrs. Elsner and Zywny even the biggest dunderhead would learn.' The Viennese press was very cordial in its tone, and when Chopin left for Prague on 19th August he could look back on a very promising début. He had thoroughly enjoyed himself in Vienna; he had heard some excellent opera performances and had made, too, the acquaintance of several notable musicians, including Carl Czerny, the redoubtable com-poser of over a thousand forgotten works. (Chopin found more feeling in Czerny himself than in his compositions.) He returned to Poland by way of Prague, Teplitz and Dresden.

In Prague he met the Dresden musician August Klengel, a composer of the old school who wrote a complete series of canons and fugues in all the keys, in emulation of Bach's 'Forty-eight.' Klengel played these to Chopin for two solid hours, much to his edification, although he did not think very highly of the older man's playing. Later (in 1830) he met Klengel again, and their acquaintance was renewed with the greatest satisfaction on both sides. 'I really feel as much friendship for Klengel as if I had known him for thirty years,' he writes, 'and he shows me hearty affection.'

Returning to Warsaw on 12th September, Chopin was mortified to find that one of the Polish papers had grossly (perhaps deli-berately) mistranslated the notice of his concert which had appeared in the *Wiener Theater-Zeitung*. The Viennese paper was now made to say: 'He is a young man whose desire to please the public comes before the endeavour to make good music'—precisely the opposite, in fact, of what the critic had said. It was a trivial annoyance, perhaps, but Frederick was in a restless and irritable mood. His future seemed more uncertain than ever; he knew that he had nothing to gain by remaining in Warsaw and that he must work hard to prepare himself for a second and longer flight abroad. Prince Radziwill had invited him to return to Berlin; he had definitely promised to return to Vienna soon; it was generally expected that he would visit Italy; and yet we find him torn by the impulse to exploit forthwith the success he had had in Vienna, and the desire to remain in Warsaw. His reasons for staying at home in Poland were confessed in a letter to his friend and confidant, Titus Woyciechowski, written three weeks after his return from abroad:

It is perhaps my misfortune that I have already found my ideal, whom I have served faithfully, though without saying a word to her, for six months; whom I dream of, to whose memory the *adagio* of my Concerto is dedicated, and who this morning inspired me to write the little waltz I am sending you. Notice the passage marked with a ✕. No one but you will know what it means. . . .

What might have been expected of a young man of Chopin's exalted temperament had happened: he was in love. On 21st April 1829 he had met his fate (for the time being!) in the person of a charming young singer, Constantia [1] Gladkowska, who appeared at a choral concert arranged by Soliva, the professor of singing at the Conservatoire. She had been born on 10th June 1810 and was the daughter of one of Warsaw's civic dignitaries. At the time we speak of she was one of six students

---

[1] Spelt Konstancja in Polish, pronounced '. . . antsya.'

of singing housed in a boarding-house attached to the Conservatoire. Being an extremely attractive girl, she had plenty of admirers. It was unlucky for Frederick that Soliva allowed his fair pupils ('encouraged,' said Elsner, who waxed indignant on the subject) to sing duets with the young officers of the garrison; for there could be no question of Chopin's competing with them on such ground, and being nervous and uncertain of himself he was forced to adore his ideal at a distance. For six months his piano alone had been the confidant of his feelings, and now he opened his heart to Titus. He was in a fever of indecision, wondering whether to go or stay. 'You wouldn't believe how dull Warsaw seems to me just now,' he writes. 'How wretched it is to have no one with whom to share one's miseries and joys; how unbearable, when something weighs upon you, not to be able to get rid of your burden.'

Finally, on 20th October, his father made him pull himself together and packed him off to the Poznan district for a visit to Prince Radziwill, who was now at home on his estate at Antonin. Nicholas Chopin attached much importance to the interest shown by the prince; Frederick himself was sceptical and, as it turned out, he proved to be right. The prince and his family were most amiable, but no financial help was forthcoming. Nevertheless, Chopin spent a delightful week with this cultivated and musical family. The two young princesses Wanda and Elise diverted his thoughts from Constantia, and for Wanda and her father he composed at Antonin his Polonaise for cello and piano (the slow Introduction being added later). It is merely a brilliant *salon* piece, as he himself admitted, useful for showing Wanda how to place her pretty fingers on the keys. The cheerful tone of the letters in which Chopin describes his visit to Antonin confirms the impression that his love for Constantia Gladkowska was, at bottom, little more than a boyish infatuation. The 'paradise' of the Radziwill estate with its two Eves completely put her out of his thoughts, and it was only on his return to Warsaw that he took up again the threads of his romance and restored his 'ideal' to her former place. What obliged him to tear himself away from

Antonin was the thought of his unfinished Concerto. This work was to be the principal feature of the concerts he intended to give during the coming season. Public curiosity was already aroused. The newspapers wrote:

Does not Mr. Chopin's talent belong to his country? Does he think that Poland is incapable of appreciating him? Mr. Chopin's works bear unquestionably the stamp of genius; among them is said to be a Concerto in F minor, and we hope he will not delay any longer in confirming our conviction that Poland, too, produces distinguished talent.

During this autumn Chopin gave no public concert, but played a good deal at private gatherings; for example, on his father's name-day (6th December) he arranged a concert at home, at which a number of classical works were performed, and on the 19th he improvised brilliantly at a private music circle, the 'Ressource.' It was not until the first week of February 1830 that he was able to try out his Concerto with full orchestra. (The preparation of orchestral parts was always a burden to him. On his journey across Europe during 1830-1 the parts of this Concerto were lost and the delay in preparing a fresh score resulted in the work's appearing as his *second* piano Concerto, Op. 21, in 1836.) On 3rd March a small orchestra was crowded into the Chopins' drawing-room, and with Kurpiński conducting, Frederick performed his Concerto and the *Fantasia on Polish Airs* before a select audience. The result was highly satisfactory. All was now ready for his public appearance, which took place at the National Theatre on 17th March.

The theatre was sold out three days before the concert. Every one was prepared to be delighted, and indeed only Chopin himself seemed to be not entirely satisfied with the effect his compositions and his playing had produced. The concert began with an overture by Elsner, after which Chopin played the first movement of his Concerto. Then came a Divertissement for horn, followed by the *adagio* and rondo of the Concerto. In the second half of the programme he played his *Fantasia on Polish Airs*. The acoustics of the hall were none too good, and there is little doubt that Chopin made a mistake in playing on his own soft-toned piano. But he could surely not complain of the press notices which his concert called forth: the papers were full of long and appreciative articles, containing not merely flattery but genuine understanding. Let us glance at one of the most spontaneous of these accounts, written immediately after the concert:

17th March 1830. 11 p.m.

I have just returned from the concert given by Chopin, that artist whom I heard playing when he was seven, when he was still only a hope for the future. How beautifully he plays to-day! What fluency! what evenness!—impossible that there should exist a more perfect concord between two hands. He plays with such certainty, so cleanly that his Concerto might be compared to the life of a just man: no ambiguity, nothing false. He plays, if I may say so, with the good manners of a well-bred person who may indeed be aware of his own significance but has no pretensions, knowing that, if he chose, anything might be permitted to him. His music is full of expressive feeling and song, and puts the listener into a state of subtle rapture, bringing back to his memory all the happy moments he has known.

There is no justification for Édouard Wolff's disparaging remarks to Niecks on the Warsaw audience's reception of Chopin's work. What could be truer than this observation from a member of that audience?

His gayest melodies are tinged with a certain melancholy by the power of which he draws the listener along with him. . . . The land which gave him birth gave him also her melody, which forces its way to the surface again and again in the work of this artist. More than once these tones seem to be the happy echo of our native harmony; Chopin knows what sounds are heard in our fields and woods, he has listened to the song of the Polish villager, he has made it his own, and has united the tunes of his native soil in skilful composition and elegant execution.

Since so many people had been turned away from the first concert a second was given on 22nd March, and Chopin's success was even greater. This time he played on a splendid Viennese

instrument (borrowed for the occasion), and every note rang out
as clear as a bell. He repeated his Concerto, but played the
Krakowiak rondo instead of the Fantasia, and ended with an
improvisation on the folk-tune 'In the town they have queer
customs.' The enthusiasm of the audience knew no bounds:
there were shouts of 'Don't be hard-hearted. Let's have one
more concert before you go!' Alas! by their extravagant tone
some of the newspaper articles did Chopin more harm than good.
The April number of the *Ladies' Journal* published a sonnet in his
honour, and when the critic of the *General Daily News* went so
far as to declare that there was no one but Mozart with whom
to compare him, an unpleasant journalistic squabble broke out.
An old feud between Elsner and Kurpiński flared up again, and
after many hard words the dispute was brought to a close by
Soliva in a sarcastic article couched in the form of an 'Appeal
to Chopin.' At the same time a third-rate musician, Orlowski,
had the impudence to take the themes of the F minor Concerto
and turn them into mazurkas and waltzes. One can imagine
how distasteful all this would be to Chopin; there could be no
question of a third concert in such circumstances.

He had still much to do before he could think of leaving
Warsaw. His new Concerto in E minor was unfinished; the
last movement—the rondo—was yet to be written, but Frederick
seems to have found it difficult to settle down to systematic work.
He could not get Constantia out of his thoughts, and his days
were often spent in a state of dreamy languor which he himself
in his calmer moments was the first to make fun of. He had met
Constantia by now, for they had many common friends, but
there is nothing to show that he ever revealed the feelings that
were tormenting him. Only to his *alter ego*, Titus Woyciechowski, and to his piano did he unburden himself, and his
compositions of this period tell the story of his hopes and fears.
The *Romance* of the E minor Concerto, the Nocturnes, Op. 9,
and the first two Nocturnes of Op. 15, the Study in E major,
Op. 10, the Nocturne in C♯ minor (*Lento con gran espres-
sione*) are evidence of his emotional state. At times, too, he took

pleasure in detecting in the poems of the Polish romantics similarities with his own position, and thus we find him setting to music Witwicki's *The Warrior* ('. . . The time has come for me to leave you. Farewell! my father, mother and sisters') and Mickiewicz's passionate 'Hence from my sight!'

> *Larghetto appassionato.*
> 'Hence from my sight!' At once I obey.
> 'Hence from my heart!' And my heart obeys at once.
> 'Hence from my memory!' Ah no! *That* command neither my memory nor thine can obey.

It is not difficult to understand why Chopin did not declare himself. What could come of it? He was only twenty and still had his name and fortune to make. He knew that he was going abroad for several years. Perhaps in his heart of hearts he realized that he was merely giving way to a craving for emotion and sentiment.

Before he left Warsaw he and Constantia exchanged rings, but there is no evidence of any promise between them. In his album she wrote: 'Remember! Never forget that we in Poland love you . . . in foreign lands they may appreciate and reward you better, but they cannot love you more.' Little did Frederick guess, when his beloved wrote those last words, that one day he would take a pencil and lightly add: 'Oh yes, they can!'

The rest of Constantia's story is soon told. On 31st January 1832 she married Joseph Grabowski and, giving up all thought of a stage career, lived quietly and happily in the country with her husband and the five children who were born to them. In 1845 a terrible blow fell upon her: she became blind. When her husband died in 1878 she led a lonely life, but bore her misfortunes cheerfully and never lost her interest in literature and music. When Karasowski's *Life of Chopin* was read to her she was amazed to discover how much she had meant to the young composer; she had no idea that his feeling for her had been so intense. But she had no regrets. 'I doubt whether Chopin would have been such a good husband as my honest Joseph,'

she said, 'for he was temperamental, full of fantasies, unreliable.'
She died on 20th December 1889, having, a few days before
her death, burnt all her letters and souvenirs of Frederick
Chopin.

The two concerts which he gave in March 1830 mark the
climax of Chopin's success in Warsaw: during the rest of the
time he spent in Poland other events occupied the public mind
and other musicians claimed a share of the limelight. On
20th May the tsar arrived for the opening, a week later, of what
was to be the last session of the Polish Diet. Feeling in the
Polish capital was tense, and the brilliant festivities only served
to emphasize the unreal, 'electric' atmosphere. A host of foreign
artists descended upon the town, the most outstanding figure
among all these singers and pianists being Henriette Sontag.
Her lovely voice and perfect technique sent Chopin into rap-
tures, for he was a real connoisseur of singing who found in
Sontag's art precisely those elements which distinguished his own
style of piano playing: exquisite gradations of tone, impeccable
accuracy and infinite charm. Then there was a young French
pianist, Mlle Belleville, who made a considerable impression.
It was she and another pianist, Woerlitzer, who were invited to
support Sontag at a gala concert given for the tsar on 31st May.
Chopin affected not to notice this slight, but we may be sure he
was not indifferent to it.

When the tsar left on 28th June, after using threatening language
to the Poles, the musical season collapsed. The public was
exhausted by the number of concerts (Sontag alone had given
eight), and by not having his new Concerto ready Chopin had
missed his opportunity. At the beginning of July his Variations,
Op. 2, arrived from Vienna and were on sale, and on 8th July
he played them at a belated concert given by a singer, Mme
Meyer. The audience was very small, and this appearance of
Chopin's passed almost unnoticed in the press. Immediately
after the concert Frederick went off to Poturzyn to see his friend
Titus Woyciechowski and to have heart-to-heart talks with him.
He felt better after he had opened his heart to Titus, but he was

back in Warsaw on 24th July for Constantia's début in Paer's opera *Agnese*, and his troubles began all over again.

It was now the very height of summer, and in order to enjoy a breath of country air Chopin paid a last visit to his native village, Zelazowa Wola. While he was there the news of the July Revolution in Paris ('The Three Glorious Days') arrived in Warsaw. Although a rigorous censorship kept details of the successful rising out of the newspapers, the city was in a ferment. Numbers of the university students were arrested and a placard appeared on the Russian grand duke's palace: 'House to let after the New Year.' However, these events seem to have passed completely over Chopin's head. He was too busy finishing his Concerto in E minor—to say nothing of studies and smaller pieces. The unsettled state of Europe affected his plans for the future, and in his letters to Titus there is continual talk of fresh dates for his departure; vague schemes are outlined, only to be dropped one after the other in his fever of indecision. At length, on 23rd September, he invited all musical Warsaw to his home for a 'dress rehearsal' of the E minor Concerto. Its success was complete and press notices appeared as though it had been a public performance:

I hasten to bring a piece of good news to all friends of music and of native talent: Frederick Chopin has completed his second grand piano Concerto. It is the work of a genius . . . and we must add that Mr. Chopin will rob the Warsaw public of a great pleasure if he departs without having publicly produced this second Concerto.

And so it was decided. On 11th October 1830 Chopin gave his last concert in Warsaw. Here is his own account of the event:

I was not the slightest bit nervous and I played as I play when I'm alone. It went well. The hall was full. Goerner's Symphony came first. Then My Highness played the first *allegro* of the E minor Concerto, which I reeled off on a Streicher piano. The bravos were deafening. . . . Soliva, very pleased, conducted, on account of his 'Aria with Chorus,' which Mlle Wolków sang, dressed in blue and looking like an angel. After this aria came the *adagio* and rondo [of the Concerto].

[In the second part of the programme] . . . Soliva then conducted the aria for Mlle Gladkowska, beautifully dressed in white with roses in her hair . . . she sang it as she has never sung anything before. . . . After the young lady had been led from the stage I went on to play the Potpourri on Polish Airs. This time I understood what *I* was doing, the orchestra understood what *it* was doing and the pit understood too. For once the final mazurka called forth terrific applause. . . . It seems to me that I have never been so much at ease when playing with an orchestra.

In spite of Chopin's success only the *Warsaw Courier* published any notice of the concert. But Frederick was too much absorbed by the preparations for his departure to trouble about the local press. On 1st November his friend Reinschmidt gave a farewell party for him. The next morning, after his sister Louise had finished making fair copies of some of his studies (her manuscript of Op. 10, Nos. 1 and 2 is dated '2 November 1830'), he bade farewell to his family and friends. (There is not a shred of evidence to support Karasowski's statement that a silver goblet filled with Polish earth was given to Chopin at the moment of his departure and that this same earth was strewn on the grave at his funeral in 1849. The whole story arose from a hazy memory of the fact that on 12th June 1850 Chopin's faithful pupil, Jane Stirling, wrote to Warsaw asking that a small box of Polish soil might be sent to Paris for the unveiling of the Chopin monument in the Père-Lachaise cemetery. There was no question of this ceremony having already been performed in October 1849.)

When the stage-coach that was to take him to Vienna reached the Warsaw suburb of Wola a surprise was in store for Chopin. Joseph Elsner had arrived there before him with a male-voice choir, which now sang, with guitar accompaniment, a short cantata especially composed by Elsner himself.

Born among the Polish fields, may your talent bring you fame wherever you go; and whether you dwell on the banks of Spree, Tiber or Seine, let there ever be heard in your music, according to the good old

Chopin

Polish custom, those tunes which delight us here: the Mazurka and the
dear Krakowiak.

> *Chorus.* Although you leave our native land
> Still will your heart remain with us,
> And the memory of the genius within you.
> And so, from the bottom of our hearts we say,
> 'Good luck wherever you go!'

A last handshake, the coach moves off, and Chopin has left
Warsaw for ever.

CHAPTER III

ALTHOUGH he had found it hard to tear himself away from
Warsaw on 2nd November 1830, Chopin was none the less
full of eager hope for the future and confident that he would prove
himself worthy of the faith that his family had in him. He
realized what sacrifices his parents were making, and it was his
ambition to be able to stand on his own feet as soon as possible.
But his youthful optimism would have been sadly shaken had
he been able to foresee the trials and anxieties which the coming
year had in store for him. From now until the end of 1831 he
was to meet with a succession of disappointments enough to
break the heart of a much more resolute young man than he, and
he was to learn what it means for an artist to have to make his
way by his own efforts in a foreign country, where the atmosphere
is generally unfriendly when not actually hostile. During this
time he did not earn a penny and was constantly obliged to
appeal to his father for money. Sometimes he scarcely had a
coin in his pocket. To make matters worse, he was tormented
by the thought that he was wasting his time and getting no
nearer to the goal he had set himself. His parents never breathed
a word of reproach, but in his father's letters there are many
traces of the worry which the people in Warsaw had to endure
on his account.

At first all went well. He met his friend Titus at Kalisz, and
the pair set off at once for Breslau, where they arrived on 6th
November. During their four days' stay Chopin played the
Romance and rondo of his E minor Concerto at a private concert, ousting from the programme an unhappy amateur who was
to have played a Moscheles concerto, but who took fright at the
rehearsal, when Chopin sat down and casually ran through a
few of his Variations, Op. 2. The worthy citizens of Breslau

were baffled by the novel effects which the young stranger produced: they were inclined to believe that there was some trickery, some sleight-of-hand involved; but Chopin did not stay to undeceive them and went on at once to Dresden, where he had made several useful acquaintances in 1829 on his way to Vienna.

His first visit was to Miss Pechwell, a pianist who had been very obliging to him when he first passed through the town. She invited him to a soirée at which she was to play. Chopin gives an amusing description of this Dresden gathering. In the concert-room he found

a crowd of ladies sitting at both sides of eight enormous tables. My eyes were dazzled not so much by the diamonds which adorned them as by the number of knitting-needles. Seriously, the number of ladies and knitting-needles was so great that one might have feared some rebellion against the menfolk which would have had to be resisted solely with spectacles and bald heads; for there was a host of glasses and as many shining pates!

He saw, too, Klengel, the organist whom he had met before in Prague, and took the opportunity to play him his concertos. Klengel remarked that his playing reminded him of Field, the Irish pianist and composer, a suggestion which Frederick took as a compliment. (We shall learn later what he thought of Field when he heard him.) Klengel also pressed him to give a concert, but he knew that Dresden could bring him neither fame nor money and so, after a week's stay, he made for Vienna, where he and Titus arrived on 22nd November, having spent a day in Prague.

Chopin was now to learn what value could be attached to the flattering assurances of those who had welcomed his first appearance in the Austrian capital with extravagant enthusiasm. In 1829 he had come as a brilliant amateur who played for nothing and gave his compositions away. This time he appeared to the Viennese musicians as a competitor for public favour and the money that goes with it. It is not surprising, therefore, that they received Chopin with some show of cordiality but left him to shift for himself in the matter of concert-giving. It was the same with the publisher Haslinger. He had not yet printed Chopin's Sonata, Op. 4, or the *Swiss Boy* Variations and did not intend to do so; as for the two new concertos, he would not look at them. It is probable that he had lost money with the 'Là ci darem' Variations, even though he had paid Chopin nothing for them, for such difficult and novel music was unlikely to sell in Vienna, where waltzes were at this time the only things that the public would buy.

Chopin was not deceived by Haslinger's suave politeness: from henceforth his motto was to be 'Pay up, animal!' (The astute publisher finally got the better of him, however! In 1841, when Chopin's fame had spread throughout Europe, he printed these early works and sent the proofs to Chopin for correction. Chopin refused to touch them: he did not wish to be reminded of his schoolboy attempts at composition. Thereupon Haslinger bided his time, and as soon as Chopin was dead he sold 'the Master's posthumous works,' which he had obtained for nothing twenty years previously.)

If the professional musicians were courteous but unhelpful, the attitude of the general musical public was likewise not at all encouraging to the young Pole. He had scarcely been in Vienna a week when news arrived of the revolt which had broken out in Warsaw on 29th November. The unhappy Poles could expect no sympathy in the capital of a country which had taken its share of the spoils in the various partitions of Polish territory, and all that Chopin could hear in the imperial city of Metternich, the sworn enemy of revolution, was: 'God made a mistake when He created the Poles.' 'If you go to Poland you'll come back empty-handed,' and so forth.

When he heard what had happened in Warsaw, Titus, a vigorous and active young fellow, at once set off for home, leaving Chopin behind, to be racked with doubts and fears for the safety of his family and Constantia. Chopin's letters of this period betray an extraordinary state of mind. To his parents he wrote in a cheerful vein, relating his experiences in the musical and artistic world of Vienna and only touching lightly on the difficulties he was meeting with. On the other hand, in his letters to Jan Matuszyński he unburdened himself in a wild and incoherent manner of all the misery which was oppressing him, but which he forced himself to hide from the outside world. His father, fearing he would do something foolish, had written urging him to stay where he was, and Frederick could do no more than send to Warsaw letters like the following, written on Christmas Day 1830:

> If it were not that I should be a burden on my father, I would come back. I curse the day I left. . . . I am up to the neck in evening parties, concerts and dances, but they bore me to death; everything is so terribly gloomy and depressing for me here. . . . I have to dress and get ready to go out; in company I must appear calm, and then when I come home I let myself go on the piano. . . . One passage in your letter made me miserable. Is she really changed? Hasn't she been ill? . . . perhaps the shock of what happened on the 29th has caused it. God forbid that it should be my fault. Reassure her; tell her that as long as there is breath in my body . . . until I die . . . and even after my death my ashes shall be strewn under her feet. . . . Shall I go to Paris? The people here advise me to wait. Shall I come back to Poland? Shall I stay here? Shall I put an end to myself? Shall I stop writing to you? Advise me what to do.

Then on the next page he goes on to give a picturesque description of the pleasant life he is leading in his charming Viennese apartment.

This violent fluctuation in his moods, from the depth of despair to gay nonchalance, is characteristic of Chopin. Throughout his life we find him reacting in this way to the events of the outside world. He could be cool, calculating and cynical, and then a moment later enthusiastic, cheerful and, at times, boisterously vulgar. It is only in his letters written in Polish that we find the real Chopin—he never wrote freely in any other language, and what he sometimes wrote in Polish would surprise those who know his character only from the sentimental utterances of his pupils and casual acquaintances.

Meeting with Thalberg

By the end of January 1831 Chopin had practically given up all hope of being able to arrange a concert of his own. Duport, the new director of the Kärntnertor Theatre, where he had played in 1829, was prepared to offer him the theatre on the usual terms —no fee and the proceeds to go to the management—but Chopin knew he could not afford to go on in this way, and the project came to nothing. At this time, too, the attention of the Viennese was being focused on another new meteor—Sigismund Thalberg (1812–70), who had the advantage of being protected by very high personages, and swept all his rivals aside until the day in 1837 when he was rolled in the dust by Liszt. Chopin heard his dazzling performance and remained unmoved.

Thalberg plays splendidly [he wrote], but he's not my man. He's younger than I and pleases the ladies—makes potpourris on La Muette [Auber's Masaniello]—produces his piano and forte with the pedal, not the hand—takes tenths as I do octaves and wears diamond shirt-studs. He does not marvel at Moscheles—no wonder, then, that only the tuttis of my concerto pleased him. He writes concertos too.

In these difficult circumstances Chopin let week after week slip by without making a determined effort to assert himself. It was not until 4th April that he appeared before the public of Vienna. The occasion was not a particularly brilliant one: a matinée in the Redoutensaal by the singer Mme Garcia-Vestris. Among the ten other artists who took part was 'Herr Chopin (piano player),' who played his E minor Concerto, as a piano solo. Such was the sum total of fame that Chopin acquired from his second visit to the Austrian capital.[1]

In the face of this complete failure of all his plans for a triumphal reappearance in Vienna, why did Chopin stay there so long? He himself did not know. His days passed in a round of futile social engagements which brought him little satisfaction. He was constantly at the Italian Opera and was a welcome guest at many of the great houses—there is a description in his letters of a musical

[1] A recently discovered programme shows that he played again on 11th June 1831.

evening at the house of Malfatti (the emperor's physician), where moonlight, fountains and flowers united for a brief hour to form a rare and ideal background for the young exile's poetical improvisations. Among the notable musicians whom he met on a familiar footing were Slawik the violinist, a second Paganini ('Ninetysix staccato notes with one stroke of the bow!'), and Joseph Merk, the principal cellist of the Royal Opera, to whom he dedicated his *Introduction and Polonaise*, Op. 3. He was frequently 'hard up,' but this does not seem to have distressed him very much. One day he cheerfully wrote in his diary: 'Today I have only one crown in my pocket, but I feel richer than Arthur Potocki whom I met just now. F. Chopin (poor devil).' But often he was devoured by regrets and anxieties, and his pleasures were poisoned by the thought of what was happening in Poland. The knowledge that the flower of Polish youth was perishing on the battlefield made him realize all the more keenly that he too was a Pole, and the emotion which the memories of his country's heroic past aroused in him found expression in the Scherzo in B minor and the Ballade in G minor, both of which were conceived at this period. In the middle section of the highly dramatic Scherzo, full of defiance and strife, Chopin lets his thoughts wander back to the familiar melodies of the Polish fireside, and we hear the old cradlesong 'Sleep, little Jesus, sleep.' Then suddenly and ruthlessly the challenge to battle banishes the dream. He also set to music a number of Witwicki's poems, and his choice is significant: *Sad River, The Bridegroom, The Messenger, Lithuanian Song* . . . always the same theme: home, friends and family, the beloved.

At last, towards the end of June, he decided to continue his journey. Italy was now out of the question, for revolt had broken out there, too. He would go to Paris. But since Chopin was legally a Russian subject the authorities at the Russian embassy were not disposed to allow him to join the rest of the Polish exiles and conspirators in Paris, that hotbed of revolution, and after a great deal of trouble he had to be content with having his passport endorsed 'To London via Paris.'

He left Vienna on 20th July in the company of a compatriot, Norbert Alfons Kumelski, and travelled to Munich by way of Salzburg. In a letter home Kumelski describes an amusing little episode that occurred at Salzburg. They arrived in the town just as the clock of the archbishop's residence was striking six, and were amazed to hear the ancient clock playing a tune which sounded strangely modern. Chopin was puzzled: had the long-dead clockmaker anticipated the nineteenth century? He would make a note of it. A day or two later when they visited the residence they discovered that the keeper of the clock, being very partial to opera, had set the mechanism to play a duet from one of Auber's operas. He chose a fresh tune each month.

Chopin found himself obliged to remain in Munich much longer than he had intended, owing to the non-arrival of the funds his father had promised him at the end of June. He was for several weeks without news of his family, for the Russians were preparing to storm Warsaw, and communication with the city was almost impossible. However, he managed to draw some advantage from the enforced delay. He was amply provided with letters of introduction and found the musicians of Munich quite willing to help him to arrange a concert. Thus, on 28th August he played his E minor Concerto and the *Fantasia on Polish Airs* to an appreciative audience at the Philharmonic Society Hall. A week later he was at Stuttgart when the news of the fall of Warsaw (8th September) arrived. This disaster to the Polish cause threw him into a state bordering on frenzy, and having no one in whom to confide his distress, he scribbled in his note-book an incoherent jumble of lamentations and curses which show how worry, fear and regret had preyed on his over-wrought nerves.[1]

---

[1] Unjustified doubts have been expressed concerning the authenticity of these note-book entries. I have read them in Chopin's album myself.

The suburbs have been destroyed, burnt down. Johnnie and William have surely perished on the ramparts. I can see Marcel a prisoner. Sowiński, that good lad, is in the hands of those villains! Paszkiewicz, one of the dogs from Mohilev, seizes the capital of the first monarchs of Europe! Moscow rules the world! Oh God, do You exist? You do, and yet You do not take vengeance. Have You not had enough of these Muscovite crimes or . . . or, are You Yourself a Russian!!!? . . . Father, Mother, where are you? Perhaps corpses . . .

and so on in the wildest strain. Less well authenticated is the story of the 'Revolutionary' Study, Op. 10, No. 12, being composed at the same time, although there is nothing improbable in it. One might mention, however, that the legend is quite off the mark in adding the Preludes in A minor and D minor to the list of pieces which Chopin composed in despair and fury at Stuttgart. We shall see that the Prelude in A minor definitely belongs to the period of Chopin's visit to Majorca (1838).

When he came to his senses Frederick was anxious to be off. He left Stuttgart forthwith, and in the middle of September arrived in Paris which was henceforth to be his home, his second *patrie* and the scene of his greatest triumphs and tragic end. Poland, the real, visible Poland of his childhood and youth, was now far away; but in Chopin's heart and mind she was destined to be transfigured, by a subtle and stealthy process, into a strange dream-country that would haunt his imagination for ever and cause to rise within him those exquisite musical shapes, full of tenderness and passionate regret, which, as the years passed, came to be the living symbol of Poland for millions who knew nothing of the reality for which the symbol stood.

CHAPTER IV

When Chopin reached Paris in the early autumn of 1831 and took modest lodgings at 27 Boulevard Poissonnière, he was at first bewildered to find himself in the midst of a whirlpool of political, intellectual and artistic activity the like of which has rarely been seen. In July 1830 Charles X and the last survivors of the *ancien régime* had been swept away by a revolutionary movement which had its source in something deeper than the mere desire for political freedom. After enduring for fifteen years the blind reactionary government which had followed upon the heroic and inspiring days of the Revolution and the Napoleonic period, the French had rid themselves for ever of the Bourbons and were rejoicing in their newly won liberty. With the younger generation, the 'Children of the Century,' this idea of absolute liberty for the individual amounted to an obsession; these ardent young men were prepared to carry their theories to the wildest extremes. The great tide of romanticism was rising towards its high-water mark and all the barriers of tradition, convention and respect for established authority were being swept away by the flood. In the arts the change of outlook was as fundamental as in the sphere of politics, and by a rare dispensation of providence a veritable galaxy of brilliant young writers and artists appeared at the critical moment to form the vanguard of the new movement.

Victor Hugo, Balzac, Vigny, Lamartine, Musset and George Sand, to name only a few, infused new life into literature and the drama —in 1830 the production of Hugo's romantic drama *Hernani* had been the occasion for a tumultuous struggle between the supporters of the new school and the die-hard upholders of the ancient theatrical conventions. Among the painters Delacroix, Ingres and Delaroche led the way; and although music (as always in France) lagged behind the other arts, the new movement had two enthusiastic representatives in Liszt and Berlioz—the latter's *Symphonie fantastique*, that perfect reflection of the spirit of the time, already existed in its first version. Indeed Paris could claim to be the musical centre of Europe, for since Beethoven, Schubert and Weber had vanished from the scene, Germany had ceased to occupy the first place. It was in Paris that the chief representatives of the older school were to be found: Rossini, Cherubini, Boïeldieu, Paer and Lesueur. Cherubini ruled the Conservatoire with a rod of iron, zealously maintaining obedience to the established rules of harmony and counterpoint. (Chopin was at first inclined to jeer at him, but later he saw the value of this discipline and profited by Cherubini's teachings.)

There were three excellent orchestras and at the opera houses, where Rossini and Auber reigned supreme, singers like Malibran, Pasta, Grisi, Cinti-Damoreau, Rubini, Lablache and Nourrit raised the standard of the performances to a level to which no other European city could aspire. The violinist Baillot and the young cellist Franchomme were among the leading instrumentalists, and as for pianists, it seemed to Chopin that every piano player in the world was to be found in Paris at that moment. Liszt stood by himself, head and shoulders above men like Hiller, Stephen Heller, Osborne and Herz; but it was Frederick Kalkbrenner, for many years the undisputed king of Parisian pianists, who attracted Chopin's attention most. Thanks to a few letters of introduction which he brought from Germany (the most useful being one from Dr. Malfatti to Paer) he was able to meet all the well-known musicians as soon as he arrived. His letters contain many shrewd and biting comments on the high and mighty personages to whom he made his bow. For Kalkbrenner he had nothing but admiration, differing in this from most of the young generation of pianists, who regarded the older man as a symbol of what they were fighting against.

If Paganini is perfection itself, Kalkbrenner is his equal, but in a quite different sphere. It is difficult to describe to you his 'calm,' his enchanting touch, the incomparable evenness of his playing and that mastery which is obvious in every note . . .

Thus Chopin, who was the last person to overpraise in these matters. Besides, Kalkbrenner was a gentleman, very dignified and very certain of his superiority to the young bohemians who might play with devastating expression, but who had not a tenth of his strict, technical mastery. Long years of ceaseless practice had given him perfection of touch and tone, and his playing of his own works and those of the school of Clementi and Hummel could not be surpassed. Chopin was quick to realize that Kalkbrenner possessed something he lacked: he was modest enough to say nothing of the qualities which he himself had and Kalkbrenner would never be able to claim—poetry and feeling, colour and rhythm. Anxious to perfect himself, Chopin approached Kalkbrenner with a view to taking lessons. After hearing him the master declared that he had talent but lacked schooling, and that he would take him for three years and turn him into something 'very, very . . .!' Three years! Such was the normal course for Kalkbrenner's pupils, and he saw no reason to relax his rule in favour of the young Pole. One is frankly surprised that Kalkbrenner did not recognize that Chopin was, to say the least, a very *unusual* pupil—a virtuoso who had already been acclaimed in some of the most critical cities in Europe. However, there is no reason to suppose, as so many writers have, that he was actuated by jealousy, any more than was Cherubini when, a few years earlier, he refused to break a sacred rule of the Conservatoire against admitting foreigners for the benefit of young Liszt. Chopin hesitated. He had to earn his living, and even if he had been able to afford the three years, he had no wish to become merely an imitation of Kalkbrenner. Apart from the technical aspects of his art he had nothing to learn from him. He knew exactly what the 'new world of music' which he intended to create would be, and when his friend Titus wrote to him seriously about his future he could truthfully say: 'Don't worry about that, my dear friend; I am going ahead in my own carriage; I have only engaged a coachman to look after the horses.'

When he wrote home to Warsaw for advice in this important matter, the effect produced on his family and on his old master

Elsner was as might have been expected: on the one hand consternation and anxiety, on the other indignation. From both quarters long letters full of advice and warning were quickly dispatched to Paris. Elsner was certain that Frederick was being duped by Kalkbrenner, and in his solemn letter of 27th November he exhorted him to follow the dictates of his own genius and seek fame as a composer rather than as a pianist (a composer of Polish national opera was what Elsner meant). Chopin listened respectfully but went his own way. Nor would he join in the chorus of denigration which his enthusiastic friends raised against Kalkbrenner. He decided, in the long run, to let the matter drop. He may have attended one or two of Kalkbrenner's classes in order to avoid offending him, but this is not proved. What is certain is that the two musicians continued on a most friendly footing, not as of pupil to master, but as colleagues and equals. When Chopin was preparing his first concert Kalkbrenner gave him what help he could. Chopin paid him the compliment of dedicating his E minor Concerto to him and Kalkbrenner responded by writing variations on one of Chopin's mazurkas. Here is a letter which reveals the cordial relations that existed between the two:

Sunday, 28th December 1834.

MY DEAR CHOPIN,

We never see you nowadays. The countless distractions and pleasures of Paris make you forget your old friends. Come along to dinner with us to-morrow. You'll find us with Liszt and a few other friends who will be delighted to see you. Addio.

FRED. KALKBRENNER.

Chopin's relations with his other colleagues (and rivals) in the pianistic world were, from the first, marked by great cordiality. The younger men welcomed him with open arms and readily acknowledged his genius, for there were few among the more thoughtful romantics who did not feel that here was the artist they had been waiting for, one who was bringing into the realm of music the new thoughts, new emotions and modes of expression which could satisfy their longing for a new world of sentiment and colour. If ever an artist appeared at the right moment in history it was Chopin. His success in the Paris of the 1830s was really never for a moment in doubt, in spite of his apparently uncertain beginnings.

Apart from his musical acquaintances Chopin naturally turned at first to the society of the many Polish *émigrés* who had made Paris their headquarters, and he soon became prominent in the aristocratic group which centred round the Hôtel Lambert on the Île Saint-Louis. Here he was in close contact with distinguished Poles like Prince Valentine Radziwill, Mickiewicz the poet, Countess Delphine Potocka, the Czartoryskis and others, who obtained for him the entrée to the great French houses in the Faubourgs Saint-Germain and Saint-Honoré. His first concern was to give a concert, and after much discussion 25th December was fixed as the date. Since Chopin was unknown to the general public some well-meaning friends had the idea of writing to *Le Temps* an open letter, representing him as an unfortunate victim of the Polish Revolution (which he was not) in order to arouse interest in the concert, but the editor declined to publish it. There was no lack of support from his musical friends: Kalkbrenner and Baillot, to name only two, promised their help. But Chopin had difficulty in obtaining singers—Rossini could not help him here without being overwhelmed by requests from other concert-givers—and his début had to be postponed until 15th January 1832. The programmes were printed and all was ready, when Kalkbrenner fell ill. Thus it was not until 26th February that the 'Grand Vocal and Instrumental Concert' took place at Pleyel's Salon, 9 Rue Cadet. After Beethoven's Quintet, Op. 29 (with Baillot and Urhan, an extraordinary viola player), and a duet, sung by Mlles Toméoni and Isambert, Chopin played his F minor Concerto as a piano solo. Afterwards the audience were treated to a monstrosity of Kalkbrenner's, a *Grand Polonaise with Introduction and March*, played on six pianos by Chopin, Hiller, Stamaty, Sowiński, George Osborne and the composer. Finally Chopin played his 'Là ci darem' Variations.

This concert placed Chopin in the front rank of pianists. Liszt and Mendelssohn, who were both present, applauded furiously. Nor was it the financial failure it has been made out to be: Chopin had the hall free and the expenses were insignifi-cant, so that with tickets at ten francs each a fair sum went to the concert-giver. Chopin's compatriot, Anton Orlowski, wrote home: 'Our dear Fritz has given a concert which brought him a great reputation and some money. He has wiped the floor with all the pianists here: all Paris was stupefied.' On 3rd March Fétis, the principal music critic, wrote in the *Revue musicale*:

Piano music is generally written in certain conventional forms that may be regarded as basic and that have been continually reproduced for over thirty years. It is one of the defects of this type of music, and our most skilful artists have not succeeded in ridding their works of it. But here is a young man who, surrendering himself to his natural impressions and taking no model, has found, if not a complete renewal of piano music, at least a part of that which we have long sought in vain, namely an abundance of original ideas of a kind to be found nowhere else. . . . I find in M. Chopin's inspirations the signs of a renewal of forms which may henceforth exercise considerable influence upon this branch of the art.

This opinion of a learned contemporary is worth bearing in mind when one considers the extent of Chopin's debt to his predecessors. Fétis was steeped in the music of his own and previous centuries: if Chopin's work struck *him* as being markedly original it is safe to assume that the resemblances to Field, Kalk-brenner, Hummel and others are less real than some writers would have us believe. After all that has happened in the world of music since 1830 it is impossible for us to-day to hear Chopin's F minor Concerto as Fétis heard it and to detect, as he did, the new note, the fresh perfume, the first glimpse of a hitherto unknown colour.

It has been mentioned that Liszt was present at Chopin's first Paris concert. On no one did the impact of Chopin's personality produce such an effect as on Liszt, and the story of their friendship is one of the curiosities of nineteenth-century musical history. Liszt's biographer, Lina Ramann, who was singularly ill informed on the subject, has much to say concerning the influence which Liszt is supposed to have had on Chopin as a composer. In order to refute the suggestion of such influence it is only necessary to compare Chopin's compositions up to 1831 with those of Liszt for the same period. It is evident that Liszt had so far achieved nothing at all as a composer. He was like a ship without a rudder for many years to come and did not find his true bearings until some years after Chopin's death. On the other hand we now know that by the time Chopin reached Paris in September 1831 his musical character was fixed, in all essentials, and his future course marked out. The changes we may observe during the remaining years which he spent in France are not to be attributed to external influences; they were brought about by the plant-like development of his musical being according to its own laws.

The two young men became friends at once, but there was more warmth on Liszt's side than on Chopin's: this was no great romantic friendship, although the popular imagination likes to link their names together. There were traits in Liszt's character that repelled Chopin from the beginning. His letters to his Polish friends and their replies to him make it clear that he could not bear Liszt's showmanship and his way of playing the *grand seigneur*, although his admiration for Liszt the pianist was unbounded. At no time was Liszt ever on the same footing as Chopin in the highest Parisian society. Something in his manner, some ineradicable trace of the parvenu, prevented his being accepted, and any headway he might make was quickly lost by some miscalculation which aroused the merriment of the quick-witted and sarcastic Parisian aristocracy. There is evidence that as early as 1835 all was not well between the two, and although for several years they appeared outwardly to be intimate friends, Chopin remained on his guard and never made Liszt the confidant of his innermost feelings. At some date before 1840 Liszt overstepped the mark by making himself at home in Chopin's apartment with a lady friend (Marie Pleyel,[1] wife of Pleyel the piano manufacturer, seems to be indicated in one of Liszt's letters), and from that time their friendship lost whatever intimacy it had had. Chopin's resentment at Liszt's behaviour communicated itself to his family in Warsaw, and Liszt's effusive urbanity did not succeed in overcoming it. Three weeks after Chopin's death in October 1849, Liszt, who knew nothing of his early life, took the liberty of sending Chopin's sister Louise a questionnaire in order to furnish himself with a few biographical facts for the *Life of Chopin* he intended writing. The nature of Liszt's questions shows how little real intimacy had existed between him and Chopin. Louise regarded Liszt's step as a piece of impertinence and the questionnaire was returned with curt answers written out by Jane Stirling, one of Chopin's pupils.

With the impetuous Berlioz, who returned to Paris from Rome at the end of 1832, Chopin formed a warm personal friendship which was not affected by the utter dissimilarity of the two men as musicians. Chopin could never overcome his aversion to Berlioz's music, but he respected his sincere and forthright character; they got on famously together and there were many lively discussions on art, literature and music among the members of their little circle. Berlioz mentions a country outing which he organized: he carried off Chopin ('Chopinetto mio'), Liszt and Alfred de Vigny to Montmartre, a quiet country village in those days, where they walked and talked endlessly. Berlioz's dramatic love affair with the Irish actress, Harriet Smithson, is well known. On one occasion, tortured by his passion, he rushed off to Saint-Ouen in a state of frenzy, and Chopin and Liszt, who followed him post-haste, had to spend the night in the open country, looking for the distracted lover. It was Chopin who helped Berlioz with the piano version of his *Francs-Juges* overture, since Berlioz knew nothing of piano writing, and on 7th December 1834 he took part in one of Berlioz's concerts, playing the *Romance*

---

[1] She was cast off by her husband for her conduct. (Details from Camille Pleyel's will—1855.)

from his E minor Concerto, a piquant contrast to the concert-giver's own highly coloured compositions.

Mendelssohn was another who was quickly attracted by the young Pole's charm and genius, although, being a level-headed fellow, he never succumbed to the Parisian mania for assuming romantic poses and was never very happy among the rebels of the boulevards. Of Chopin's playing he wrote, in 1835:

There is something so thoroughly original and at the same time so very masterly in his piano playing that he may be called a really perfect virtuoso. I was glad to be once again with a thorough musician, not one of those half-virtuosos and half-classics who would like to combine in music the honours of virtue and the pleasures of vice, but one who has his own perfect and clearly defined style.

(Mendelssohn's opinion of Chopin as a composer was not so unqualified.) The two friends must have spent some agreeable hours together in Paris. There exists a three-voice canon written by Mendelssohn in April 1832, just after Frederick's first concert: perhaps to prove that he, too, had had a thorough musical education, Chopin added a neat bass part in free counterpoint, which Mendelssohn acknowledged to have been 'composed by Sciopino.'

It is pleasant to think of this band of brilliant young men in the Paris of the early 1830s. Their world is the tiny kingdom of the boulevards from the Madeleine to what is now the Place de l'Opéra. Here they see each other daily; to be far from this delectable region is to be banished from civilization! One day in Chopin's handsome apartment, just round the corner in the Chaussée d'Antin, Liszt sits down at the splendid Pleyel piano and dashes off Chopin's studies in incomparable style, interrupting his playing to join in the writing of a letter to Ferdinand Hiller. When Chopin's turn to write a sentence comes he observes:

I write to you without knowing what my pen is scribbling because at this moment Liszt is playing my studies and putting honest thoughts out of my head: I should like to rob him of the way to play my own studies! . . . Heine sends his heartiest greetings. . . . Love from Berlioz.

But we are anticipating. The handsome apartment did not materialize until Chopin had established his position and had begun to earn the money he so sorely needed. On 20th May 1832 he took part in a charity concert arranged by the Princess Moskowa, in the hall of the Conservatoire, and played the first movement of the F minor Concerto. It was an important occa-sion, for 'all Paris' was there; but Chopin failed to impress the audience as he had hoped. His playing was lost in the large hall and the *Revue musicale* blamed the unsatisfactory orchestration of the Concerto as well as the small tone which the pianist drew from his instrument. This failure depressed Chopin greatly. How was he to live? Paris was swarming with pianists and pupils were hard to obtain. It is said that he intended going to America. (England, not America, is mentioned in his father's letters.) However, a turning-point in his fortunes was reached when he was introduced to the Rothschilds by Prince Valentin Radziwill. The power of the Paris Rothschilds was immense; failure was impossible for an artist whom they chose to patronize, and as soon as Chopin was heard by the fashionable world which centred round this great house his success was assured. The first important result of his conquest of the aristocratic *salons* was that he was asked to give lessons to the daughters of the noble families. In a short time his income from teaching became the envy of his less fortunate compatriots. It is no slight to Chopin to admit that social and snobbish considerations played a large part in his enormous success as a teacher. It was something of a novelty for the aristocracy to find a piano teacher who besides being a superb virtuoso and composer was also a gentleman who lent distinction to a *salon* and did not have to be admitted by the back door, the treatment commonly meted out to professional musicians, even of the standing of Rossini.

For his lessons Chopin received the high fee of twenty francs (the money being discreetly left on the mantelpiece!), and as he could give five or six lessons a day his money troubles vanished, and he was soon reckoned as one of the richest Poles in Paris. He moved from his lodging in the Boulevard Poissonnière to the

In Aristocratic Circles

Cité Bergère, and thence to an apartment in the Chaussée d'Antin. He had a man-servant (unheard of for musicians in those days) and a carriage, and his clothes, hats and gloves came from the most exclusive shops. When he chose to give a concert of his own (as in 1841) he could play for three-quarters of an hour and make six thousand francs. After his death most of his furniture was sent to Warsaw and there destroyed by the Russians in 1863 (together with his letters to his family, covering the period 1831–9), but there survive a handsome carved and gilt boot-cupboard, a beautifully fretted ivory comb and other things which allow us to re-create in imagination the atmosphere of luxury and distinction in which Chopin lived from the time when his position in Paris was established. At the beginning of 1833 he describes his situation thus:

I have gained the entrée to the first circles; I have my place among ambassadors, princes, ministers, but I really don't know by what miracle it has happened, for I have not pushed myself forward. All that is absolutely indispensable for me to-day, for on it *bon ton* depends: you at once have greater talent if you have been heard at the English or Austrian embassy; at once you play better if the Princess Vaudemont has taken you under her protection. . . . In Paris I enjoy the friend-ship of the musicians although I have only been among them a year . . . even men of the highest reputation dedicate their compositions to me before I dedicate mine to them. . . . You think perhaps I am making a fortune! My carriage and white gloves cost more than I earn; with-out them I should not be *de bon ton*. I am for the Carlists, I hate Louis-Philippe's men. I'm a revolutionary, money means nothing to me.

Without this fortunate change in his circumstances Chopin might well have foundered in Paris, for no one was less fitted than he, both physically and temperamentally, for the strain and vicissitudes of the concert virtuoso's life. He knew that the deli-cate nuances, the intimate poetry of his music and his playing were totally unsuited to large halls and crowded audiences. When this had been finally brought home to him as a result of continued failure to achieve a real success with the wider Parisian public, it cost him no regrets to withdraw from the arena, to follow his natural inclinations and reserve himself for those small circles of sympathetic listeners who spread his fame abroad quite as effec- tively as the largest audiences that were ever dominated by Liszt or Thalberg. Indeed his impenetrable seclusion finally called into existence during his own lifetime a Chopin legend which aroused public curiosity to the highest pitch on the rare occasions in later years when he did condescend to give a concert. 'In those days,' cried Liszt, 'it was not so much a question of the *School of Chopin* as the *Church of Chopin.*'

On 3rd April 1833 he took part in a concert arranged by the Herz brothers, playing with them and Liszt a quartet for eight hands on two pianos, and on 15th December he joined Liszt and Hiller in a performance, at the Conservatoire, of movements from Bach's Concerto for three pianos. After various appearances in 1834, both public and private, which were of no great im- portance, Chopin received a serious set-back on 4th April 1835, when he played at a grand concert given at the Italian Opera for the benefit of the Polish *émigrés*. Habeneck conducted; Nourrit, the famous tenor, sang songs by Schubert; Liszt and Ernst, the violinist, were there, and Chopin played his E minor Concerto and a duet with Liszt. The Concerto was received with perfunctory applause by the restless audience and even the well-disposed *Gazette musicale* could not hide the fact that Chopin's appearance had been a failure.

This defeat convinced Chopin that he was not cut out for the task of securing the attention and arousing the enthusiasm of large audiences. However, three weeks later, on 26th April, he played his *Andante spianato and Polonaise* (Op. 22) for piano and orchestra at Habeneck's benefit concert at the Conservatoire, and scored a rather cheap success with the brilliant Polonaise. Nevertheless he was not deceived, and never again did he expose himself to rebuffs from the general public in Paris. On 9th April 1836 he played a duet with Liszt at the latter's 'farewell concert,' and after this he was not heard in public again until 3rd March 1838, when he took part in a two-piano (eight hands) arrangement of Beethoven's seventh Symphony, which was played at his friend

Alkan's concert. Three weeks later he broke his self-imposed
rule in order to help a compatriot, Orlowski, and went to Rouen,
where he played the E minor Concerto with great success. But
properly speaking his last public appearance in Paris was on
26th April 1835; the remaining three concerts which he gave in
1841, 1842 and 1848 were really private affairs for which the
audience (never more than three hundred) was selected with great
care, and criticism, in the ordinary sense of the word, was excluded.

Chopin's aversion to appearing in public as a performer did
not prevent him from attending the concerts given by other
musicians, and he was always ready to make the acquaintance
of new musical personalities. At the end of 1832 John Field,
originator of the nocturne, came to Paris and gave two concerts,
the second being far less successful than the first. Chopin, who
had long desired to hear the Irishman and had been flattered by
being compared to him, was extremely disappointed when he at
last made his acquaintance; but it must be admitted that Field
was by this time long past his best. What Chopin thought of
him is to be gathered from a letter written by one of his friends,
Édouard Wolff, to Joseph Nowakowski. Wolff writes:

> Chopin and you are right, he plays like a beginner; no speed, no
> elegance, and he is incapable of executing difficulties. In a word,
> feeble. But he has his merits; steady German playing, easy-going,
> one, two, three. . . . He's an agreeable and decent fellow.

This is the only evidence we have of Chopin's opinion of Field
as a pianist, but it is certain that he thought highly of him as a
composer. From him he took the form and name of the small-
scale lyrical or elegiac piano piece to which Field gave the title
'Nocturne.' But having adopted the general idea of the nocturne,
Chopin transformed it into something very different from the
original model. Apart from one or two of his early efforts (such
as Op. 9, No. 2) Chopin's nocturnes belong, as regards their
musical content, to a world unknown to Field. A gulf separates
Field's pleasant pieces from specimens of the *genre* like Chopin's
Op. 27, No. 1, in C♯ minor, or his Op. 48, No. 1, in C minor.

During 1832 Chopin's name was made, as we have seen, by his playing of his own works in public concerts and in the aristocratic *salons* of Paris, and by the end of the year he could think of publishing the works he had brought with him from Poland. So far only his Op. 2 (the 'Là ci darem' Variations), published in Vienna in 1830, had been brought to the notice of the outside world. The music critic of the Leipzig *Neue Zeitschrift für Musik*, Robert Schumann, aged twenty-one, had saluted these Variations with an outburst of enthusiasm culminating in the words 'Hats off, gentlemen! A genius!' and, what was of greater practical value, had induced the brilliant young pianist Clara Wieck to perform them at Leipzig (July 1832), so that Chopin's future productions were awaited with some curiosity. He was able to make a beginning in December 1832, when his first sets of Mazurkas, Opp. 6 and 7, were published by Probst-Kistner of Leipzig. (The B♭ major Mazurka of Op. 7 soon achieved an extraordinary popularity.) During 1833 and 1834 Chopin had no difficulty in disposing of his numerous manuscripts which were already awaiting a publisher.

In France his works were brought out by Maurice Schlesinger, who besides being a music publisher owned the influential *Gazette musicale*. He naturally made sure that his journal did not fail to applaud each of Chopin's compositions as it appeared, and we must therefore beware of taking the *Gazette's* laudatory reviews too seriously. Schlesinger's rivals, such as Herz, who owned *La France musicale*, were scarcely likely to advertise their competitor's wares; one might speak of a conspiracy of silence, for Chopin's name was not mentioned at all in *La France musicale* until February 1838, when a venomous and sneering review of the A♭ major Impromptu appeared in its pages. The feud between Herz and Schlesinger brought a certain amount of unpleasantness for Chopin in its train, for it led to a duel between Schlesinger and one of Herz's pupils, and on 29th April 1834 Schlesinger was sued in the courts, Chopin being cited as one of the witnesses. M. Maurice Schlesinger lost his case and had to pay fifty francs damages.

Chopin was well paid for his compositions. He was a shrewd business man and had no intention of selling his work in the cheapest market. In this connection we obtain a glimpse of another side of his complex nature: the dreamer of dreams was capable of driving a hard bargain and of entering upon prolonged and prosaic discussions about money and terms of payment. When he was in such a mood he would come down to earth with a vengeance and sometimes say incredible things about his own manuscripts and those who he thought were trying to swindle him.

With his English publishers he had trouble from the beginning. Messrs. Wessel of Regent Street, who undertook to publish his works, had their own way of doing business; they understood the English market perfectly and found it advisable to provide these novel compositions of an unknown writer with attractive titles and other advertising devices which enraged Chopin when he heard of them. Thus the Mazurkas were described as *Souvenir de la Pologne*, the Nocturnes, Op. 9, as *Murmures de la Seine*, those of Op. 37 as *Les Soupirs* (in London in 1848 Chopin was often asked to play his 'second Sigh'!), the B minor Scherzo as *Le Banquet infernal*, the G minor Ballade as *La Favorite*, and so on. It was a surprise to the composer to learn that he had dedicated his F minor Concerto to 'Mrs. Anderson' (a London pianist) and his Mazurkas, Op. 50, to 'Mr. Henry Field, of Bath,' and that he had had Messrs. Wessel in mind in 1829, since his Fantasia, Op. 13, and other works had been 'expressly composed for their collection.' In truth, Wessel at first made nothing out of Chopin's works. He had to beg Liszt to play a few of them during his English concert tour of 1840, complaining that *he* had been taken in!

Chopin's compositions were, on the whole, very favourably received by the music critics in France and Germany. Schumann's notices in the *Neue Zeitschrift* showed undiminished enthusiasm, and it was only in the influential Berlin journal *Iris in the Realm of Music* that Chopin was attacked, by Ludwig Rellstab, who took a spiteful pleasure in tearing each new work to shreds. This went on until Rellstab realized that he stood alone and was making himself look foolish. He then changed his tone, and by 1839 was finding words of praise for what he had previously condemned. Speaking of the Nocturnes, Op. 9, he had said: 'In short, if one holds Field's charming romances before a distorting concave mirror, so that every delicate expression becomes coarse, one gets Chopin's work.' In 1839, however, he wrote of Op. 9, No. 2: 'It is gracefully ornamented and replete with subtle harmonic effects . . . and may rightly add to the fame of its celebrated composer.' In 1843 Rellstab came to Paris, furnished with a diplomatically worded letter of intro-duction to Chopin from Liszt. One wonders how he was received. (His paper had ceased to appear in 1841.)

At Ferdinand Hiller's invitation Chopin visited Aachen in the second half of May 1834 for the Lower Rhineland Music Festival. Mendelssohn came from Düsseldorf to meet them, and an interesting account of the occasion is to be found in his letters. Before returning to Paris, Hiller and Chopin paid flying visits to Düsseldorf and Coblenz. This was the only time that Chopin attended one of these festivals: in December 1848 Hiller wrote inviting him to come at Whitsuntide 1849, but the dying man could not think of such a journey.

From 1833 to 1835 a warm friendship existed between Chopin and Vincenzo Bellini, composer of *Norma* and *The Puritans*. They had much in common, both as men and musicians, but to speak of Chopin's 'indebtedness' to Bellini is to ignore historical fact. It is not difficult to show that the very elements in his style that Chopin is supposed to owe to the Italian—the luscious thirds and sixths, the curve of his melody and the *fioriture*—were already being exploited by Chopin long before he had heard a note of Bellini's music, or even his name.

Bellini and Chopin—in certain aspects of his work—may be said to have drawn their water from the same well. When one considers how little music other than that of the Italian operatic school was to be heard in Warsaw during Chopin's youth, it is indeed surprising that he was able to free himself to the extent he did from this powerful influence. The 'Bellini' argument is generally supported by reference to Chopin's early nocturnes and the slow movements of his concertos: a comparison between the *dates* and *places* of the production of Bellini's works, the times when Chopin could have become acquainted with them (or extracts from them), and the chronology of the compositions in which Bellini's influence is said to be discoverable, soon establishes the fact that although Chopin's debt to Italian opera in general was enormous, he owed nothing to Bellini *specifically*.[1] Even in later works like the *Barcarolle* there is no element which can be attributed to Bellini himself: the obvious Italianisms are not essentially different from those which we find in works Chopin had composed before leaving Warsaw. The story that Chopin expressed a wish to be buried near Bellini at Père-Lachaise is without foundation. It is more appropriate that his grave should, in fact, be close to that of Cherubini, whose musical treatises he studied assiduously and with profit.

[1] One writer on Chopin's 'Italianism' points out how the principal melody of the *Allegro de Concert* (published 1841) might have come straight from *The Puritans* (1835). Actually Chopin's melody dates from 1832. It might be added that a Bellini opera was not heard in Warsaw until ten years after Chopin had left.

CHAPTER V

MARIA WODZIŃSKA

WE HAVE noted Countess Delphine Potocka among Chopin's friends during his first years in Paris. Although he strenuously denied to Liszt and others that she had ever been more than a friend, after his death a story gained currency about his relations with her, based on an alleged scabrous correspondence between the two. In 1945 a Polish woman produced a typescript purporting to give extracts from the 'letters,' and for a time imposed her fake on the musical world. However, in 1961, a conference of experts called by the Chopin Institutes of Warsaw pronounced the documents spurious.

There is nothing to show that the countess's relations with Chopin went beyond a warm and sincere friendship. The arguments against the existence of a closer liaison are so strong (cf. footnote, p. 116) that we need not take it seriously, but pass on to Chopin's second affair—his ill-starred love for Maria Wodzińska. Thanks to the romantic imagination of a member of the lady's family, Count Wodziński, the whole story has been distorted out of recognition. *The Three Romances of Frederick Chopin*, a kind of novelette which Count Wodziński published in 1886, is unfortunately the basis of most accounts of this significant episode in Chopin's life; but now that the facts are known they may be presented without the usual sentimental and fanciful background.

Among the high-school pupils who lived with Nicholas Chopin in Warsaw were the three brothers, Anton, Casimir and Felix Wodziński, sons of a wealthy landowner of Sluzewo, an estate not far from the capital. Frederick Chopin formed a boyish friendship with these lads and sometimes spent his holidays at their home. On such occasions he saw a good deal of their sister Maria, who was nine years younger than he. He gave a few piano lessons to the little girl and remained on friendly terms

with the family. When the revolution broke out at the end of
1831 the Wodzińskis left Poland and went to live at Geneva,
while an uncle of theirs, Matthew Wodziński, settled down at
Dresden. Early in 1834 Chopin was invited to visit Geneva,
but he could not accept; on 18th June, however, he sent Maria
a copy of his newly published Waltz, Op. 18, with a dedication:
'To Mlle Marie, from her former teacher.' He had not seen her,
of course, since 1830, when she was a mere child, but during the
summer of 1835 the Wodzińskis came to join their uncle at
Dresden (Anton had gone to Paris), and Chopin met them there
in the following circumstances:

During that same summer of 1835 his father and mother made
their first excursion abroad—to Carlsbad, and after spending a
week or two with the Marquis de Custine at Enghien, Chopin
hastened to join them there. They all met on 16th August and
spent a happy month together—it was the last time that Chopin
was to see his parents—and in the second week of September they
went to Tetschen, where for a few days they were the guests of a
rich and cultivated family, the Thun-Hohensteins. On 14th
September Nicholas and Justyna Chopin left for Poland, but
Frederick stayed on until the 19th. He was in excellent spirits.
On the 15th he wrote out for the Thun-Hohenstein ladies his
splendid A♭ major Waltz, later published as Op. 34, No. 1.
Afterwards he travelled to Dresden accompanied by one of the
sons of the family and put up at the Stadt Gotha Hotel. Count
Thun-Hohenstein describes Chopin's visit as 'strictly incognito,'
and so indeed it was. One of the royal princesses, Louise, wrote
him several notes asking him to play to her and met with an absolute refusal. The fact is that Chopin had no time for any one but
the Wodzińskis. As soon as he arrived he had gone to visit
them and had been thunderstruck by the change time had wrought
in the little girl Maria: she was now a most attractive and accomplished young woman. In Geneva the poet Slowacki had fallen
in love with her and had been inspired to write one of his finest
poems, *In Switzerland*, and she had made a deep impression on the
future emperor of the French, Napoleon III. She had Italian

blood in her veins, which may account for her dark, languorous
eyes and insinuating ways.

With Chopin it was almost a case of love at first sight, although
once again, as with Constantia Gladkowska, he did not express
himself in words, but rather let his music be the interpreter of his
feelings. Maria was an excellent pianist,[1] and the two young
people spent many blissful hours under the indulgent eye of
Countess Wodzińska and the amiable old uncle who has, quite
unjustifiably, been transformed by some writers into the 'wicked
uncle' of a fairy-tale. On 22nd September Chopin gave Maria
a card on which he had written the first bars of the E♭ major
Nocturne, Op. 9, accompanied by the significant words 'Soyez
heureuse,' and a day or two later he composed (or at any rate wrote
out) for her the famous A♭ major Waltz (published as Op. 69,
No. 1). The legends associated with the improvisation of this piece
at the moment of Chopin's departure are without foundation.

When he left Dresden the Wodzińskis missed him sorely, but
there is no indication that any one save Maria's mother guessed
how far he had surrendered himself to this new passion and what
hopes he was already beginning to build upon his cordial reception by the girl's family. An old Warsaw friend, Mme Linde,
was at Dresden on 22nd September, and she may have noticed
something, for later, when Chopin's sisters were trying to find
out what their brother intended doing during the summer of 1836,
she was able to hint knowingly that he would return to Dresden
'... if certain persons are there. Oh, we know Maria has won his
heart, but, of course, you and I, madame, who know him ...'

The misinterpretation of a paragraph in the *Neue Zeitschrift für
Musik* and of a passage in one of Mendelssohn's letters has caused
some confusion in the story of Chopin's movements at this time.
He left Dresden on 26th September and arrived that night at
Leipzig, putting up at the Hôtel de Saxe. Although he stayed
a week it was only at the last moment that he saw Mendelssohn
and Schumann. They met at the house of Clara Wieck's

[1] In March 1843 she appeared at a concert in Warsaw, playing a
Chopin ballade 'in really masterly fashion and with great talent.'

father, and Chopin's playing of his nocturnes and studies aroused the enthusiasm of all who heard him. For his part he was full of admiration for Clara Wieck, 'the only woman in Germany who can play my music.' Next day he returned to Paris via Heidelberg, where he called on the parents of his pupil., A. Gutmann. Unfortunately he fell ill while there and was looked after by Mme Diller and her sister. He made the great mistake of hiding his illness from his parents and by so doing gave colour to the rumours that began to fly about when, for weeks after his return to Paris, no news was heard of him. On 8th January 1836 the Warsaw *Courier* announced:

We wish to inform the many friends and admirers of the eminent talent of the virtuoso, Frederick Chopin, that the report of his death which has been circulating during the last few days is without foundation.

What were the Wodzińskis, who were now in Poland, to think of this? How deeply interested they were is revealed by Nicholas Chopin's letter of 9th January:

MY DEAR CHILD, MY GOOD LAD,

Never was a letter so eagerly, so impatiently awaited as the one we have just received. For more than three weeks the rumour has been going round. . . . M. Wodziński was here before the Christmas holiday . . . by his eagerness in asking for news of you we saw he had heard the rumour, and under pretext of waiting for the post to see whether you would send news of Antoine, he put off his departure for two days.

Here we have an explanation of the ultimate ruin of Chopin's hopes; not family pride but common prudence governed the attitude of Maria's father and uncle towards him, for if the rumour of his death proved to be false, his serious illness was a fact which parents with any sense of responsibility could not overlook. Mme Wodzińska was not so cautious, and if she did not encourage him outright she nevertheless allowed him to live in a fool's paradise instead of making him realize, before it was too late, that there was little chance of the men of the family being reconciled to the idea of Maria's becoming the wife of a man whose health gave cause for anxiety. Maria herself appears to

have been strangely passive in the matter; her letters to Chopin
are quite negative in character; they are merely amiable; there is
no life or warmth in them at all. Was she unaware of the depth
of Chopin's feelings towards her or was she simply following the
current convention which demanded the greatest discretion and
reserve from young ladies when writing to men?

On 28th July 1836 Chopin joined the Wodzińskis at Marien-
bad. Mme Wodzińska was there with her daughters only, the
father and sons being away, and for the moment Chopin's happiness was untroubled. Maria painted his portrait, and the whole
of August was spent in walks and music-making. By the end
of the month he still had not declared himself, and instead of
returning to Paris he followed the Wodzińskis back to Dresden.
At this time he presented her with copies of two of his recently
written *Études*, Op. 25, Nos. 1 and 2, and composed the song *The
Ring*, whose words are curiously prophetic ('I loved you always but
you became another's wife'). At last, on 9th September, at the 'grey
hour' (twilight) he proposed and was accepted, Mme Wodzińska
making it a condition that nothing should be revealed until she
had brought her husband and uncle round to her way of thinking.
In the meantime Chopin was to submit to a period of probation;
he was to take the greatest care of his health ('Keep well; everything depends on that'), and avoid the fatigue of late nights in
the Parisian *salons*; and Mme Wodzińska ended: 'I bless you,
from the bottom of my heart like a loving m . . .' (mother).

Confident that his future happiness was assured, Chopin left
Dresden on 11th September and spent a day with Schumann
at Leipzig before returning to Paris. He played to him his
two new studies. Schumann has left a vivid description of the
occasion (see p. 121). But once in Paris he found it next to
impossible to keep his promise about 'early to bed,' and Mme
Wodzińska was not slow to upbraid him. She and her husband
had called upon the Chopins in Warsaw, a sure sign that Count
Wodziński was not absolutely opposed to the engagement, and
Maria presented them with a lithograph of the water-colour
portrait she had painted ('Maria Wodzińska to his parents, in

gratitude for their gracious kindness'). Chopin's mother wrote
in support of Mme Wodzińska's grievance: 'She told me that
you had not kept your given word' and did her best to make
Frederick realize that he was under observation. Alas! he took
little notice. During the winter of 1836–7 he was down again
with influenza. This must have settled matters as far as the
Wodziński menfolk were concerned, and Mme Wodzińska was
left to extricate herself from an awkward situation. She did so
by simply not answering Chopin's letters. He sent gifts to their
home, Sluzewo; Christmas and New Year came and went, but
no letter reached him. At last, on 25th January 1837, Mme
Wodzińska wrote a cold, embarrassed letter, avoiding all mention of the engagement and saying nothing of the family's plans
for the coming spring and summer. Maria's postscript is quite
colourless: Chopin must have known that something was wrong.
But it was not in his nature to assert himself as an ordinary man
would have done, when his happiness was at stake. Instead of
demanding an explanation he merely attempted to find out by
broad hints when and where he might hope to see the family
again. He received no satisfaction, however, for the Wodzińskis
felt it would be diplomatic to stay where they were, and in a
miserable state of mind and body he allowed himself to be persuaded to make a trip to London with his friend Camille Pleyel.
On his return he gave a final hint to Mme Wodzińska: 'I thought
I might go on from London to Germany [i.e. Dresden, if they
were there], but I have come back home; the season is coming
to an end and will probably end for me in my room.' This was
the end, too, of all his hopes. He received a few more laconic
letters from Countess Wodzińska, but the subject of the 'grey
hour' was quietly dropped. In 1840 Maria became engaged to
Joseph Skarbek — son of the Frederick Skarbek after whom
Chopin was named—and on 24th July 1841 she became the
Countess Skarbkowa. The marriage was unhappy and ended
in a divorce in 1848. Maria's second husband, Wladyslaw
Orpiszewski, was, like Chopin, a consumptive, but he lived
for many years. Maria Orpiszewska died in 1896. His rejection,

and especially the manner of it, was a bitter blow to Chopin. He gathered together all the letters he had received from the Wodzińskis and made of them a packet on which he wrote: 'Moja Bieda'—My Misery. This was discovered among his papers after his death. In later years he had plenty of hard things to say about his former friends ('imbeciles and heartless fools'). As for the *Farewell Waltz*, he gave copies of it to several of his Parisian lady-friends, which shows that the depression caused by his disappointment was not lasting.

There is no need to assume that considerations of family pride caused Count Wodziński to withhold his consent to the marriage: he knew quite well that the wife of Frederick Chopin would have her place in the most distinguished society in Paris. What weighed most with him was the question of Chopin's health, and in the end he was proved to be right. The only one who could be blamed was Mme Wodzińska, and then only for having been too hasty in encouraging Chopin. It will be noticed that Maria herself has scarcely been mentioned in this account, but that is hardly surprising. As the daughter of a noble Polish family she was absolutely ruled by her parents and did not question their right to arrange her life for her. Convention forbade her to reveal her feelings, so that we have no means of telling for certain whether she returned Chopin's love with an ardour equal to his. She remains a somewhat shadowy figure in his life-story and was soon to be supplanted by a woman of incomparably greater fascination—George Sand.

It was during the anxious waiting period of the summer of 1837 that Chopin paid his first visit to England. His friend Camille Pleyel noticed that he was looking ill and worn, and persuaded him to accompany him to London for a fortnight. On their arrival they were met by Stanislas Kozmian, one of Chopin's Polish acquaintances, who joined with Pleyel in attempting to cheer Chopin up. In a letter to his family Kozmian shows how they set about it:

Chopin has been here for two weeks incognito. He knows no one and does not wish to know any one but me. I spend the whole day with him and sometimes even the whole night, as yesterday. He is here with Pleyel, famous for his pianos and for his wife's adventures. They have come to 'do' London. They are staying at one of the best hotels, they have a carriage, and in a word they are simply looking for the chance to spend money. So one day we went to Windsor, another to Blackwall,[1] and to-morrow we are off to Richmond. . . . I often go to the opera. Pasta was marvellous in *Medea* and *Romeo*,[2] but I did not see *Hildegonde* [2] because Chopin refuses to go to hear boring music. The concert for the Beethoven memorial was a failure. . . . Moscheles played a long concerto; Chopin says his playing is 'frightfully baroque.'

Chopin made no attempt to meet Moscheles and Mendelssohn at this concert, and during his fortnight's stay no one saw anything of him. He dined once at James Broadwood's house in Bryanston Square, being introduced to the family as 'Monsieur Fritz.' As soon as he touched the piano, however, his identity was disclosed: only one artist could evoke such poetry from the instrument; it must be, it was—Chopin!

At the end of July he returned to Paris. He was now in his twenty-eighth year. The eager, carefree youth who left Warsaw in 1830 had changed into a serious and self-reliant artist, calmly confident in his own powers and yet modest and unassuming. He had lost many of his illusions; seven years spent in the most brilliant and corrupt society in Europe had made short work of them, and the final blow to his hopes of a happy marriage had left him empty-hearted and somewhat cynical. In this mood he was ready to take things as they came, and where was he more likely to find consolation for a vanished dream than in the intoxicating atmosphere of Paris—*his* Paris, where he lived not as an unknown exile, but as a prince among the *élite* of beauty and fashion?

[1] Celebrated at this time for the extraordinary 'fish dinners' to be obtained there.

[2] The three operas mentioned are by Cherubini, Bellini and Marliani (*Ildegonda*).

CHAPTER VI

CHOPIN AND GEORGE SAND

IN relating the story of Chopin's liaison with George Sand it is no longer necessary, at this time of day, to rake up from the biographies and commentaries written during the late Victorian period all the spiteful abuse and cruel words which were then showered upon the head of that 'wicked woman' or to edify the reader with specimens of the kind of whitewashing which her champions have performed on her behalf. We are not concerned to point a moral, nor are we called upon, as was, for example, Frederick Niecks, writing during the 1880s, to skate carefully over a 'doubtful' episode in our hero's career. The position to-day is surely this: Chopin and George Sand belong to history; we are interested in both of them as human beings and in him more particularly as a unique musician. In considering their relationship it will be well to bear the following points in mind:

The accusation which has most readily sprung to the lips of those who regard George Sand as Chopin's evil genius is 'Hypocrite!' and it is difficult to acquit her of the charge *as a writer*. But because she wrote like a hypocrite in later years when, under the eye of her adored son, Maurice (a man who hated Chopin), she compiled her *Story of my Life*, it does not necessarily follow that she had acted in bad faith when she gave free rein to her passionate impulses in 1838. Take for example the following passage which 'explains' why she began to live with Chopin: 'One duty more in my life already so full and so laden with weariness seemed to give me a better chance of attaining to the austerity to which I felt drawn with a kind of religious enthusiasm.' This may well strike the reader as a piece of nauseating hypocrisy. but it is fairly certain that no such calculations did, in truth, influence her relations with Chopin, and by writing like this George Sand unwittingly placed a deadly weapon into her

enemies' hands. In short, one can never trust her memoirs when
it is a question of analysing her motives: when she sat down to
write them, she felt herself under the necessity of living up to her
reputation as a writer and a thinker, and she could not resist the
temptation to 'preach.' Hence many of the simplest and most
natural things she did in her younger days are explained and
justified by long-winded and pompous arguments which convince no one. Moreover, it should not be overlooked that when
Chopin's early biographers had recourse to George Sand's published correspondence they could not know that the precious
Maurice had tampered with his mother's letters and had suppressed many important passages which tended to show that
between 1838 and 1846 she and Chopin had led a happy life
together, a life about which there was nothing sordid or mean.
One can only hope to reach something approaching the truth in
this story by leaving aside the tittle-tattle and hearsay of 'mutual
friends.' When the lies, distortions and spite have been cleared
away there remains abundant proof of the genuine love and devotion which united the pair; and although the end of the story
was tragic for Chopin, his life was enriched by the experience of
a great love which gave a finer and deeper poetry to his music.

At the time she came into Chopin's life George Sand was
thirty-two and had already crammed into that brief space of time
more adventure and experience of the world than would normally
fall to the lot of two or three ordinary mortals. Unhappily
married at eighteen to a dull, unsympathetic husband, Casimir
Dudevant, she had soon grown weary of the monotonous existence
she was forced to lead at Nohant, their country house near Château-
roux, in the Berry province of France, and in 1831 had come to
Paris resolved to put into practice the idea of total freedom which,
as we have seen, was a common currency among the young
romantic set of the capital. 'What I want,' she wrote to her
mother, 'is not society, noise, theatres, clothes . . . it 's liberty.
Here I can go out when I like, at ten o'clock or midnight, that 's
my business.' Such an attitude implied, naturally, a series of
love affairs of varying duration and importance, but whatever

judgment one may pass upon the Baroness Dudevant for her unusual outlook and its consequences, one cannot deny that she was at least sincere in her belief that genius places its owner above all moral and social laws and that a truly artistic life is, indeed, incompatible with the conditions of an ordered existence. This, as René Doumic points out, 'is rubbish. An irregular life is neither the cause nor the mark of genius: all the rag-tag and bob-tail of Bohemia are there to prove that if this mode of existence cannot create genius, it is, on the other hand, quite capable of paralysing talent.'

Left to fend for herself in Paris, Mme Dudevant plunged un-restrainedly into the swirling flood of literary and artistic activity. For a time she wore men's clothes in order to emphasize her independence and to enable her to mix freely with men, but too much stress should not be laid on this temporary pose. Suddenly she found that she could write, and almost before she was aware of it she had become one of the foremost novelists of the day with a European reputation (or notoriety). To-day the works which first brought her fame and money are unreadable and unread, but when they appeared, *Indiana* (1831) and *Lélia* (1833) created an immense sensation by their thinly disguised attacks on the accepted social institutions, chiefly marriage, and in a very short time the name of George Sand (the pen-name she adopted for the publication of *Indiana*) was associated in the minds of the guardians of public morals with libertinism, revolution and the break-up of family life. In England she was regarded with peculiar horror: already in 1837 a pamphlet was published attacking the 'immorality' of her early novels, and later she did not fail to appear in *Punch*, waving the banner of socialism and revolution.

Her Venetian escapade with the poet Alfred de Musset during the winter of 1833–4 had been the sensation of the season. True to type, both partners had lost no time in making literature out of their joys and sufferings. It is too easy, however, to jump to the conclusion that men and women living in such a theatrical and unreal atmosphere must have been insincere in their emotions.

They were not; they were in dead earnest, and we shall do them an injustice if we do not take into account the power of the imagination over such a woman as George Sand in her dealings with exceptional men like Musset and Chopin. She deceived no one more than herself, and on looking back over her career we must smile to think that it was precisely when she was leading the life of a steady, humdrum bourgeois that she produced that portion of her work which alone has a chance of surviving.

During the summer of 1836 the legal processes of her separation from her husband were completed. She was left completely mistress of her actions and of a respectable fortune which included the Nohant estate; she was likewise given the custody of her two children, Maurice and Solange. She had by this time met Liszt and was very thick with the Countess d'Agoult, Liszt's mistress and the mother of his three children, the second of whom, Cosima, afterwards became Wagner's wife. Mme d'Agoult's *salon* at the Hôtel de France in the Rue Lafitte was the rendezvous of all the literary and musical celebrities. It was here in the autumn of 1836, that is, just after he had become engaged to Maria Wodzińska, that Chopin was introduced to George Sand by Liszt himself. If Chopin's friends are to be believed, his first impression was distinctly disagreeable. Since his thoughts were occupied by Maria he may well have been repelled at first by a personality so different from that of his 'ideal' of the moment, and what he had heard of George Sand's adventures would tend to heighten this feeling. It did not last, however. 'Lélia' had not the kind of beauty to attract a man immediately; her features were regular, but heavy, her complexion was swarthy and dull, and her short, compact figure lacked grace. But she had beautiful arms and hands, and dark eloquent eyes, and a strange charm which many men found irresistible. In society she often gave the impression of being stupid, for she had none of the Parisienne's gift for witty repartee; but she knew how to listen, and if she spoke it was because she had something to say. She was as accomplished as most women (one of the best portraits of Chopin was made by her), and her interest in music was genuine. In

Chopin

this connection one of her complaints (in 1825) against her dull husband is of interest: 'I saw that you did not like music and I ceased to play because the sound of the piano drove you away. I longed for a good piano.' It has often been denied that she had any technical knowledge of music. Nevertheless she was able, in 1850, to write out a whole set of Berry folk-tunes (including a bourrée 'Chopin was particularly fond of'), which she sent to Paris to a conductor, M. Vaillant. She was capable of playing Chopin's easier pieces and made copies of a number of them.

Very little is known of the early days of her acquaintance with Chopin, but we have details of a soirée which he gave in December 1836 at which she was one of the small number of guests. Joseph Brzowski, who was also invited, writes:

Madame G. Sand, dark, dignified and cold . . . regular features, calm, or rather inanimate in their expression, in which one could only perceive intelligence, reflection and pride. Her dress fantastic (obviously proclaiming her desire to be noticed), composed of a white frock with a crimson sash and a kind of white shepherdess's corsage with crimson buttons. Her dark hair parted in the middle, falling in curls on both sides of her face and secured with a ribbon around her brow. Nonchalantly she took her place on the sofa near the fireplace and, lightly blowing out clouds of smoke from her cigar, answered briefly but seriously the questions of the men sitting beside her. . . . After Liszt and he had played a sonata, Chopin offered his guests ices. George Sand, glued to her sofa, never quitted her cigar for a moment.

And what of Chopin? Is there any justification for the common notion that George Sand completely dominated him and that he was, as it were, the passive victim of a scheming and unscrupulous woman? The answer must be no, none at all. In 1836 we see him as a man of exceptionally slight physique. He had fair hair, blue-grey eyes [1] and irregular but distinguished features, his nose being markedly aquiline. His whole person was characterized by refinement and high distinction. He was

[1] For once Liszt was right—confirmed by an official description of Chopin, below which is the composer's signature. In later years every one 'remembered' his eyes were brown.

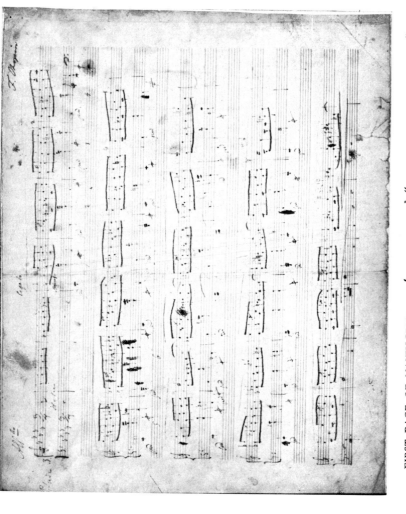

FIRST PAGE OF MANUSCRIPT OF 'STUDY IN D♭' ('TROIS NOUVELLES ETUDES')

undoubtedly a dandy, but it has yet to be proved that dandyism in men is always the result of effeminacy. In any case his effeminacy was superficial, not fundamental. In him we have the unusual spectacle of a proud, reserved and passionate spirit housed in a frail and ailing body. Again and again those who knew him expressed their conviction that his spirit consumed his flesh and that something of his life was burnt away every time that he surrendered himself to the torrent of passionate music which flowed from the piano when he abandoned himself to his inspiration. Jane Welsh Carlyle particularly felt this when she heard him in 1848. Chopin is a tragic, not a merely pathetic figure. Owing to his almost impenetrable reserve where all but his Polish intimates were concerned, scarcely any of those who have described his character ever penetrated beneath the charming and polished exterior. The gentle, amiable and ineffectual Chopin of a thousand legends never really existed. Instead there was a man incapable, indeed, of standing up to life in a sturdy, forthright manner, but intelligent, exacting, intolerant, shrewd and sarcastic, unexpectedly resolute and implacable on occasions, and not above being downright coarse when in a fury. In his liaison with George Sand he had none of the attributes of the average aggressive and enterprising lover, but there were keen observers who realized that her apparent masculine domination was very deceptive. The poet Mickiewicz, who saw them at close quarters, stated categorically: 'Chopin is her evil genius, her moral vampire, her cross; he tortures her and will probably end by killing her.' There is doubtless a certain amount of exaggeration in this, but Mickiewicz's opinion is none the less highly significant.

George Sand quickly submitted to the fascination of Chopin's personality and music. Perhaps she saw in his polite reserve a challenge to her own powers, which so many other men had acknowledged. She began to see much of him and in April 1837 invited him to Nohant with Liszt and his countess. He did not go; but as soon as he knew that his engagement to Maria Wodzińska would come to nothing, he had no longer any reason for keeping her at a distance, and their friendship quickly ripened into something deeper. One day she sent him a note: 'I adore you. George.' He treasured it in his pocket-book to the end of his life. During the summer of 1838 she frequently came to Paris, living almost incognito as Mme Dupin in an attic in the Rue Lafitte, and Chopin saw her constantly. When he hesitated to take the final step she wrote to his friend, Albert Grzymala, an extraordinary letter, a pamphlet in fact, setting forth the situation as she saw it, and enlisting Grzymala's aid to overcome Chopin's last scruples. The gist of it was: 'If he still loves this other person [Maria Wodzińska], very well, I withdraw, but if not . . .' This letter is a perfect example of George Sand's habit of talking to convince herself that what she is saying is true. Her weakness in this respect is so obvious that it is unreasonable to accuse her of cold-blooded hypocrisy. Chopin required little persuasion, and he soon loved her with long-pent-up and ardent passion.

Circumstances compelled them to get away from Paris as quickly as possible. George Sand was directly threatened by the lover whom she had thrown aside for Chopin, one Mallefille, a dramatist who, so far from suspecting what was going forward, had just published a rhapsodical effusion: 'To M. Frédéric Chopin, on his Polish Ballade,' offering it to the composer 'as a proof of my affection for you and my sympathy for your heroic country.' When Mallefille's eyes were opened a duel between him and his 'harmonious rival' could scarcely be avoided. One day he chased George Sand down the street as she was leaving Chopin's apartment, and if she had not been able to escape in a cab he would have attacked her there and then. Such scandal and violence were the last thing that Chopin could bear. He would be made the laughing-stock of his elegant friends in the Faubourg Saint-Germain, who had no idea that he was seriously involved with 'that dreadful woman.'

Other reasons were not lacking for an immediate departure from Paris. George Sand's son Maurice was suffering from rheumatism and needed a holiday in a dry, warm climate, and

Chopin's health was beginning to show disturbing signs of deterioration. Having heard, from people who had never been there, that Majorca was an ideal spot for sunshine and fresh air, for writing, studying and love-making, they decided to spend the winter and spring of 1838–9 on what they imagined to be an enchanted island. The arrangements were made in great secrecy: only two or three trusty friends knew what was afoot. On 18th October George Sand left Paris quietly; Chopin was due to join her at Perpignan on 29th or 30th October. In order to procure funds for the expedition he sold his Preludes to Camille Pleyel for 2,000 francs, receiving 500 francs on account, and borrowed another 1,000 francs from his friend, the banker Leo. Most of the Preludes were already in existence (No. 7 was given to Delphine Potocka in 1836), but a few were still needed to complete the cycle of twenty-four, and these (certainly Nos. 2 and 4) were written in Majorca.[1] In excellent spirits, 'fresh as a rose and rosy as a turnip,' says George Sand, Chopin made his appearance at the appointed time at Perpignan. He was looking forward to a long-needed rest from the fatigues of Paris. He had brought with him his volumes of Bach, his own unfinished manuscripts and plenty of music paper, and was no doubt already dreaming of the music he was going to write. From Perpignan they made their way to Barcelona, and at five in the evening of 7th November 'Mme Dudevant, married; M. Maurice, her son, minor; Mlle Solange, her daughter, minor; and M. Frédéric Chopin, artist,' with the maid, Amelia, went on board *El Mallorquin* which was to take them to Palma. They had only a vague notion of what they would find there, but the sea was calm and the night warm, and the steersman sang quietly to himself as the ship made her way through the darkness.

[1] A. Gutmann was simply lying when he told Niecks that he had copied out *all* the preludes long before Chopin left Paris. Almost every statement made by Gutmann in later years can be proved to be false.

CHAPTER VII

MAJORCA AND NOHANT

THE travellers were enchanted with their first sight of Majorca, but no sooner had they set foot on shore than they found unpleasant reality staring them in the face. There was nowhere for them to stay, no inn or hotel, and it was with great difficulty that they managed to find a couple of depressing and noisy rooms above a barrel-maker's workshop. Yet they felt so cheerful in the warm sunshine that they made light of their troubles. George Sand could write light-heartedly on 13th November:

When you arrive here you begin by buying a piece of land, then you build a house and order the furniture. After that you obtain the government's permission to live somewhere and finally at the end of five or six years you begin to open your luggage and change your shirt, while awaiting permission from the customs to import shoes and handkerchiefs.

About the same time Chopin was writing to Fontana:

I am at Palma among palms, cedars, cactuses, olive-trees, oranges, lemons, aloes, figs, pomegranates, etc.: everything the Jardin des Plantes has in its hothouses. The sky is like turquoise, the sea like emeralds the air as in heaven. In the daytime, sunshine; every one goes about in summer clothes and it's hot: at night, guitars and songs for hours on end. Enormous balconies with vines overhead; Moorish walls. In a word, a superb life! . . . I am close to what is most beautiful. . . . I feel better.

After a few days they found a partly furnished house in the village of Establiments near Palma, and a further offer of accommodation in the deserted monastery of Valldemosa, six miles away in a wild and romantic spot. George Sand writes on 15th November:

I have also reserved a cell, i.e. three rooms and a garden, for thirty-five francs a year in the monastery of Valldemosa—a huge and splendid deserted convent in the mountains. Our garden is strewn with oranges and lemons; the trees are cracking beneath their burden. . . . Vast cloisters of the most beautiful architecture, a delightful church, a cemetery with a palm-tree and a stone cross like the one in the third act of *Robert le Diable*. The only inhabitants of the place, besides ourselves, are an old serving-woman and the sacristan, our steward, doorkeeper and major-domo rolled into one. I hope we shall have some ghosts. My cell door looks on to a huge cloister, and when the wind slams the door it rumbles like gunfire through the convent. You see that I shall not lack poetry and solitude.

For the time being, however, they remained at their villa, Son-Vent; but while George Sand was writing so cheerfully trouble was brewing for them. A day or two previously their little party had gone for a long walk, three leagues, over very rough ground, and on the way back they had to fight against a violent wind which completely exhausted Chopin, whose lungs were weak. Almost at once he was down with acute bronchitis, and this before they had been there a fortnight. Conditions in the villa were wretched. The furniture was primitive, they had to fend for themselves as far as food was concerned, and to make matters worse the weather suddenly broke and the rain poured down. The bare plaster walls swelled like sponges, causing a deadly chill inside the house, while outside there was steaming heat. In the foul stench of the braziers which they lit to keep themselves dry Chopin began to cough alarmingly. Three local doctors were called in. All they could suggest was that the patient should be bled, but George Sand would not hear of this and tended him in her own way. He was indeed miserable: the postal service was so bad that he had received nothing from Paris, and there was no sign of the piano which Pleyel had promised to send him. Thanks, no doubt, to the gossip of the three doctors the rumour soon flew round that Chopin was consumptive, and in an instant he found himself an object of horror and fear to the local inhabitants. When the news came to the ears of Señor Gomez, the owner of the house, he insisted that the polluter of his dwelling should quit it forthwith and pay for replastering and whitewashing. The bed and bedding would be burnt and paid for, that was the law. More dead than alive, Chopin was removed to the French consul's house for a few days until the monastery cells could be got ready, and on 14th December George Sand wrote:

He is recovering, and I hope he will soon be better than before. His goodness and patience are angelic.[1] We are so different from most of the people and things around us . . . our family ties are only more strengthened by it and we cling to each other with more affection and intimate happiness.

On the same day Chopin wrote to Fontana:

I have heard only to-day that the piano has been put on board a cargo vessel at Marseilles. . . . I suppose the piano will spend the winter in the port . . . and I shall have the pleasure of packing it up and sending it off again. In the meantime my manuscripts sleep, but I can't. . . . To-morrow I'm off to that wonderful monastery at Valldemosa, to write in the cell of some old monk who perhaps had in his soul more fire than I, but stifled it, stifled and put it out because he had it in vain. . . . I expect to send you my Preludes and the Ballade soon. Go and see Leo. Don't tell him I'm ill or he'll get alarmed about his 1,000 francs.

(In all his letters Chopin insists that his correspondents should say as little about him as possible to his Parisian acquaintances. He knew only too well what comments his disappearance had caused and what remarks would greet the news of the fiasco of the 'honeymoon.')

On 15th December they took possession of their new quarters, and in spite of discomforts were not too badly off. Had Chopin been strong and well they would have enjoyed themselves. The two children were in their element, and George Sand was able to make progress with her latest book, *Spiridion*, and to give lessons to little Solange. Chopin had hired a poor local piano and set to work to complete the Preludes. On one sheet (dated 28th

---

[1] Suppressed by Maurice Sand. When she came to write her *Story of my Life* George Sand said: 'The poor great artist was a detestable patient'!

November) he had written down Nos. 2 and 4, as well as the Mazurka in E minor, Op. 41. He also finished the F major Ballade, giving it a different ending from what it had had when he played it to Schumann in 1836. He may have written other preludes, but we have no evidence of that. It is very unlikely that the more elaborate preludes or those containing elements of virtuosity, such as Nos. 8, 16 or 24, were written in such conditions with the aid of such a poor piano.

We shall not repeat here the too celebrated story of the composition of the 'Raindrop' Prelude in melodramatic circumstances. If a prelude *was* written in anything like the circumstances described by George Sand many years later, it was probably No. 15, which best fits the novelist's highly coloured account.

Here is a letter from Chopin to Fontana:[1]

PALMA,
28th December 1838.

Or rather Valldemosa, a few miles away. Between the cliffs and the sea, a huge deserted Carthusian monastery where, in a cell with doors larger than gates ever were in Paris, you can picture me, my hair uncurled, without white gloves, as pale as ever. The cell is shaped like a high coffin, the enormous vaulting covered with dust, the window small; outside the window are orange-trees, palms, cypresses, opposite the window my bed on straps, under a Moorish filigree rosette. Close to the bed an old, square, grubby writing-desk which I can scarcely use; on it a leaden candlestick (a great luxury here) with a candle in it, Bach, my scrawls and someone else's old papers . . . silence . . . you can yell . . . still silence. In short, I'm writing to you from a queer place. . . .

I can't send you the Preludes yet; they're not finished. I feel better now and I'll hurry up. . . . What's my servant doing? Give the *concierge* twenty francs from me as a New Year's present when you get that money and pay the chimney-sweep. . . . The moon is marvellous to-night; I've never seen it like this before. But, but! you write that you have sent me a letter from home; I've neither seen it nor received it. . . . Nature here is kind, but the people are rogues. They

---

[1] Translated from the original in the author's collection.

Chopin

never see strangers, so they don't know how much to charge; you can have oranges for nothing, but they make you pay fantastic sums for a trouser-button. But all that is a mere grain of sand compared with this sky, the poetry which everything breathes here and the colouring of this most wonderful scenery, still uncontaminated by the eyes of men. Few are those who have startled the eagles which daily soar over our heads.

It is clear that Chopin was not miserable during the whole of the time he spent at the monastery: he had his good and bad days. George Sand cooked all his meals herself and did what she could to make him comfortable, and in the middle of January the Pleyel upright piano was delivered. This was a blessed relief to Chopin, and on 22nd January he was able to send off the completed manuscript of the Preludes,[1] after which he finished the Polonaise in C minor, Op. 40, No. 2 (the famous one in A major was written before he left Paris), and began the Scherzo in C♯ minor. At the beginning of February he sent to Paris the fair copies of the second Ballade and the two Polonaises, Op. 40 (the first dedicated to Titus Woyciechowski and the other to Fontana —when they were published Titus's name was omitted). He was completely confined to the immediate neighbourhood of the monastery; only George Sand paid one or two courtesy visits to people at Palma, for whom she had letters of introduction, and showed herself once at the theatre. They were glad when the fine weather returned and allowed them to leave the island which they now loathed. Chopin could not have endured it much longer. From every point of view, sentimental and practical, their expedition had been, as George Sand admitted, 'a complete fiasco.' When they left on 13th February Chopin's health was much worse than when he had arrived. Neither he nor George Sand had accomplished half of what they had hoped to do; only the children had benefited by the trip. To set the

[1] The letter to Fontana announcing the dispatch of the Preludes is always shown as being dated 12th January, i.e. before the Pleyel had arrived. Actually the original is undated.

seal on their bad luck, the boat on which they returned to Barcelona carried a cargo of live pigs, the crossing was rough and
Chopin had a haemorrhage of the lungs which caused him to
lose a great deal of blood. He was half dead when they reached
port, and had to be transferred from the ship to a French sloop,
where the ship's doctor gave him proper attention and stopped the
bleeding. Such was the pitiful homecoming of the enthusiastic
couple who had set sail for the enchanted island three months
before.

After some days spent at Arenys de Mar, a village near Barcelona, they continued their journey to Marseilles, where they
decided to stay for some weeks, in order to give Chopin a chance
to recover from the effects of his ordeal. They put up at the
Hôtel de Beauveau, but George Sand discreetly arranged to have
her letters sent to the address of Dr. Cauvières, who was attending
Chopin. In spite of everything Chopin recovered quickly and
busied himself with the sale of his manuscripts, showing a talent
for involved negotiations and prolonged haggling that one would
scarcely have suspected. His letters (in Polish) to Fontana form
an amusing and revealing contrast with those which he wrote to
his publishers in Paris. For example, on 13th March he writes
thus of Pleyel, who had undertaken to publish the Preludes:

> I did not count on such a Jewish way of doing business on Pleyel's
> part, but since it is so, please hand him this letter . . . don't let
> Schlesinger take you in like Pleyel. . . . Scoundrels! And this
> Pleyel, my God, who adores me so! Perhaps he thinks I shan't return
> to Paris? I'll return sure enough, and both he and Leo shall receive
> their thanks from me!

Here is 'this letter' (now published for the first time): [1]

MONSIEUR C. PLEYEL,
                    PARIS.

I am vexed, my dear friend, that Fontana has been troubling you with
my affairs—I had considered myself authorized to entrust him with
that message for you because you had offered to publish my music.

---

[1] By kind permission of the owner, Miss S. Brookshaw.

I am writing this very day to tell him not to bother you any more with this business. I wrote two letters to you from Majorca and was grieved at receiving no reply. I learn from Fontana that you are still unwell and that grieves me still more than your silence. As for myself, at the time when I wrote I was dangerously ill; I can tell you that now I am out of danger and well on the way to recovery.

The piano remained behind at Palma. I have sold it, or practically sold it, for *twelve hundred francs*, which will be paid over to you by Messrs. Canut and Mugnerot, bankers at Palma, or by me, if it is to me that these gentlemen make payment. I have just written to tell them that if they have decided to keep this piano, as they more or less definitely announce, they are to pay the money over to you directly. I await their answer. Should they send the instrument back to me I will receive it here and have it dispatched to you. I expect to return to Paris when the fine weather comes; I am waiting for it here where the climate is mild and where I am completing my convalescence.

Au revoir, then, my dearest friend.

Yours devotedly,

F. CHOPIN.

Furious and impatient letters followed fast upon each other to the long-suffering Fontana, who was looking after his friend's affairs; he could hardly keep pace with Chopin's imperious instructions. Frederick was evidently making a rapid recovery. On 27th March he writes to his other obliging friend, Grzymala:

I am feeling much better and can thank you all the more warmly for the funds you have sent. . . . My love has just finished a most admirable article on Goethe, Byron and Mickiewicz. It will do you good to read it. I can see you enjoying it. And it is all so true . . . without any distortion or endeavour to bestow praise.

The presence of two such celebrities soon became known at Marseilles, and the local dilettanti began to seek them out; but George Sand was firm and the door remained closed to the inquisitive Marseillais. The little household kept to itself and relied on its own resources for entertainment. 'Luckily Chopin with his piano dispels boredom and brings back poetry to the house,' wrote George Sand. Only once did they show themselves to the Marseilles public—on 24th April, when Chopin

played the organ at the memorial service for his friend Adolphe
Nourrit, the celebrated tenor, who had committed suicide at
Naples. Chopin made no attempt to 'show off' on the wheezy
old organ, and the large congregation went away disappointed,
after having paid sixpence for their seats and heard a simple little
tune which any one might have played!

In May they made a short trip to Genoa (a place of bitter-sweet
memories for George Sand, who had been there with Musset in
1833) and then, after a rough return journey, travelled by easy
stages to Nohant, George Sand's country home, where they
were to spend the rest of the summer and complete Chopin's
convalescence.

Nothing is more distasteful in George Sand's memoirs than the
passages in which she explains away how Chopin came to be
installed at Nohant as a member of the family. She claims that
she 'felt alarmed at the task' which she was about to undertake,
i.e. of looking after him with maternal care and devotion, and
that it was only by a decree of fate that they drifted into a liaison
which lasted several years. It would have been well if she had
never written these pages, for they certainly appear to justify the
accusations of 'hypocrite and liar' which, when she is judged by
her *actions*, she does not in general deserve.

Everything goes to show that Chopin was her lover, in the
accepted sense of the word, only for the very briefest period, and
passion was replaced, on her side at least, by a calmer affection
to which she was pleased to give the name 'maternal.' With
Chopin it was otherwise. In spite of physical weakness he continued to love her intensely and jealously; his life was bound up
with hers; her presence was necessary to him, and when at last
fate separated them his life fell to pieces, the fountain of music
dried up within him, he was lost. We shall explain in some
detail, later, how that separation came about, and it will be seen
that cruel misunderstandings rather than deliberate design were
the cause of a break that was so tragic in its consequences. But
for the present let us return to sunny Nohant in the summer of
1839.

As soon as they arrived George Sand sent for her doctor, Dr. Gustave Papet, and had Chopin thoroughly examined. The worthy doctor declared that he was suffering from a chronic affection of the larynx and that what he needed was rest and fresh air. Thus reassured, Chopin could take stock of his new surroundings and settle down to work. He was delighted with Nohant at first and enthusiastic about its nightingales and flowers. But having always been accustomed to the bustle of Paris and the exhilarating atmosphere of its society, he soon became bored with the quiet, monotonous existence one led at Nohant and was forced to confess that he was 'not cut out for country life.' George Sand thus describes how they spent their time (15th June 1839):

We lead the same monotonous, quiet, gentle life. We dine in the open; friends come to see us, now one, now another; we smoke and chat, and in the evening when they have gone, Chopin plays to me at twilight, after which he goes to bed like a child at the same time as Maurice and Solange;

and on 15th August: 'He has a splendid piano and delights us from morning till evening. He has written some ravishing things since he has been here.'

Among many happy days, one especially, 19th June, stood out for George Sand; she noted it at the side of her window where, years before, she had written, in English, a poetical passage on the setting sun. As for Chopin, he was again in the right mood for composing. During this summer he wrote the first movement, the scherzo and the finale of the Sonata, Op. 35 (the funeral march had been composed long before), three Mazurkas of Op. 41, the F♯ major Impromptu and the G major Nocturne, Op. 37. He also spent some time correcting his copies of Bach, modestly and fearfully picking out what he judged to be the errors of Bach's editors.

When the autumn came round it was time to think of returning to Paris, where his pupils were awaiting him, and letters went off almost every day to Fontana, instructing him about this and that in connection with new rooms, furniture and fittings, and new clothes for Chopin himself. From these letters misleading generalizations have often been made; a man who has been out of town for over a year may surely ask his friend to buy him a hat, a waistcoat and trousers, and see that his room is decently papered, without being considered morbidly fussy and helpless. After much searching George Sand took rooms at 16 Rue Pigalle, a fashionable new quarter in those days, and Chopin was installed at 5 Rue Tronchet, some distance away. Nothing in Chopin's or George Sand's outward behaviour gave any clue to the relationship existing between them. To the outside world they were friends, colleagues; and Chopin's family were kept equally in the dark, George Sand being for them, as for every one else, 'Pani Domu'—the lady of the house. Indeed Chopin's father wrote: 'We are reassured now that you are so well looked after, as you tell us; but we should be curious to learn something of this intimate friendship.' As the winter advanced Chopin found his rooms in the Rue Tronchet too cold. He quietly moved to the Rue Pigalle, where George Sand lived in what Charles Gutzow described as 'a little enclosure in the heart of Paris, to love, to write and to scorn the world.' Here Chopin had his own quarters where he could receive his pupils and friends, and one of his first visitors was Ignace Moscheles, who had missed him in London in 1837. Chopin played him his new B♭ minor Sonata and other pieces, and Moscheles declared that now for the first time he understood his music. A few days later they both played at the court, at Saint-Cloud, before Louis-Philippe and his family, and Chopin especially was treated with great cordiality by the royal party. Moscheles also extracted from Chopin a promise to compose three short studies for the Piano Method which he and Fétis intended to publish. The studies, known as the *Trois Nouvelles Études*, were written before the end of the year. Moscheles received the autograph manuscripts as a souvenir of his association with the composer.[1]

In the summer of 1840 Chopin and George Sand did not go to

[1] In English concert programmes these studies are almost invariably described as posthumous works.

Nohant—her play *Cosima*, produced in April at the Comédie Française, had been a complete failure, and she could not afford to invite guests to a three months' stay at her country house—but during the remaining years until 1846 their programme did not vary: when the concert and teaching season was over they set off for Nohant and stayed there until October or early November, while guests joined them for a few weeks. Thus it comes about that Chopin's life for the next few years appears to be entirely uneventful; his two concerts in 1841 and 1842, the death of his father in 1844 and a visit from his sister Louise in the same year are the only happenings which deserve mention in a short biography. But it is precisely because his daily life was so undisturbed that his mental and spiritual life was free to develop unhindered, and during these tranquil years his genius came to splendid maturity in an almost unbroken series of masterpieces, nearly all of which were written at Nohant; for during the winter in Paris Chopin was too much taken up with his teaching and social engagements to be able to give himself to the exhausting task of filing and polishing his musical ideas until they satisfied his acute critical sense.

At Nohant, as in an English country house, the guests were not forced on each other's company; it is a waste of time to imagine how Chopin must have suffered by the presence of some of George Sand's less select friends. (As a matter of fact he got on very well with men like Louis Blanc, the prophet of socialism; these visitors treated Chopin with great deference and he was not inconvenienced by them at all.) Naturally he preferred the company of artists like Eugène Delacroix, who was one of the few people, other than Poles, to become intimate with him; or Pauline Viardot, a most accomplished member of the Garcia family, with whom he went through dozens of operas and music of all periods.

Delacroix's letters give an impression of life at Nohant during the summer of 1842:

When you are not assembled for dinner or lunch or billiards or for walks, you can go and read in your room or sprawl on your sofa. Every now and then there blows in through your window, opening on to the garden, a breath of the music of Chopin, who is at work in his room, and it mingles with the song of the nightingales and the scent of the roses. . . . I have endless conversations with Chopin of whom I am really very fond and who is a man of rare distinction. He is the truest artist I have ever met, one of the very few whom one can admire and value.

If he *had* to avoid some of the visitors, Chopin could do so without bad manners or unpleasantness; but alas! it was not always easy to escape the company of Hippolyte Châtiron, George Sand's loud-voiced half-brother, smelling of drink and full of revolting cordiality.

Those who have been so quick to denounce George Sand as the evil genius of Chopin's life would do well, before listening to the malicious gossip of those friends who never moved a finger to help the ailing man, to consider what he actually owed to her. His debt, and consequently that of the world of music, may be summarized thus:

From 1839 to 1846 he enjoyed complete exemption from material worries. His daily life was organized for him, leaving him free to devote himself to his pleasures and his art. At Nohant he had the best and sunniest room and was waited on hand and foot; he was never pressed to do what did not appeal to him. Think of Wagner's titanic struggle to win this freedom from care! Yet Chopin had it all without having to ask.

George Sand looked after his health with amazing devotion, and often when he was ill she made herself ill by nursing him. There exists a letter from her to his doctor, Molin, which gives but one example of the trouble she took when he was unwell, and we shall later quote one written by her to his sister Louise which shows the same womanly devotion. After her care and attention were withdrawn his fate was sealed, for she alone knew what he needed and could make him take the precautions necessary to preserve his life.

For Chopin the musician George Sand had a respect bordering on reverence. Never did she attempt to interfere with his work,

or presume to give him advice 'in the choice of his chords.' [1]
Besides all this there was something else which mere physical
comfort could not replace for Chopin: the presence near him of
someone who loved him and understood him, and who gave him
the warm feeling of companionship and security. These things
George Sand gave; if she did not 'inspire' him (his dream-
Poland did that!), she at least created the conditions in which
his genius was free to blossom forth, and every time we listen
to the F minor Ballade we might give a grateful thought to
the woman but for whom such works might never have been
written.

George Sand and he had in common far more intellectual
interests than has generally been acknowledged. It was he who
introduced her to Polish literature (an absolutely unexplored territory), of which he was an ardent student, and he translated for
her the works of Mickiewicz to enable her to write her essay
on *Goethe, Byron and Mickiewicz.* In December 1840 they both
followed the Polish poet's course of lectures on Slavonic literature at the Collège de France, and the celebrated Mme Sand
was applauded when she appeared in the lecture hall with
Chopin.

Only twice during this period, on 26th April 1841 and
21st February 1842, did Chopin play in public, before exclusive
audiences composed of members of the aristocracy and his pupils
and their friends. On these occasions, at Pleyel's rooms, he was
at his best: he had the stimulus of public performance, yet the
atmosphere was not that of an ordinary concert with a curious,
staring and perhaps indifferent audience, but of a private gathering
of well-bred people anxious to do homage to his genius and eager
to let him carry them away by the poetry of his playing. Liszt
published in the *Gazette musicale* a brilliant account of the first
concert, stressing the social rather than the musical side of it, and

[1] In this connection one's thoughts turn at once to poor Liszt, embarrassed by the tiresome exhortations of the Princess Sayn-Wittgenstein,
who had her own ideas on how his symphonies should end.

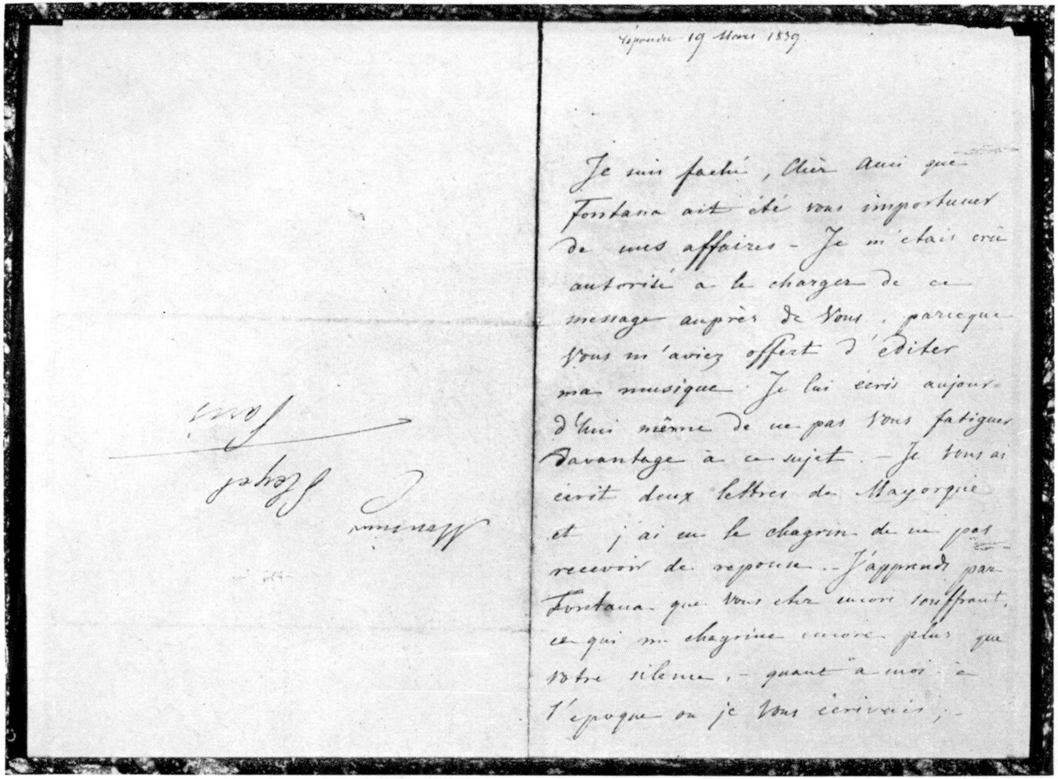
répondu 19 Mars 1839

Je suis fâché, Cher Ami que Fontana ait été vous importuner de mes affaires — Je m'étais cru autorisé à le charger de ce message auprès de Vous, parceque Vous m'aviez offert d'éditer ma musique. Je lui écris aujourd'hui même de ne pas Vous fatiguer davantage à ce sujet. — Je Vous ai écrit deux lettres de Mayorque et j'ai eu le chagrin de ne pas recevoir de réponse. — J'apprends par Fontana que Vous êtes encore souffrant, ce qui me chagrine encore plus que votre silence, — quant à moi à l'époque où je Vous écrivais, —

Monsieur
Pleyel
Paris

LETTER TO CAMILLE PLEYEL (I), 12TH MARCH 1839

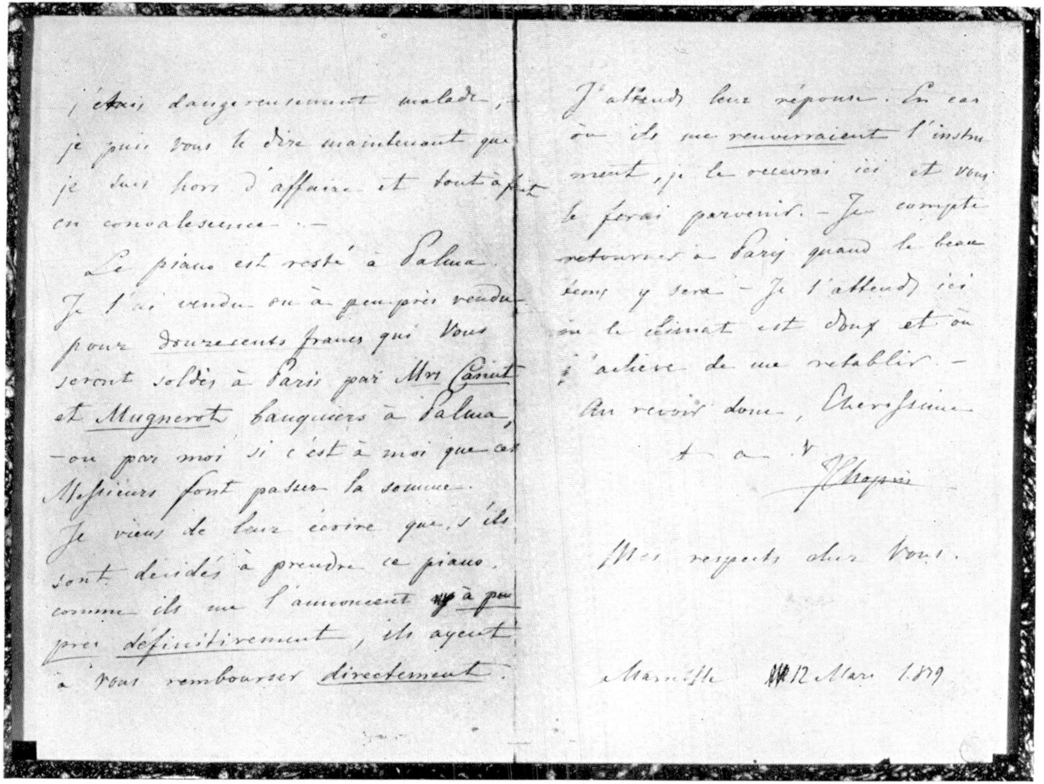

j'étais dangereusement malade ;
je puis vous le dire maintenant que
je suis hors d'affaire et tout à fait
en convalescence. —

Le piano est resté à Palma.
Je l'ai vendu ou à peu près vendu
pour douze cents francs qui vous
seront soldés à Paris par Mrs Canut
et Mugnerot banquiers à Palma,
ou par moi si c'est à moi que ces
Messieurs font passer la somme.
Je viens de leur écrire que, s'ils
sont décidés à prendre ce piano,
comme ils me l'annoncent à peu
près définitivement, ils ayent
à vous rembourser directement.

J'attends leur réponse. En cas
où ils me renverraient l'instru
ment, je le recevrai ici et vous
le ferai parvenir. — Je compte
retourner à Paris quand le beau
tems y sera. — Je l'attends ici
où le climat est doux et où
j'achève de me rétablir. —
Au revoir donc, Chérissime

t. a. v.
FChopin

Mes respects chez vous.

Marseille 12 Mars 1839

LETTER TO CAMILLE PLEYEL (2)

Chopin was not too well pleased. (His father wrote: 'I am curious about one thing: did you see Liszt after his article and are you on as friendly a footing as you used to be?' Chopin's answer was evidently negative, for some months later his father came back to the topic: 'So you met Liszt at a dinner? I know how tactful you are: you are quite right not to break with him completely, in spite of all his boasting; you used once to be friends.')

La France musicale, in its notice of the concert, made up for Liszt's omission by saying that

Chopin is a composer from conviction. He composes for himself and performs for himself. . . . One may say that Chopin is the creator of a school of pianism and of a school of composition. . . . In truth nothing equals the lightness, the sweetness with which this artist preludes on the piano; moreover nothing can be placed beside his works, full of originality, distinction and grace. Chopin is a pianist apart, who should not be and cannot be compared with any one.

For this concert he had had the assistance of Mme Cinti-Damoreau of the Opéra and of Ernst, the violinist. In 1842 Pauline Viardot sang for him, while he played works like the Ballade in A♭ major, the Impromptu in F♯ major, several mazurkas and four nocturnes. The character of the audience is vividly portrayed by this extract from *La France musicale's* notice:

And so Chopin has given in Pleyel's rooms a charming soirée, a fête peopled with adorable smiles, delicate and rosy faces, small, shapely white hands; a splendid fête where simplicity was wedded to grace and elegance, and good taste served as a pedestal to wealth. Gilded ribbons, soft blue gauzes, strings of trembling pearls, the freshest roses and mignonettes, in a word, a thousand of the prettiest and gayest hues, mixed and crossed in endless ways on the perfumed heads and silver-white shoulders of the most charming women for whom the princely *salons* contend.

Let us beware, however, of thinking that this represents the whole of Chopin. He appreciated his success with the fashionable world, but knew quite well that his best and most serious work was beyond the comprehension of this elegant throng, who

would have been sorely puzzled by the F♯ minor Polonaise or
the D minor Prelude.

In May 1844 Nicholas Chopin died. This was a heavy blow
to Frederick, whose health was gradually failing as consumption
strengthened its hold upon him. He was so downcast that
George Sand wrote to his mother in Warsaw in the hope that a
visit from some of the family might do him good. Louise and
her husband decided to come to Paris during the summer, and
Mme Sand at once wrote offering them the use of her town house
(Chopin and she had moved in 1842 to splendid apartments in
the Square d'Orléans). We may quote a part of her letter, if
only to show that by 1844 her relationship with Chopin was
indeed almost that of mother to son, and his relatives could visit
her with perfect propriety.

DEAR MADAME,

I await your arrival at my house most impatiently. I think Fritz will
reach Paris before you, but if you do not find him there I am arranging
for a friend of mine to hand over to you the keys of my apartment and
I beg you to make use of it as though it were your own. You are
bound to find my dear boy very frail and much altered since you saw
him last! But don't be too alarmed about his health. It has con‑
tinued pretty much the same for the last six years, during which I have
seen him every day. I hope that with time his constitution will be
strengthened, but at least I am sure that with a regular life and care it
will last as well as any one else's. . . . I ask you to make sure that
little Chopin (for that is what we call the great Chopin, your brother)
shall have plenty of rest before setting off for Berry with you. . . .

Louise and her husband came, then, to Nohant and saw for
themselves how matters stood between Frederick and George
Sand. They could return to Warsaw entirely reassured and
give the lie to the rumours that had reached Poland. When
they left, the most cordial relations had been established with
Mme Sand; henceforth she was an honoured friend of the family.
She presented Louise with the manuscript of her latest novel,
La Mare au Diable, and sent a valuable rosary to Chopin's mother.

Moreover she frequently wrote and kept them informed about the state of his health.

This summer of 1844 marks the culminating point of Chopin's happiness at Nohant; from that moment the sky began to cloud over by imperceptible degrees, and when the storm finally burst it did not surprise those who had marked the gradual change in the atmosphere and had sensed the electrical tension which precedes the lightning flash. Time was passing; the boy Maurice and little Solange were leaving childhood behind and beginning to assert themselves as individuals. 1844 was not 1838, and George Sand was soon to discover that children who begin by loving their parents often end by judging them.

But for the moment Chopin was untroubled by thoughts of what would happen to *him* when that ill-omened day arrived. His B minor Sonata, written now, at the summit of his creative power, stands as a milestone at this turning-point in his life. In the impassioned melody of the first movement, in the rippling gaiety of the scherzo, the quiet rapture of the *largo* and the virile exultation of the finale we may mark the essential Chopin and join with Schumann in declaring him to be 'one of the proudest spirits of the age.'

CHAPTER VIII

THE BREAK WITH GEORGE SAND

BEFORE giving his account of the break between George Sand and Chopin, Frederick Niecks, who in 1888 had practically no first-hand material to work on, wrote:

It is nevertheless an undeniable fact that we are not at the present moment, nor, all things well considered, *shall be even in the most distant future* [my italics], in a position to speak on this subject otherwise than conjecturally.

Such an attitude on the part of a biographer towards his subject is incomprehensible. However, since those days of the eighties much new evidence has come to light regarding this crisis in Chopin's life, and 'conjecture' is no longer a fitting word to apply to the judgment which may be formed from the mass of material now available, which can only be summarized here.

In 1844 Solange, George Sand's daughter, was sixteen. Her character, which was to bring misfortune to herself and those around her, was already formed. As a result of the unsettled life her mother led, she had been brought up in an utterly haphazard fashion, now dressed in boy's clothes, now handed over to the care of a waiting-woman, sent to boarding-schools or turned over to a series of dubious tutors, so that when she finally returned to the bosom of her family in 1844 she was a well-made, but head-strong, undisciplined and knowing girl, thoroughly spoilt, selfish and vain. As early as 1841 her mother had had to lecture her before she came home for the holidays:

Your brother and I love you, but we have no illusions about certain faults which you must correct and which you will surely try to eradicate: self-love, a craving to dominate others and your mad, stupid jealousy. . . . Good night! Chopin sends you a kiss and is waiting to spoil you, but I won't let him.

Her brother Maurice had been just as badly brought up. His mother adored him and let him have his own way in everything. He trifled with painting, and George Sand persuaded herself that her conceited son really had the makings of a great artist.

In the early days of their association Chopin did his best to win Maurice's affection. He gave him presents (including a handsome gold watch) and went out of his way to be friendly with the difficult youth, putting up with his churlishness for the sake of peace and quiet. But Maurice, instead of making things easy for his mother by tactfully accepting the presence of Chopin, grew more and more resentful of the devotion which she showed towards him. He imagined that Chopin was imposing on her generous nature, wearing her out and taking liberties by interfering in private family matters—in a word, that this stranger in the house was a menace to the harmony of the family circle and must be put in his place.

To back him up in his plan of resistance to Chopin he found an ally in the person of George Sand's adopted daughter, Augustine Brault. Mme Sand had good-naturedly taken in this child of a somewhat disreputable distant relative (against Chopin's advice) and endeavoured to bring her up on the same footing as Solange, in order to please Maurice, who was attracted by his pretty cousin. Solange was by no means disposed to allow Augustine to forget her humble origins, and since Maurice chose to take the newcomer under his protection the house was soon divided into two camps: Maurice and Augustine became natural allies against Chopin and Solange, with George Sand holding a midway position between the two sides. Solange could be charming when she chose; she plagued Chopin to give her music lessons and tried to play the coquette with him, much to her mother's annoyance.

During the summer of 1845 (which in other respects was uneventful) Maurice found a way to attack Chopin through his Polish servant, John. He and Augustine set the other domestics against poor John and caused such trouble in the household that Chopin was forced to dismiss him, although he was a good worker. Chopin hated such changes, and John was the only person at Nohant with whom he could speak his mother tongue; to lose him was a great blow. Thus the atmosphere grew heavy and tense, at least within the confines of Nohant: in Paris the situation was easier. Unless George Sand was deliberately lying in her letters to Chopin's sister Louise, there is no evidence that she was a partner to the intrigues against Chopin or that she had any thought of getting rid of him. To support this view it will be necessary, at this point, to quote from one such letter written at the end of March 1846,[1] that is *precisely at the time* when she was writing the novel *Lucrezia Floriani*, so generally considered to be a proof of her intention to break with Chopin and, indeed, a preparation for the final step:

MY DEAR AND WELL-BELOVED LOUISE,

. . . Our dear boy has been exhausted by the rigorous winter which lasted so long here, but since the fine weather has come he looks much rejuvenated and restored to life. A fortnight's fine warmth has done him more good than all their remedies. His health is bound up with the state of the atmosphere and so I am seriously thinking, if I can earn enough money this summer to travel with my family, of carrying him off for the three severest months of next winter [i.e. 1846–7] and taking him to the south of France. If one could protect him from the cold for a whole year, with summer following he would have eighteen months' respite to get rid of his cough. I have to torment him about it because, in spite of what he says, he loves Paris. But so as not to deprive him too much and not keep him too long from his pupils, I could let him spend September, October and November here, then come back in March, and still give him till the end of May before returning to Nohant. These are my plans for this year and next year [1846–7]. Do you agree to them?

It will be noticed that in this letter she looks forward to the year 1847. Why should George Sand write in this strain to

[1] George Sand's biographer places this undated letter in the spring of 1845; Hoesick, who saw the original, in the spring of 1846, which is confirmed by Chopin's letter of 11th October 1846, in which he states that the plan for wintering in the south was vetoed 'by the children.'

Chopin's family if she were planning to get rid of him? When this letter was written the great psychological crisis in their relations had not yet come. But it was not far off, for George Sand was now attaching more and more importance to Maurice's opinions, and Chopin was sailing dangerously near the wind. It cannot be over-emphasized that the meek, angelic Chopin of the story-books never existed. He could be a most difficult man to live with; the merest trifle would arouse him to fury, especially when his nerves were overwrought, and in these days he was indeed on edge most of the time. George Sand had already had samples of this kind of behaviour since the earliest days of their liaison. For example, in June 1841 he had occasion to be annoyed with Mlle de Rozières, Solange's governess and piano mistress. (It was a trivial matter, not worth relating here.) George Sand was not allowed to know what the trouble was, but she had to suffer for it. On 20th June 1841 she writes:

He wanted to leave the house. . . . I have never had and shall never have any peace with him. . . . The day before yesterday he spent the whole day without speaking a word to a soul. Was he ill? Has someone annoyed him? Have I said something to upset him? I shall never know, no more than a million other similar things which he does not know himself. . . . I must not let him think he is the master here—he would be all the more touchy in future.

On this occasion Maurice took it upon himself to speak to Chopin 'firmly and sharply.'

As time went on and his health failed rapidly (especially after the severe winter of 1844-5) he became more touchy than ever. In April 1846 he paid a short visit to Tours and came back 'cured of his cold, but more teasing and fault-finding than usual.' Before George Sand left for Nohant he gave a soirée for her with 'music, flowers and a good feed,' and shortly afterwards joined the family at Nohant. Augustine Brault, whom Chopin now loathed, although she was a harmless sort of girl, had been officially adopted during this spring and had returned with the family from Paris. The situation was critical; all nerves were on edge. It was obvious that an explosion was imminent, and it seems that it came on 29th June, just before Maurice's birthday. There were high words between him and Chopin, and George Sand openly sided with her son. The two men made it up immediately, but untold harm had been done. More important than the outward event was the inner change which accom panied it. Both Chopin and George Sand seem to have realized that this incident definitely marked the end of the old feeling between them. They could and did remain friends, but they now looked at each other with different eyes and both were disillusioned by what they saw, or rather, they exchanged one illusion for another. Already on 25th June 1846 George Sand had begun the publication (in serial form) of her novel *Lucrezia Floriani,* so long held to be 'the cause of the rupture.' The book was rather the *result* of the slow change of the last two years. We need not heed George Sand's protest (made some years later) that the resemblance between Chopin and 'Prince Karol' was fortuitous. This was not the first time that she had drawn portraits from the life: she was, indeed, in capable of *inventing* characters for her novels, and 'Prince Karol' is a penetrating psychological study of the 'distinguished neuras thenic' that Chopin had now become. George Sand did not analyse her own character so well in the portrait of Lucrezia, but that was scarcely to be expected. In the later chapters of the book, written towards the end of the year, is to be found a thinly dis guised account of actual happenings at Nohant—the moral crisis which determined George Sand's future attitude to Chopin. Did the latter recognize himself in the part of Karol? We can not say. At all events he took it calmly and showed no sign of having been hurt by the allusions to his strange and difficult character; he may even have acknowledged to himself the truth of the portrait, which, after all, is not a wholly unflattering one.

Leaving on one side the purely illustrative and inessential episode of the novel *Lucrezia Floriani,* we pass on to the immediate causes of the break. The explosion in June had stunned Chopin, and George Sand was so misled by his reactions as to be able to write, on 20th September: 'His nerves have calmed down, he has turned the corner and his character has become calmer and more equable.' There was a crowd in the house that summer, but he avoided company and preferred to stay in his own room. 'When I'm tired I don't feel cheerful. I become a wet blanket, and the children don't enjoy themselves so well.' He was depressed and filled with forebodings. He could not tell his family of what was gnawing at his heart: his letters are filled with meandering gossip about nothing in particular—a strange melancholy is stamped on these pages.

At the end of the summer a suitor for Solange's hand had presented himself—a young country gentleman of good family and sincere, upright character, Fernand de Préaulx. Solange light-heartedly accepted him. Chopin was pleased, and he left Nohant early in November, little imagining that he would never return. But dramatic events were preparing. On 16th March 1846 George Sand had received an enthusiastic letter from Auguste Jean Baptiste Clésinger, an ex-soldier turned sculptor and an *arriviste* of the worst type, who wrote to ask permission to call one of his statues 'Consuelo,' after the heroine of one of her novels. When the Sand family returned to Paris early in February 1847 for Solange's betrothal, the sculptor made haste to be introduced to the famous Mme Sand and was soon busy making busts of her and her daughter. He did more: he set about the conquest of Solange and was so successful that when the time came for her to sign the marriage contract with Préaulx, she refused point-blank. All was in an uproar and George Sand hurried back to Nohant with her impossible daughter. But she had reckoned without the enterprising sculptor. He followed them to Nohant, and while Madame Sand was making inquiries about him (he was known to be heavily in debt) he settled the matter by seducing Solange and attempting to carry her off. These events were kept completely secret; no one was allowed to know, not even Maurice, who was in Holland; least of all Chopin, who was still in Paris. After her experiences of the previous summer George Sand was resolved that he should be kept out of these family affairs. Frankly, one cannot blame her—intrigues of this kind were not Chopin's domain—but her decision was to cost her his love and friendship.

On 16th April she wrote to Maurice in Paris: 'Not a word of all that to Chopin; it does not concern him, and when once the Rubicon has been crossed the "ifs" and "buts" only do harm.' She was impatient for the marriage to take place: 'This marriage must be concluded impetuously, as if by surprise.' Now that there was no going back she determined to put on a bold face and she wrote defiantly to her friends, extolling Clésinger's virile, resolute character and pretending to be confident that Solange would be happy with him. She realized how Chopin must feel at not being consulted, and knew that he was probably blaming her for wilfully handing over Solange, his favourite, to a disreputable stranger concerning whom the most dreadful stories were circulating. Since he could not be told the truth she wrote, on 12th May, to his friend Grzymala a letter which has always been considered a monument of hypocrisy, yet which, when fitted into the pattern of events and the body of corroborating evidence, appears (to the present writer at least) as a fairly reasonable summing-up of the situation *as she saw it at that moment*—making allowance for the fact that even to Grzymala she had to pretend to have some faith in Solange's chances of happiness with Clésinger. In her letter she asks Grzymala to talk to Chopin and persuade him not to worry if he does not learn all that is going on, not to trouble his head about Solange and Clésinger—all will turn out well; let him only trust *her*. At the same time she wrote to Chopin, no doubt diplomatically, breaking the news of what was preparing at Nohant. Chopin thanked her, without any show of ill will. On 20th May 1847 the marriage took place; there had been no time for elaborate preparations, and the wedding announcements were badly printed on cheap paper, Solange Dudevant being described as Solange Sand. Two days before, George Sand made over to her daughter a considerable portion of her property. As soon as they were possessed of it the 'diabolic couple' proceeded to go through the money like wildfire. For the moment Mme Sand was well rid of them: 'It's over and we can breathe again,' she wrote on 21st May. While all this was happening Chopin was ill in Paris, miserable and anxious, and yet glad, in a way, to have escaped the embarrassment of being present at the wedding.

During Solange's honeymoon Augustine too had found a husband: one of Maurice's friends, Théodore Rousseau, had fallen in love with her and asked for her hand. By 7th June the engagement was settled and a modest, happy future seemed in store for the inoffensive girl. But when Solange arrived on the scene with her cavalier she was filled with insane jealousy of Augustine's happiness, and out of devilish spite she declared to Rousseau that his bride-to-be had been her brother Maurice's mistress! When her mother rounded on her for uttering such calumnies and ruining poor Augustine's life (for Rousseau took fright and withdrew), Solange with brazen impudence defied her and accused her, too, of an amorous intrigue with another of Maurice's friends, Victor Boric. This was too much. Indescribable scenes occurred: murder was nearly committed, for Maurice would have shot Clésinger on the spot if George Sand had not rushed between them, punching her son-in-law in the face and receiving a blow from him in return. In the end the Clésingers were literally thrown out of the house. Solange, unabashed, took refuge in the nearby village of La Châtre and thence wrote a lying account of the disturbance to Chopin, begging the use of his carriage for part of the journey to Paris. In good faith Chopin answered: 'Yes, by all means. I have written to your mother, telling her to let you have it.' One may imagine what George Sand felt on receiving this letter from Chopin. So that was the reward of all her love and devotion! He was prepared to think the worst of her! At that very moment he was receiving the wicked and ungrateful girl who had not hesitated to slander her own mother. She took up her pen and wrote him such a letter as he had never yet received. The letter is lost; all we know is that Delacroix, who saw it on 20th July, said it was 'cruel,' which is probably true.

George Sand had been violently outspoken; nevertheless she

expected Chopin to reply, to take her side, to break with the Clésingers and come to Nohant. Chopin did not stir, for Solange had done her work too well, and evidently he was not unwilling to believe her. On 25th July her mother became alarmed and wrote to Paris:

MY DEAR FRIEND,—I am anxious, frightened. . . . I haven't heard from Chopin for several, I don't know how many, days. He was ready to come here; suddenly he does not turn up and does not write. Has he left? Is he held up, ill, somewhere? [1]

Finally Chopin wrote, and she was as indignant about his letter as Delacroix had been about hers. This was the end. As long as Chopin maintained contact with Solange there was not the slightest hope of reconciliation.

It is of little use to refer to his letters for enlightenment on these events; in them he merely recounts what he learnt from Solange. At first, although he accepted the daughter's version, he would not run the mother down, and a letter written by Pauline Viardot to George Sand in November 1847 clearly reveals the resigned but dignified attitude which he adopted.

There is a passage in your letter which I cannot possibly pass over in silence; the one where you say that Chopin belongs to Solange's faction, which makes her out to be a victim and runs you down. This is absolutely false, I swear, at least as far as he is concerned . . . for God's sake don't believe those officious friends who come and tell tales.

Later, however, Chopin's resistance broke down, and in the summer of 1848 he was prepared to believe that there was truth in a libellous pamphlet (a kind of biography of George Sand) which Augustine's disappointed and revengeful father published, and

[1] Many writers have chosen to see a further proof of duplicity in the fact that she wrote savagely to Chopin when she was worked up just after Solange's departure and yet expressed anxiety about him on 25th July when he gave no sign of life. Why duplicity? George Sand was a woman, not a calculating machine. She had been deeply outraged by Solange's behaviour and was maddened by the thought of Chopin joining in the plot. When she had cooled down she would feel sure that he would be true to his past love for her.

which the police immediately suppressed. In December 1848 the property which Solange had received as a dowry was seized and sold for a song to pay Clésinger's debts, in spite of frantic efforts by George Sand to save it. Chopin was told by Solange that her heartless mother had put the bailiffs in. And so it went on. Had the right friends been there to straighten out these misunderstandings the final rupture need never have taken place and Chopin's life might have been prolonged by several years. He need not, for example, have undertaken the journey to England and Scotland which exhausted his already undermined constitution. Only at the last, when utterly prostrate amid the London fogs in November 1848, did a cry break from him. 'Never have I cursed any one, but everything is now so unbearable that I think I should feel easier if I could curse *Lucrezia*.' He had seen her for the last time on 4th March 1848; they met accidentally and exchanged a few words. But they were not the right words to break down the barrier which calumnies and misunderstandings had raised between them.

George Sand was at Nohant when Chopin died in 1849. At the back of his diary they found a small envelope embroidered with the initials 'G-F' (George-Frederick); it contained a lock of her hair. He had not forgotten her. And she neither forgot, nor forgave Solange for what she had done in 1847. They became reconciled, but the reconciliation was superficial—love and trust were dead; and often, in the years to come, the old resentment would rise in George Sand's heart as she thought of the harvest of cruel accusations and bitter scorn which her blind love for her children had brought her.

CHAPTER IX

THE LAST YEARS

DURING his last stay at Nohant, in the summer of 1846, Chopin had tried to settle down to work, but when his thoughts were occupied by external events and troubles he could not fall into the right mood, he could not find 'the blue note' which his friends described as the herald of his most inspired moments. 'I do my best to work,' he wrote, 'but it just won't do, and if I go on like this my new works will neither remind you of *warbling birds* nor even of *broken china*.' He managed to finish the *Barcarolle* and the *Polonaise-Fantaisie* and one or two smaller things, but when it came to his Sonata for piano and cello he could make no progress.

There is no reason to suppose his creative powers were exhausted; indeed the *Polonaise-Fantaisie* shows that he was breaking new ground and is for that reason one of his most interesting works. But after November 1846 he never again found exactly the right conditions for working, and the last three years of his life were frittered away uselessly.

He continued to live at No. 9 Square d'Orléans while George Sand's apartment at No. 5 was shuttered, locked and, in due course, re-let. His lessons, his 'mill,' as he called them, took up most of his time, for in spite of the serious decline in his health he seemed busier than ever. It did him no good to spend the hot summer months of 1847 in Paris, and when the winter came he had no reserve of strength with which to meet it. After the turn of the year his friends persuaded him to give a concert, for he had not been heard in public since 1842. It was destined to be his last appearance in Paris; and as though his admirers had felt that this would be the end, not only of Chopin's poetic career but also of a period of elegance, good manners, ease and refine- ment (the throne of Louis-Philippe was already tottering), they

CHOPIN SHORTLY BEFORE HIS DEATH
Daguerreotype made in 1849

rushed to buy the tickets, of which there were only three hundred at twenty francs each (the best seats at the Opéra cost twelve francs).

On Wednesday 16th February this unique concert took place at Pleyel's rooms. With Franchomme and Alard Chopin played a Mozart trio, and with Franchomme the last three movements of his cello Sonata. Among the other works he played were the *Berceuse*, the *Barcarolle* and the Db major Waltz, Op. 64. The only trace of weakness that his playing showed was his taking *pianissimo*, and with marvellous pedal effects, the two *forte* passages in the *Barcarolle*. For the rest, it was the same Chopin—he who had never failed to hold his listeners spellbound by the mysterious fascination of his personality and his playing.

For some time past his Scottish friend and pupil, Miss Jane Stirling, and her sister, Mrs. Erskine, had been urging him to come to England and to visit them in Scotland, and he had made up his mind to accept their invitation. Even before the revolution broke out (a week after his concert) the papers had mentioned his intention of leaving Paris. The success of the revolt and the king's flight meant that Chopin's world had come toppling down. His lessons were at an end. There was no telling when he would be able to earn money again. Chopin must have felt that Paris was no place for him at this moment, and he was anxious to be gone. The *Gazette musicale* announced his impending departure on 2nd April, and in the evening of 20th April (the day before Good Friday) he arrived in London, well provided with letters of introduction and with his good Scots ladies to make every arrangement for his comfort. His first lodging was at 10 Bentinck Street, just off Wigmore Street, but in a few days he moved to a handsome apartment at 48 Dover Street, a few steps from Piccadilly and the heart of the fashionable world . . . hence very expensive, as he soon found out.

Chopin's reputation had preceded him to London, although his music was not very well known, except in purely musical circles. For over ten years Wessel of Regent Street had published all his works; this they would not have done had there been no sale for them. We may therefore dismiss the suggestion that his music was 'totally unknown.' In 1841 his Mazurkas, Op. 41, had called forth some heavy sarcasm from the *Musical World*. Wessel, to counteract this cold blast, engaged J. W. Davison, high priest of the Mendelssohn cult in England, to write a pamphlet, *Essay on the Works of Frederic Chopin*, which appeared in 1843. This rubbishy production is not to be taken seriously—Davison admitted that he had written it with his tongue in his cheek—but at least it mentions the names of several well-known pianists who frequently performed Chopin's music. His concertos had attracted attention, and it is significant that almost as soon as Chopin arrived he was invited by the Philharmonic Society to play one of them at its concerts. Such a direct invitation was a great honour, but Chopin was not impressed by it; all he knew was that time was money in London and that consequently only *one* perfunctory rehearsal (with a large percentage of 'substitutes' in the orchestra) would be granted. He refused, therefore, and his refusal gave great offence.

But if the official musical world stood on its dignity, the highest social circles were immediately opened to the newcomer, and he gave himself not the slightest trouble to placate the powerful and well-established music critics or the acknowledged magnates of the concert world. He rather enjoyed being in a class by himself, and if his health had been reasonably good he would have had little to complain of.

They don't chatter while I am playing [he writes], and it seems that they speak well everywhere of my music; considering that they are accustomed to pushing my poor little colleagues about, I appear to them as a kind of amateur and soon I shall be a kind of *grand seigneur* because I have clean shoes and don't carry around cards with the inscription: 'Pupils accepted. Available for evening parties, etc.'

It is surprising that Chopin survived this London season at all. He was really dangerously ill, frequently spitting blood and obliged to cancel his engagements, and yet he contrived to be everywhere—at the opera, at dinners and receptions, where he met every one worth knowing, Dickens, Carlyle (who later wrote of him in moving terms), Emerson — then lecturing at Exeter Hall — and all the musical notabilities. Among the latter one may single out Jenny Lind. She was then at the height of her fame, and when she met Chopin a bond of friendship and mutual esteem was at once formed between them. In his large drawing-room Chopin had three pianos—an Erard, a Pleyel and a Broadwood, but he found little time to play on them. He gave a number of lessons to a queer collection of pupils who seemed more anxious to gratify their curiosity than to undertake serious study, and he was ready to play at private houses for a fee of twenty guineas. He only obtained very few such engagements, and even those were at the cost of a kind of haggling which must have been utterly dis-tasteful to a man who in Paris had been notorious for his aloofness and exclusiveness. He took it all in good part, however, and on his return to Paris gave his friend Grzymala an amusing account (with all his incomparable mimicry) of the sort of performance which he had to go through:

The Lady. Oh, Mr. Chopin, how much do you cost?
Chopin. My fee is twenty guineas, madam.
The Lady. Oh! but I only want you to play a little piece.
                              [*Holding up her fingers.*
Chopin. My fee remains the same, madam.
The Lady. Oh! Then you'll play a lot of things?
Chopin. For two hours if you so desire, madam.
The Lady. Oh! Then that's settled. Oh! Are the twenty guineas to be paid in advance?
Chopin. No, madam; afterwards.
The Lady. Oh! Very reasonable, I'm sure.

Add a Mayfair French accent to the lady's role and the scene is complete!

He played at Lady Gainsborough's, the Marquis of Douglas's and on 15th May at Stafford House, now known as Lancaster House. Of this latter occasion he writes:

I played at the Duchess of Sutherland's before the Queen, Prince Albert, the Prince of Prussia, Wellington and all the *élite* of the

Garter—a select gathering of eighty persons. . . . Her Majesty addressed some very gracious remarks to me.

What did Chopin play on these occasions? None of his more important works except, once or twice, the B♭ minor Scherzo or the Ballade in F. He usually confined himself to works for which his perfect finger technique and beautiful singing tone would suffice: Studies, Op. 25, No. 1 ('*leik water*, all the ladies say'), No. 2 and No. 7, the *Andante spianato*, the inevitable E♭ major Nocturne, the *Berceuse* and a selection of waltzes and mazurkas. For this reason no particular interest attaches to the various accounts which exist regarding his playing in England in 1848. Moreover, many of these 'authoritative' accounts were written twenty-five, thirty, even fifty years after the event, when to have heard Chopin play a couple of waltzes in a piano shop in '48 was taken as a certificate of competence to judge in what manner *all* his compositions should be performed or to proclaim how the composer *never* played them. No one has rendered the task of Chopin's biographer more difficult than these 'favourite pupils,' 'inseparable companions' or 'intimate friends' with their incredibly good memories. To remember in 1880 'exactly how he played every bar' of the D♭ Waltz in 1848 is no mean feat! Fifty-five years after Chopin played in Glasgow a lady remembered distinctly that it had been 'a cold, ungenial day.' Chopin himself was convinced it had been fine and that he had felt 'quite revived.' The fact is that few of these 'memories' will stand the test of being compared with contemporary records. Put together, these efforts of imagination on the part of such friends and acquaintances cancel each other out.

His public appearances during the first part of his London sojourn were limited to two brilliant matinées which he gave on 23rd June at 99 Eaton Place (Mrs. Sartoris's) and on 7th July at 2 St. James's Square (Lord Falmouth's house—bombed and destroyed during the 1939–45 war). All told, four hundred people heard him at these concerts, and he made about £300, which was soon eaten up by the expense of living in the West End at the height of the season. The second of these matinées was more successful

than the first: Chopin felt stronger and was able to do justice to the
B♭ minor Scherzo. Besides, Pauline Viardot assisted him and
sang with great effect her arrangements of some of his mazurkas.
(Chopin had no objection to his melodies being sung if it were
well and tastefully done.) We may quote from a little-known
notice which appeared in the *Daily News* on 10th July to show
how he impressed his hearers at this second matinée:

There was a numerous and fashionable assembly, who were delighted
with the entertainment provided for them. M. Chopin performed an
Andante sostenuto and a Scherzo from his Opus 31, a selection from his
celebrated studies, a Nocturne and a *Berceuse* and several of his own
Preludes, Mazurkas and Waltzes. In these various pieces he showed
very strikingly his original genius as a composer and his transcendental
powers as a performer. His music is as strongly marked with individual
character as that of any master who has ever lived. It is highly finished,
new in its harmonies, full of contrapuntal skill and ingenious con-
trivance; and yet we have never heard music which has so much the
air of unpremeditated effusion. The performer seems to abandon himself to the impulses of his fancy and feeling, to indulge in a reverie and
to pour out unconsciously, as it were, the thoughts and emotions that
pass through his mind. . . .
He accomplishes enormous difficulties, but so quietly, so smoothly
and with such constant delicacy and refinement that the listener is not
sensible of their real magnitude. It is the exquisite delicacy, with the
liquid mellowness of his tone, and the pearly roundness of his passages
of rapid articulation which are the peculiar features of his execution,
while his music is characterized by freedom of thought, varied expression and a kind of romantic melancholy which seems the natural
mood of the artist's mind.

Nothing came of Chopin's hope to play at court. This was
probably his own fault, since he would make no move in the
matter and the director of the royal concerts was not used to
running after musicians. Yet the rumour soon went round Paris
(and was taken seriously by Liszt) that Queen Victoria had
come to him incognito for piano lessons!
This success brought little satisfaction to him. His meeting
with Pauline Viardot, who was still intimate with George Sand,

had opened the old wound, for it is inconceivable that they should not talk over old times. He discovered that Mme Viardot had been asked to report on his situation, which only served to increase his bitterness. The money with which he had hoped to tide over a difficult period in Paris was vanishing before his eyes; his miserable state of health killed all optimism for the future, and he felt lost and bewildered among the hospitable, friendly but uncomprehending English.

By the end of July the season was over. London was soon empty. Revolution on the Continent prevented fashionable society from taking its holidays abroad; instead, every one followed the Queen and Prince Albert to Scotland, and Chopin too, greatly in need of rest and fresh air, made for the north, arriving at Edinburgh in the first days of August. After a day's sight-seeing in the capital he went to Calder House, Midlothian, where he was the guest of Lord Torphichen, the brother-in-law of his pupil, Miss Jane Stirling. Her devotion to Chopin has become a legend, and indeed there is nothing which she did not do to ensure his comfort and happiness. He received every morning the latest newspapers from Paris, his note-paper was beautifully engraved with views of Edinburgh, a splendid Pleyel and a Broadwood were at his disposal, every wish of his was antici-pated; but nothing could overcome his gloom and the sensation of being utterly alone in a strange and remote country. He was not insensitive to the romantic atmosphere of Calder House, with its memories of John Knox and its centuries-old trees and lawns, but he had no inclination to compose; he could not find, he said, 'a single decent musical idea.' His break with George Sand and the revolution in Paris had brought his world to an end. From this time he seems to have lost all interest in life, to have given up the struggle, and in his letters we find only a pathetic harking back to the past and a mournful anticipation of the fast-approach-ing end. To Fontana he wrote:

We are two old cembalos on which time and circumstances have played out their wretched trills. Yes, two old cembalos, even if you protest at being included in such company—that means no disparagement to beauty and respectability. The *table d'harmonie* is perfect, only the strings have snapped and some of the pegs are missing. The sole trouble is this: we are the creation of a celebrated maker, a Stradivarius of his kind, who is no longer there to mend us. In clumsy hands we cannot give forth new sounds and we stifle within ourselves all those things which no one will ever draw from us, all for lack of a repairer. I can hardly get my breath: I am just about ready to give up the ghost. I don't know why thoughts of Johnny and Antoine, Witwicki and Sobanski should come into my head. Those with whom I was in most intimate harmony are dead for me; even Ennike, our best piano tuner, has been drowned, so that I have not in the whole world a piano tuned to suit me. Moos has died and no one can make me such comfortable shoes. . . . I am writing this rubbish because I have not a sensible idea in my head. I am vegetating, patiently waiting for the winter, dreaming now of home, now of Rome. . . .

Eager to earn what he could, he had accepted an engagement to play at Manchester on 28th August, at one of the 'Gentlemen's Concerts,' and for a few days he stayed with a wealthy and cultivated manufacturer, Salis Schwabe, at Crumpsall House in the suburbs, away from the smoke of the town. The concert was a miscellaneous one: Chopin played the same few pieces that he had played in London. While at Calder House he had narrowly escaped being killed when the horses bolted and his carriage was overturned; thus he could not prepare any new works, and at the last minute he had to delete from the programme the F major Ballade. There was a large audience (twelve hundred people) and 'of course the lustrous-eyed and liquid-voiced Alboni was the chief attraction of the concert'; but Chopin had no reason to be dis-satisfied with his reception. We are told that he 'elicited a rapturous encore and . . . treated the audience to what appeared to be a fragment of great beauty.' It was generally agreed, how-ever, that his playing was too delicate for a large hall. One critic missed 'the astonishing power of Leopold de Meyer, the vigour of Thalberg, the dash of Herz,' while appreciating the great finish of his playing.

After this concert Chopin spent a day or two at Edinburgh with the family of Dr. Lyszczyński, a Pole who had settled in the town. It was a great joy to him to be with someone with whom he could speak his native tongue and who could also give him medical advice; but he was for ever on the move, and at the beginning of September he went to Johnstone Castle, eleven miles from Glasgow, where he stayed with Mrs. Houston, Jane Stirling's widowed sister. He was not the only guest there: 'There is a crowd of various ladies and seventy⁄to⁄eighty⁄year⁄old lords, but no young folk—they are out hunting'—but he was more lonely than ever. To his friend Camille Pleyel he wrote thus: [1]

JOHNSTONE CASTEL [*sic*].
NEAR GLASGOW

Sept. 11th.

MY DEAR FRIEND,

Instead of a letter I am sending you M. Telefsen who is going to spend a few days in Paris; M. Ed. Rodrigues spoke to you about him before the '48 revolution. He is my pupil; he has been most helpful to me and will be still more so by sending me news of you. He will tell you also all that I am doing—I wish he could tell you what I shall do, but I don't know that myself—all I know is that I shall always love you, always.

Your most sincerely devoted

F. CHOPIN.

Do be kind to him.

After a trip to Strachur on Loch Fyne, where he visited his pupil Lady Murray, he hastened back to meet his old friend Princess Marcelline Czartoryska and her husband, who had arrived in Edinburgh. How pathetic was his eagerness to seek out anything or any one that might recall to him the Poland that he would never see again! 'I felt myself somewhat restored to life under the influence of their Polish spirit,' he wrote, 'and it gave me strength to play at Glasgow, where a number of the nobility had come to hear me.' This Glasgow recital took place on 27th September and was not unlike his London matinées, for the time of day (2.30 in the afternoon) and the price of the tickets

---

[1] Unpublished. Original in the author's collection.

(half a guinea) kept away the ordinary citizens of the town, and only aristocratic county people formed the audience. Chopin played his usual programme and made £90. (The criticisms in the Glasgow press merely repeat what had been said at Manchester.) For once he was really cheerful: the Czartoryskis came to the concert and dined at Johnstone Castle, and Chopin declared that that day had done him a world of good. He then went to stately Keir House, near Bridge of Allan and Stirling, the home of Jane Stirling's uncle, where there was a large house-party. His hosts did everything to make his stay agreeable, but the weather was unsettled and the beautiful scenery remained shrouded in mist. He felt weak and helpless.

All the morning until two o'clock I am good for nothing; later, when I am dressed, everything wearies me and I gasp until dinner-time—after which I must remain at table for two hours with the men, watching them talk and listening to them drinking. . . . Bored to death I go to the drawing-room where it takes all my strength of mind to pull myself together a little, for they are then curious to hear me; then my good Daniel carries me upstairs to the bedroom, undresses me, puts me to bed, leaves a candle and I am free to gasp and dream until morning, when the same thing begins all over again.

Chopin's diary for 1848 has been preserved; in it there is a pencil sketch, made about this time, which shows into what depths of despair the sick and weary man had fallen. It represents part of a churchyard—a low gate, a few graves with crosses and in the midst of them one grave marked with a larger cross; on the inside of the cover are a few stray bars of music.

On 4th October he gave an evening concert in Edinburgh at the Hopetoun Rooms, and for once, exceptionally, he did not have the assistance of a singer. His programme remained as before, but he added one of the ballades, an impromptu and several preludes and mazurkas. It was 'remembered' (forty years afterwards) that Miss Stirling, fearing the hall would be empty, bought a hundred tickets and gave them to her friends. One may be allowed to doubt this, for it is certain that the audience 'was select and highly fashionable,' the tickets were 'limited in number' and 'the rooms were filled.' Chopin himself wrote: 'All the distinguished society of the neighbourhood had assembled for it. They say it went well—it meant a little success and some money.'

By this time the winter was at hand. Chopin dreaded it and expected to be compelled to remain fixed wherever the cold weather caught him. Yet he went to Wishaw (Lady Belhaven's house) and in mid-October was at Hamilton Palace for a few days. On the return journey to Edinburgh he caught a cold which confined him to his room at Dr. Lyszczyński's and made him desperately anxious to get away from Scotland. He was at the end of his tether—killed by kindness and pestered to death by the excessive attention and fussiness of his Scottish friends. He learnt that there was a rumour that he intended to marry Jane Stirling. The mention of it only served to call to his mind bitter memories of what he had lost:

What has become of my art? And my heart, where have I squandered it? Scarcely can I remember what songs they sing at home. This world seems to slip from me, I forget things, I have no strength.

There can be no doubt that Jane Stirling was in love with him. During the remaining months of his life she was never far from him, and after his death she devoted herself to the cult of his memory. Jane Welsh Carlyle describes how she saw her in London—'like Chopin's widow,' pale and dressed in deepest mourning.

On 31st October Chopin returned to London—to 4 St. James's Place, off St. James's Street, where he was forced to stay indoors, fighting for breath and exhausted by suffering, for three weeks. Only once did he go out—on 16th November, to play at the Guildhall, at a concert and ball given for the benefit of the Polish refugees. This was destined to be his last public appearance. His intense patriotism and strong sense of duty roused him to make this effort on behalf of his fellow countrymen, but it went unnoticed: there is scarcely any mention of his playing in the accounts of the event which appeared in the press. Happily

Chopin was unaware of the tragic significance of this final concert; he simply writes of playing 'at that Polish concert and ball
which was very brilliant.'

Impatient to escape from London, where the fog was choking
him, he wrote to Grzymala begging him to get his rooms
ready and not to forget a bunch of violets for the *salon*: 'Let me
have a little poetry around me when I return—as I go through to
my bedroom, where I am sure I shall have to stay in bed a long,
long time.' On 23rd November, a day eagerly noted in his
diary, he left 'this hellish London' and returned, more dead than
alive, to Paris.

Chopin's brief career was over: from now until October 1849
his life was nothing but a hopeless struggle with consumption,
a disease in the presence of which medical science was at that
time helpless. His decline did not follow a regular course, for
on certain days he would feel stronger. Then his optimism
returned. But these short periods of apparent recovery became
rarer and rarer. By the spring of 1849 it was clear that he was
doomed. For years his financial position had been secure, but
now with startling suddenness it became precarious. He could
neither compose nor take pupils. He had never saved money,
having always spent to the limit of his income, and the little
that he brought back from England soon went in doctors' fees
and in the expenses of his apartment at the Square d'Orléans.
Realizing what a cruel situation he was in, Jane Stirling endeavoured, with magnificent generosity, to help him without
wounding his pride. On 8th March she sent him, anonymously,
a packet of bank-notes to the value of 25,000 francs. Unfortu-
nately for all concerned, the packet was handed to Chopin's
concierge, Mme Étienne, who took it and hid it, unopened, in her
room. It was not until the end of July that Miss Stirling discovered that Chopin had never received the money! Then, with
the help of a clairvoyant, Alexis, the untouched bank-notes were
recovered. Chopin did not know what to make of the whole
affair. At first he refused to accept such a princely gift from his
pupil, but finally he was persuaded to keep a portion of it, noting

in his diary on 28th July: 'Mrs. Erskine [Jane Stirling's sister] left 15,000 francs.'

During these last months time hung heavily on Chopin's hands, in spite of the unfailing devotion of friends like Eugène Dela, croix, who did their best to keep up his spirits by their visits and interesting conversation. On rare occasions he felt an impulse to compose, and the Mazurkas in G minor and F minor, Op. 67, No. 2 and Op. 68, No. 4, were jotted down at this time. Delphine Potocka sometimes sang for him, and in her album he wrote his last song, to words by Krasiński, *A Melody* ('Afar they saw the promised land'). He also began to write a piano method, but did not proceed very far with it. Some fragments were published in 1898.

At the beginning of summer he moved to a spacious and airy abode at 74 Rue de Chaillot, in a quiet suburb of Paris. Here he felt his isolation more than ever, and on 25th June he wrote to his sister Louise in Warsaw, begging her to come. From other sources the Chopin family learnt that he had not long to live, and Louise, accompanied by her husband and daughter, at once began her preparations for the difficult journey across Europe. On 8th August they reached Paris and their coming was a godsend to Chopin, who welcomed them with a pathetic outburst of emotion.

At this point George Sand reappears for the last time in Chopin's story. A friend of Mlle de Rozières had written to her in July, describing Chopin's state and suggesting that she should offer him the hand of friendship again, before it was too late. George Sand refused to make any such advance. She said she was not sure he wanted it, and thought that the emotional strain of meeting her would do him more harm than good. However, when she learnt of Louise's arrival she could not resist writing to her thus:

NOHANT,
1st September.

DEAR LOUISE,

I hear you are in Paris: I did not know of this. At last I shall obtain through you some real news of Frederick. Some people write that he is much worse than usual, others that he is only weak and fretful as I have always known him. I venture to ask you to send me word, for one can be misunderstood and abandoned by one's children without ceasing to love them. . . . Your memories of me must have been spoilt in your heart, but I do not think I have deserved all that I have suffered.

Yours from the bottom of my heart,

GEORGE.

Louise did not reply to this letter, and George Sand made no further attempt to approach Chopin. The stories which have been told concerning a dramatic visit she is said to have made when he was on his deathbed are untrue.

On 30th August three of the most famous French doctors had decided, in consultation, that Chopin must not think of undertaking a journey away from Paris. In preparation, therefore, for the coming autumn and winter, his friends sought out for him a splendid, sunny apartment at 12 Place Vendôme. It was handsomely fitted up, and in September he moved in. Notwithstanding his desperate state he took a keen interest in the furnishing of his new home; even at this stage he had not entirely given up hope. But by the beginning of October it was evident that the end was not far off.

On 12th October his doctor, Cruveilhier, thinking that Chopin would not last the night, sent for the Abbé Jelowicki in order that the dying man might receive the sacraments of the church. In later years the worthy abbé published a highly coloured account of Chopin's last moments, designed to edify his readers rather than to give a true picture of the event; but his failings in this respect are as nothing compared with the glaring falseness of the stories told, years afterwards, by Chopin's friends and acquaintances. Gutmann, in particular, excelled himself when he came to give his version to Niecks. These accounts have one thing in common: they generally omit to mention the very persons whose presence at Chopin's bedside can be proved by contemporary documents.

One 'romantic' incident may be mentioned: on 15th October Delphine Potocka arrived from Nice, and Chopin asked her to sing to him for the last time. What she sang is not known, but it was probably Stradella's *Hymn to the Virgin*,[1] which he had often heard from Pauline Viardot.

His sister Louise, Princess Marcelline Czartoryska and Solange Clésinger were with him when he died at about two o'clock on the morning of 17th October 1849. Prostrate with grief, Louise at once wrote to inform her husband, who had returned to Warsaw, and Princess Czartoryska added a few words to the letter:

> *Tuesday–Wednesday 17th.*
> *Two o'clock in the morning.*

Oh, my darling, he is dead! Little Louise and I are well; I embrace you tenderly. Remember mother and Isabelle. Adieu. [Princess Marcelline continues.] Our poor friend's life is over—he suffered greatly before the final moment came, but he suffered with patience and angelic resignation. The way your wife nursed him was exemplary. God gives her immense physical and moral strength. . . . I am too exhausted to write any more, but I can say from the bottom of my heart that I will fulfil conscientiously the promise I made to you and to our dying friend and will look after your wife as though she were my own sister. . . .

MARCELLINE CZARTORYSKA (*née* RADZIWILL).

During the morning the sculptor Clésinger came and took casts of Chopin's face and hands, and the artist Kwiatkowski made several pencil sketches of his head. One of the best of these, given to Camille Pleyel, is published here for the first time. In accordance with Chopin's last wish a post-mortem examination was held (the results of it are unknown) and his heart was sent in an urn to Warsaw, where it was placed in the church of the Holy Cross.

The funeral, which did not take place until 30th October, was a ceremony of unusual splendour. Mozart's Requiem was sung (with Mme Castellan, Pauline Viardot, Dupont and Lablache)

[1] The very fact that the countess was asked to sing by the dying man *after* he had made his full confession and received absolution, and in the presence of his sister and confessor, should be sufficient to discredit the unfounded stories of a previous sexual relationship between them over several years.

during the service at the Madeleine, and the Funeral March from Chopin's B♭ minor Sonata, orchestrated by Réber, was performed as an introit. The church was packed, for the Requiem had not been heard since 1840, when Napoleon's remains were brought to the Invalides from St. Helena, and public interest had been stimulated by knowledge of the difficulties which had had to be surmounted in obtaining permission for women singers to take part in the church service. Chopin himself had asked that the Requiem should be performed, and his friends carried out his request; but in doing so they turned his funeral into a social event. (To cover the expenses Miss Stirling and her sisters advanced a loan of about 5,000 francs to Chopin's sister Louise.) During the intervals of the Mass, Preludes Nos. 4 and 6 were played on the organ by Lefébure-Wély.

From the Madeleine the long funeral procession made its way along the Grands Boulevards to the cemetery of Père-Lachaise. Contrary to custom, no speech was made at the graveside; when all was over the crowd dispersed in silence. Shortly afterwards, a committee, headed by Camille Pleyel, opened a subscription among the composer's friends for the erection of a monument to his memory, and Solange Sand's husband, Clésinger—the cause of the mischief which ruined Chopin's life—was entrusted with the design and execution of it. The monument, a mediocre piece of work, was unveiled in 1850 on the first anniversary of Chopin's death; it represents a weeping Muse, with a broken lyre. A small box of Polish earth had arrived from Warsaw just in time for the ceremony. The priest murmured a prayer in Polish as he sprinkled it on the grave.

More than once it has been proposed that the remains of Poland's greatest composer should be taken to Cracow and there placed in solemn state among the tombs of the Polish kings in the historic Wawel. Fitting as this might be, it is yet no less fitting that he should rest in a green and quiet spot overlooking the Paris which he came to love as his second *patrie* and spiritual home, where from the beginning his genius was acclaimed and where his fame has ever been secure.

CHAPTER X

CHOPIN AS A PIANIST AND TEACHER

As a pianist Chopin must be classed apart: he cannot be fitted, like Liszt and his heirs, into any 'royal line,' nor can his name be associated with any 'school.' His style of playing was so personal, so elusive, so little susceptible of definition, that it could not have been handed down to disciples, even if Chopin had been more fortunate in his pupils than actually was the case. When he vanished from the scene nothing of his art as a pianist was left; there remained only a legend—and the protests of those who best knew his playing, when they heard his music interpreted by others, even by sensitive artists like Tausig and Rubinstein: 'No, no! Not like that!'

Although he was soon acknowledged as the creator of a new piano style, Chopin never set himself to systematize and classify his discoveries in the realm of piano technique; only towards the end of his life did he jot down a few ideas for a 'Piano Method.' These pages are not without interest, but they are too meagre to be of much use in helping one to understand how he produced those breath‑taking effects which had hitherto scarcely been believed possible. How valuable it would be, for example, to have an exact account of Chopin's theory and practice in the matter of pedalling, a branch of piano playing in which he was both an explorer and an unsurpassed master!

The descriptions of his playing left by his contemporaries are often unsatisfactory and contradictory. All agree that his performance was unique and unforgettable, but few define his characteristics with any precision. The account from the *Daily News* (already quoted from on page 107) was evidently written by a discerning critic and reveals the main impression that Chopin's playing made

We have never heard music which has so much the air of unpremeditated effusion. The performer seems to pour out, unconsciously

as it were, the thoughts and emotions that pass through his mind. . . .
He accomplishes enormous difficulties, but so quietly, so smoothly . . .
that the listener is not sensible of their real magnitude.

The harmony between Chopin's physical make-up and his
style of playing was complete.   On the whole he chose to convey
his intentions by subtle refinements of execution rather than by a
broad and comprehensive treatment of the instrument.   He was
physically incapable of consistently achieving the powerful effects
which many of his works call for and for that reason had to give
up playing them towards the end of his life; but this does not
mean that he never produced an emphatic *forte* or could not play
with dramatic fire.   Nothing could be farther from the truth
than to imagine that a gentle murmur was all that he ever cared
to draw from the piano, and that his works are heard in their
true setting if they are tinkled on small square or cottage pianos.[1]
His friend and pupil Georges Mathias, speaking of him at his best,
declared:

Those who have heard Chopin may say that nothing approaching it
has ever been heard.   What virtuosity!   What power!   yes, what
power!   But it only lasted a few bars; and what exaltation and inspiration!   The man's whole being vibrated.   The piano was animated by
the intensest life: it sent a thrill through you!

And Ernest Legouvé, who often heard him in Paris, shows us
how Chopin could carry his listeners away:

Once at the piano Chopin played until he was exhausted.   In the
grip of a disease that knows no mercy, dark rings appeared around his
eyes, a feverish brightness lit up his face, his lips turned to a vivid red
and his breath came in short gasps.   He felt, we felt that something

---

[1] The book *How Chopin Played*, based on the recollections of A. J.
Hipkins, has given a new lease of life to some of the most deplorable
of the Chopin legends.   Just how much of Chopin's playing Mr. Hipkins was acquainted with has lately been revealed to the writer by the
acquisition of his annotated copies of Chopin.   Mr. Hipkins was in
no position to make *ex cathedra* pronouncements on the subject.

of his life was flowing away with the music; he would not stop and we had not the strength to stop him. The fever which consumed him took possession of us all!

It would have been strange indeed if the creator of the Polonaise in A♭ and the A minor ('Winter Wind') Study had never evoked from his piano more than a delicate murmur. His own indications on his music, such as the *fff—con più fuoco possibile* at the end of the C♯ minor Étude of Op. 10 and the *appassionato— il più forte possibile* of one passage in the G minor Ballade, are not to be set aside merely because Chopin himself rarely had the physical strength to do justice to his own most virile works. By comparison with some of the hammer-and-tongs virtuosi of his day Chopin was indeed a quiet player; yet as Mikuli, who was also with him in Paris, points out:

> The tone which Chopin drew from the instrument, especially in *cantabile* passages, was immense . . . a manly energy gave to appro priate passages an overpowering effect—energy without coarseness; but, on the other hand, he knew how to enchant the listener by delicacy —without affectation.

It is to be feared that the notion of Chopin's playing being in variably characterized by excessive delicacy and effeminacy has been prejudicial to the comprehension of a considerable portion of his work. Many have hesitated to accept as the manifestations of a virile and enthusiastic spirit compositions which, it has been thought, should properly be performed with feminine charm and simpering prettiness. On occasions Chopin strove to avoid such misunderstanding by having his new works played by his pupils when he felt too weak to do them justice. Thus in 1839 his pupil Gutmann was called upon to play the C♯ minor Scherzo to Moscheles, so that the latter might not get a wrong idea of the work.

To attempt to conjure up in words the magic of Chopin's poetic playing was beyond the power of most of those who heard him, but one sensitive listener, Schumann, has left a vivid description of his rendering of the A♭ and F minor studies of Op. 25, which he heard at Leipzig in 1836:

Let one imagine that an Aeolian harp had all the scales and that an artist's hand had mingled them together in all kinds of fantastic decorations, but in such a way that you could always hear a deeper fundamental tone and a softly singing melody—there you have something of a picture of his playing. It is wrong to suppose that he brought out distinctly every one of the little notes: it was rather a billowing of the chord of A♭, swelled here and there by the pedal; but through the harmonies could be heard in sustained tones a wonderful melody, and only in the middle section did a tenor part once stand out more prominently from the chords and the principal theme. When the study has ended you feel as you do after a blissful vision, seen in a dream, which, already half-awake, you would fain recall . . . and then he played the second, in F minor . . . so charming, dreamy and soft, just as if a child were singing in its sleep.

When we come to inquire into the means by which Chopin accomplished his miracles, rather than the miracles themselves, we are on firmer ground. His hands, though not large, were extraordinarily supple and ideally proportioned for piano playing. The widespread chords and arpeggios which abound in his works presented no difficulty to him: he overcame these problems with such unconcern that one can only compare him, in this respect, with Thalberg, who made it a point of honour to vanquish the greatest difficulties with the minimum visible signs of effort.

To obtain, as it were, a bird's-eye view of the technical domain of which Chopin was master, one has only to glance at his twenty-seven Studies and the Preludes. He could execute every one of these pieces with absolute perfection—an achievement which not even the most blasé of modern pianists will underrate. The metronome marks which he placed on the studies are authentic (*his* metronome, unlike Schumann's, worked reliably) and are a guide to his own interpretation, in so far as they indicate the speed at which he could perform, with every refinement of shading and accent, works like the Study in A♭, Op. 10, No. 10, of which Hans von Bülow wrote: 'He who can play this Study in a really

finished manner may congratulate himself on having climbed to
the highest point of the pianist's Parnassus.' The earliest records
of Chopin's playing call attention to the evenness of his touch
and the independence of his hands: each of his fingers seemed to
be controlled by an individual will. His scale-playing caused
people to ask: 'What is his secret for making scales *flow* like
that?' and in the style of playing which the French call *jeu perlé*
he could produce ravishing effects of delicate limpidity.

Always keeping in view the end he was aiming at—pure
singing tone, a fine *legato* and carefully moulded phrasing, Chopin
did not hesitate to throw overboard the classical rules of fingering
whenever they hindered his purpose. He was radically original
in this respect and his defiance of the well-established conventions
aroused the indignation of the pundits. In order to keep the
hand quiet and 'flow over the difficulty' he would slide one
finger over several adjacent keys or unobtrusively pass his fourth
finger over the little finger, thus—his own fingering of a passage
in the *Berceuse*:

Or again, he would play a sequence of notes (*legato*) with the
thumb (Study in F minor):

Such 'liberties' seem nothing to us to-day, yet in Chopin's time
they were regarded as outrageous. From his earliest days (perhaps because he was never subjected to any discipline by a strict
piano mentor) he boldly asserted a demand for complete freedom
for the pianist. It is in one of his first studies that we find him
setting forth his new ideas (see Op. 10, No. 2). To make sure
there should be no misunderstanding, Chopin marked the
fingering of almost every note for the right hand.[1] The famous

[1] Hugo Leichtentritt points out that Chopin was here harking back
to 'an old fingering method of the pre-Bach period.' The Oxford

'Black-Key' Study, Op. 10, No. 5, in which the thumb joins the other fingers in sporting on the black keys—a practice frowned on by the older school of pianists—may be quoted as another example of his breaking away from tradition.

Although many pianists before Chopin had realized the importance of pedalling, none went so far as he in exploring the rich new territory which the invention of the sustaining pedal had opened up. Every page of his music clearly shows how much he relied upon its use for obtaining those wonderful effects by which the piano was transformed under his hands into a new instrument, and his listeners were carried away into the 'strange spaces' where he confessed he often wandered. (If, as a single example, the reader will look at the *Barcarolle*, Op. 60, it will be most strongly brought home to him just how much the pedal meant to Chopin: without the sustaining pedal this music is unthinkable.)

Knowing that without the pedal his imagination would have been tied down to earth, Chopin was careful—in his manuscripts at least—to make clear his intentions regarding its use. Unfortu-nately his publishers were not so particular. In many cases the engraver took no notice of what the composer had written, but applied his own rule of thumb when sprinkling pedal marks over the printed page. Even in those cases where we can be quite sure that the pedal marks are authentic[1] the problem of correct pedalling is not solved for the modern interpreter of Chopin. The pianos of his time had far less sustaining power than ours: consequently Chopin could, without prejudice to clarity, hold down the pedal in longish passages which, if played thus on a modern instrument, would be hopelessly blurred.

When Chopin was playing it was often observed that his foot seemed literally to vibrate as he rapidly pedalled certain passages.

---

edition of Chopin gives the fingering of the first French edition, as inserted by Chopin himself in the proof-sheets.

[1] No edition of his works so far published gives all the original pedallings.

Chopin

Here is an example of his practice, taken from the A major Polonaise (Chopin's original manuscript):

No element in Chopin's style of playing has aroused more discussion than his celebrated *tempo rubato* and none, it is safe to say, has been more responsible for false interpretation of his music. How many pianists, resolved on differentiating between the piano styles of, say, Beethoven and Chopin, have been content to pull Chopin's notes to pieces, completely disregarding the composer's indications of measure and rhythm, in order to produce the coveted 'Chopin *rubato* effect'! With whatever freedom Chopin may have 'leaned about with his bars,' one thing is certain: his use of *rubato* was more restricted than is commonly thought and could never be reduced to a mere recipe for adding a novel flavour to the music. With him, the give and take in the matter of time-values which *rubato* implies was always subject to the discipline of the 'presiding measure.' In a considerable portion of his work the use of *rubato* is quite out of place and may even make nonsense of the music. The worst of all is to hear Chopin's phrases distorted by those clumsy *accelerandi* and *ritardandi* (within the space of a bar or two) which so often pass for *rubato*. Where Chopin himself produced wonderful effects of lingering, of hesitation or, on the other hand, of eager anticipation, was in those passages where no harm is done to the rhythmic and harmonic structure if, *over a firmly controlled bass*, the player allows the melody to vacillate in response to the mood of the moment, to hover, as it were, in the air, or to bound forward to meet the next accent. In pieces like the *Andante spianato*, the Nocturnes, the *Berceuse*, the A♭ Study of Op. 25, to name only a few examples that spring at once to the mind, Chopin produced inimitable effects—effects

124

which no system of notation could record.[1] In the following
passage from the F minor Ballade he for once succeeded in
conveying his intention by means of the ordinary notation:

Since such happy thoughts varied with the player's mood, it is
not surprising that many listeners received the impression that
he 'never played a piece twice in the same way.' Besides, he
would often improvise fresh ornaments on the spur of the moment
and scatter them freely over such pieces as the Nocturnes: his
inventiveness in this direction was inexhaustible.

When Chopin played Bach or Mozart he could be as 'steady
as a metronome.' We need not pay too much attention to
Berlioz when he says that Chopin *could not* play strictly in time
—Berlioz was sensitive to the slightest departure from the beat.
He was admirably equipped to perform the works of these
masters, and brought to the task a loving understanding as well
as his subtly refined technique. On one occasion he played to
his pupil, Friederike Müller, fourteen of Bach's Preludes and
Fugues from memory. Usually, of course, it was his own music
that people wished to hear, but it was not uncommon for him to
perform those works of Beethoven, Weber or Hummel which
came closest to his own type of musical thought. Thus we hear
of him playing Beethoven's Op. 26 in A♭, the 'Moonlight'
Sonata or the 'Appassionata,' never the later sonatas, which,
besides being completely over the heads of the frequenters of the
Parisian *salons*, were enigmas to Chopin himself and many of
his musical contemporaries. We may well believe W. von Lenz
when he declares that Chopin's interpretation of Beethoven's

[1] The very special rhythm of a Chopin mazurka is not to be confused
with the *rubato* described here.

works made them sound 'small.' Although Chopin was by no means unaware of the significance of Beethoven,[1] he had so little in common with him that he could bring to the interpretation of his music not much more than a perfectly finished technique—too perfect, perhaps, for Beethoven's rugged masterpieces.

Chopin need not be blamed for his failure to get to the heart of Beethoven. Like most *creative* geniuses he was dominated by the urge to project outside himself the music that was within. His mind was in many ways sealed against external impressions. In this respect he was the exact opposite of Liszt, the supreme interpreter of other men's music. It was his characteristic aloofness from that which did not harmonize with his own outlook that prevented Chopin from seeing any attraction or merit in Schumann's work. There is something almost pathetic in Schumann's early hero-worship and devotion to the 'Glorious One,' for Chopin could never bring himself to take an interest in his friend's compositions.[2] Let us remember, however, that but for this preoccupation with the world of his *own* imagination, Chopin might have lost some of his essential quality. If his sympathies had been wider he might have dissipated his powers over a wider field of endeavour, instead of concentrating the riches of his mind into the handful of masterpieces which have earned him his own special place in the history of the musical art.

There is not a great deal to be said of Chopin as a teacher. His pupils were, on the whole, undistinguished, which is not surprising when one considers whence they were drawn. For eighteen years he was the piano teacher *à la mode*, and the majority of his pupils were ladies of the high aristocracy who wished to perfect themselves in their 'accomplishments.' When, exceptionally, he had a serious, professional pupil, Chopin was prepared to devote himself generously to his interest. Thus he

---

[1] In 1833 he made Elsner a present of Fétis's *Beethoven Studies: a Treatise on Harmony and Composition*.

[2] Schumann's enthusiasm cooled down considerably in later years.

appealed to the Grand Duke of Baden to obtain exemption from military service for Adolph Gutmann, declaring himself anxious 'that the career of an artist who gives so much promise should not be blighted at its outset' (unpublished letter of 25th November 1839). Gutmann, however, achieved nothing later on. Among Chopin's better pupils may be mentioned Charles Filtsch, an infant prodigy who died very young ('I shall shut up shop when that young man sets out on his travels,' said Liszt), Friederike Müller, who made a name for herself in Germany, Georges Mathias, who became a noted professor at the Paris Conserva-toire, and Mikuli, who later published an edition of Chopin's works. The rest are of small account. (We shall say nothing of the irrepressible 'last pupils' who came forward with unfailing regularity until well into the twentieth century to initiate aspiring pianists into the 'secret of Chopin.') Princess Marcelline Czar-toryska herself seems to have been the one whose playing most nearly approached that of her master. She was one of Chopin's most intimate friends, and the temperamental affinity between them made it possible for her to interpret his music with rare fidelity to his own conception.

However advanced his pupils were when they came to him, Chopin made them all go back to Clementi's *Gradus* and Cramer's studies: he set a high value on these for teaching purposes. In the matter of scale-playing he made his pupils begin with the scale of B major. He considered that when the hand was lightly placed on the keyboard with the fingers covering the notes E F♯ G♯ A♯ B (for the right hand), it was in the ideal playing position. Until this easy and graceful position had become second nature to the pupil no attempt was to be made to practise the scales containing more white notes. Chopin was well aware that, although easiest to read, the scale of C major is the most difficult to play perfectly. The scale of C therefore came last. A glance at the following basic exercises, which Chopin sent from Paris for his young niece Ludwika, will convey better than any description some idea of the principles he worked on.

Elbow level with the white keys. Hand neither towards the right nor the left.

Such were the exercises he prescribed for obtaining maximum fluency and evenness of touch. Notice the instruction: *Elbow level with the white keys*—a complete contrast with the 'high seat' adopted by most of his contemporaries.

Octaves were to be played freely from the wrist, but without sacrificing fullness of tone. As the pupil progressed he was put through the usual routine of studies and 'pieces.' Above all, Bach's Preludes and Fugues—'l'indispensable du pianiste' in Chopin's estimation—had to be studied with the greatest care. Afterwards came his own studies and preludes. And all the time Chopin called for pure, round tone, perfect *legato* and graceful ease. 'Facilement, facilement,' he would repeat. He had few hard and fast rules, knowing that no two players have the same shape and size of hand. He had a horror of his pupils' becoming dull and mechanical and discouraged them from practising more than three hours a day. Although he was opposed to the use of mechanical contrivances, finger stretchers and the like, he does not seem to have objected to dumb keyboards, which is surprising. Jane Stirling, for whom his word was law, possessed one.

It was quite in keeping with Chopin's character that there should be 'stormy lessons' when his pupils were particularly dense and annoying. On the other hand, when the lesson went well Chopin might, if his pupil were studying a concerto, chime in with a delicious accompaniment on a second piano. He generally used Pleyel pianos, preferring their light touch and silvery tone. Camille Pleyel did his best to meet his wishes, and Chopin responded by encouraging his pupils likewise to use Pleyel's instruments. When he was in England in 1848 Broad- wood provided him with pianos for his concerts—the time had not yet come when travelling virtuosi made an elaborate show of transporting their own extra-special instruments all over the country. Thalberg seems to have been the first to begin that practice.

The reader who is interested in the evolution of piano pedagogy will have noticed how, after the black period of nineteenth- century German virtuosity of the sledge-hammer school, a return has been made in our own time to the natural and unconstricted manner of playing the piano which Chopin taught and practised. As one reflects on the contortionist methods which were inflicted on the musical world by the German professors of the sixties and seventies of last century, one can only wonder how Chopin's works fared at the hands of those steel-fingered 'giants of the keyboard.'

CHAPTER XI

THE COMPOSER

IT is generally acknowledged—even by those to whom his music makes little appeal as such—that the esteem in which Chopin is held is justified by qualities of a peculiarly distinctive kind, not easy to define with precision, but unmistakable and inimitable. Serious criticisms can be and have been levelled against him. One writer after another has pointed out his shortcomings—his limited range, his aloofness from common humanity, his inability to handle the larger musical forms, his preoccupation with the narrow world of his own personality, and so forth. These are well-founded criticisms; yet when the discussion is over and Chopin's faults have been duly recorded, we are left face to face with the phenomenal fact that a handful of works written by the most reserved and exclusive of musicians continues to exercise a powerful attraction on men and women of every nationality and of the most varied types of mentality. The artist who shunned the crowd during his lifetime has become the prophet of his own nation and the very incarnation of the spirit of poetry in music for the rest of the world. No comparable small body of music has been subjected, in the course of a century, to such unceasing, relentless performance; yet the charm endures and the CHOPIN RECITAL, even when given by an indifferent performer, still draws crowds of the faithful to the concert hall. Eighty years ago it was suggested that Chopin's works should be 'put away and not touched for twenty years.' This exhortation fell on deaf ears; nor is there any sign that it would be obeyed to-day.

While the admirer of Chopin attributes this popularity to the composer's good qualities—the beautiful *sound* of his music, his gift of melody, his iridescent harmony, and above all his power of touching the listener's heart and stirring his imagination—there have not been lacking those of a severer cast of mind who

Victorian Misunderstandings

have regarded such attractions with suspicion. The history of
Chopin's reputation need not be discussed here—it may be mentioned that he has always stood higher in France and Germany
than in this country—but one cannot proceed far in a discussion
of him as a composer without referring to the reactions which his
works have provoked in certain English musical circles. Preju-
dices die hard, once they have established themselves, and it is
still not uncommon for the Victorian misconceptions of the nature
of Chopin's genius to make their way to the fore whenever his
name is mentioned. Nothing is more instructive than to look
back at what was written about Chopin a generation or two ago,
and to note with what mistrust so many worthy people made
the acquaintance of a new and rare beauty in art. Often the
experience affected them more than they felt was good for them
and they instinctively turned to an old and well-proven weapon
of defence: the atmosphere surrounding Chopin's work was
declared to be 'unhealthy.'

As soon as that fatal word had been uttered the rest of the
vocabulary of condemnation was not slow to follow: 'morbid,'
'exotic,' 'diseased,' 'feverish and unwholesome'—such were the
terms frequently applied to his art. The very musical apparatus
by which the composer produced some of his most enchanting
effects was often dismissed as 'enervating chromaticism.' It was
possible for a biographer to write of the first movement of the
Bb minor Sonata: 'The music grows more and more passionate
and in the concluding portion *transcends the limits of propriety.*'
Similarly we are told that the *Polonaise-Fantaisie* (now generally
admitted to be one of Chopin's finest works), 'on account of its
pathological contents stands outside the sphere of art.' Another
advises us to keep away from one of the Nocturnes: 'Let us not
tarry in the treacherous atmosphere of this Capua—it bewitches
and unmans.' Perhaps the most amazing (and ludicrous) example
of this attitude is to be found in Kleczyński's *Chopin's Greater
Works—How they should be understood.* It turns out that the way
to understand the second Prelude is *not to play it,* 'as it is bizarre.'

In the face of such misunderstandings, which have inevitably led to false interpretations of his music, it becomes necessary to assert that as a musician and an artist no one was ever 'healthier' than Frederick Chopin. Those who examine his works with the object of detecting 'pathological symptoms,' reflections of the composer's admittedly deplorable physical state, are only deceiving themselves when they claim to discover in one of the Ballades the sad effects of consumption or traces of neurotic hysteria in one of the Scherzos. From first to last Chopin's musical imagination was as healthy as any man's. He never ceased to be the reverent student of Mozart and 'the serious artist nourished on Bach.' The notion of his 'using his art only to recount to himself the story of his own tragedy'—a characteristic phrase in the Chopin picture created by Liszt—will not bear investigation.[1] Chopin was one thing only—a musician working with musical materials for purely musical ends; his first concern was the solution of *musical*, not sentimental problems. Where romantically minded commentators see 'blood and passion' or 'love and hatred' the composer himself insisted that there were only chords, modulations, progressions. There was more than that, of course, but he did not choose to reveal what it was, and the clues to the mystery are few. Yet whatever may have been the source of his inspiration—in many cases it can have been no more than the feel of the keyboard beneath his hands or the sudden fascination of a new sound pattern, accidentally lighted upon as he improvised—as soon as Chopin set to work to give a final shape to his ideas the craftsman in him took charge, and everything was subordinated to the imperious need for achieving the utmost perfection in the utterance of his thought. No composer has ever gone through such agonies of striving as did Chopin, when the time came for him to commit irrevocably to paper a musical idea that may have visited him, as it were, from nowhere. If we grant that certain ideas may have come to him in a mood of depression or tense emotion, it is clear that the 'morbidity' of the original impulse must have soon been lost in the labour of polishing and perfecting.

[1] Paul Egert has demonstrated the falsity of much of the Schumann-Liszt assessment of Chopin's art.

Attitude to Romanticism—Titles

To dispose of Chopin by unhesitatingly classing him among the aggressive 'Romantics' with Schumann, Berlioz and Liszt is easy, but inexact. For their part they readily counted him as one of their number: they were sure he was completely on their side. Schumann hailed his G minor Nocturne, Op. 15, as 'the most frightful declaration of war against a whole epoch,' and for a time, in the early 1830s, Chopin may have persuaded himself that he was one of the vanguard in the battle against the old order. But soon he stood aside, cool, detached and ironical, from the hubbub that went on around him. Artistic manifestoes, pro-grammes of reform, the quarrels of the rival schools—all this left him indifferent. In 1831 he was unsophisticated enough to be dazzled by Meyerbeer's *Robert le Diable* with its romantic para-phernalia, but by 1849 he could scarcely sit through a performance of *Le Prophète*. Capable of experiencing every romantic emotion to the highest degree, Chopin was likewise capable of enshrining the memory of these experiences in music which has a truly classical finish. But for this felicitous concord between heart and head his work would not have survived: it would have passed into oblivion with those other effusions which fill the countless 'Albums des Pianistes' so dear to the sentimentalists of the nineteenth century.

Even in the relatively unimportant matter of titles for his works Chopin stood aside from the trend of fashion. Apart from such pieces as the *Berceuse* or the *Barcarolle*, he avoided encumbering his works with romantic titles. 'Prelude,' 'Scherzo,' 'Study'—such are the non-committal names of many compositions of great emotional content. There is not a single completely authenticated example of Chopin himself attaching a *story* to one of his works. Picture-painting and story-telling of the ordinary romantic kind have a very small place in his music. When we are tempted to hear the 'thunder of horses' hoofs' in the A♭ Polonaise, 'the wind sighing over the graves' in the finale of the B♭ minor Sonata or the murmur of a brook in the G major Prelude, we shall do well to see in such passages the logical working-out of a purely musical conception rather than the conscious endeavour to paint a picture.

133

If it is objected that in his four Ballades, at least, Chopin may be supposed to have adhered to a definite programme, the answer is that the evidence for the existence of a programme in the case of three of these works is of the flimsiest kind. The Ballade in F minor, with its elements of rondo, variation and sonata form, does not owe its logic to the fortunate sequence of incidents in any story, but to Chopin's craftsmanship in developing his thematic material. The only tale that the A♭ Ballade tells is how

is transformed into

Only in the F major Ballade does Chopin seem to have had his hands tied by a programme (Mickiewicz's legend of the haunted lake 'Switez'), and that work is, as a result, somewhat less coherent.[1]

Musical logic was, however, far from being Chopin's only preoccupation. Quite as important was that whatever he wrote should be perfect for the piano: mere scholastic correctness meant nothing to him if violence were done to the essential genius of his instrument. Happily he had little need to worry. He and his piano formed one being—to write perfectly for it was second nature to him, and quite often his music has little other substance than the suave and multicoloured sonorities of his Pleyel grand. How many passages there are whose *raison d'être* lies in the sheer beauty of their sound! For example, at the end of the F major

[1] It is significant that Chopin took several years to make up his mind regarding the form of this Ballade, and in its final form the work shows traces of patchy construction.

Prelude there is an unexpected E♭ which leaves the music suspended in the air:

This stray note, pointless when considered only on paper, becomes pure poetry when realized on the piano—a delicious floating away into space. On the other hand, when his imagination dictated it to him, Chopin could write passages whose 'ugliness' (as it seemed to his contemporaries) is equally pianistic. No one before him had ventured so far into the unknown, where the piano is concerned. Sometimes in his audacity he stretches out his hand to the twentieth century. Audacity was indeed required to publish in 1840 (shades of Mendelssohn!) that weird finale of the B♭ minor Sonata. Of this Hugo Leichtentritt observes:

We can now understand this as a boldly prophetic movement, a piece of musical impressionism coming seventy-five years before its time. Written in the *genre* 'unisono' which is only a stepchild in European art-music, this finale makes one of the most decisive steps forward towards a new goal, and many of the procedures of the moderns, like Schoenberg, are here anticipated.

Not for a moment would one suggest that Chopin was all novelty. His art was firmly rooted in the heritage of the past, and even a casual examination of his works (especially the early ones) will show to what extent he made use of the common musical currency of his period. But nearly always he transformed that which he borrowed into something finer. A piece of musical small change like the Alberti bass becomes unrecognizable when Chopin uses it. As for the ornamentation which he used so lavishly, its source should be sought, not so much in the standardized cadenzas and *fioriture* of the older keyboard writers, as in the Italian opera which formed the staple musical diet of

Warsaw in Chopin's time. The atmosphere of the capital was saturated with this Italianism, and it would have been impossible for Chopin to remain unaffected by it. As it was he revelled in it, and his early works are full of echoes of the opera house. Nevertheless, however he might borrow or adapt, Chopin instinctively transferred this 'vocalism' to the piano on the instrument's own terms; that is, he stylized it and achieved his purpose without attempting to produce a naïvely realistic imitation of the *bel canto* of the operatic stage. Gerald Abraham has well summed up Chopin's gift in this direction:

He had an instinct amounting to genius for inventing melodies that would be actually ineffective if sung or played on an instrument capable of sustaining tone but which, picked out in percussive points of sound each beginning to die as soon as born, are enchanting and give an illusion of singing that is often lovelier than singing itself.[1]

The reader may be again reminded that long before he made the acquaintance of Bellini's operas Chopin was writing music that is full of Italianisms.[2] This element is most easily recognized in compositions of the nocturne type, and no fewer than eight such pieces [3] (beginning with the posthumous Nocturne in E minor, published in 1855) were already written before Chopin arrived in Paris. As the years went by his harmony became more and more refined, but the old favourite turns of melody remained with him till the end. Instead of considering Chopin as indebted to Bellini for melodies of the type to be found in the Db Nocturne, Op. 27, we have only to look back at the Eb Polonaise, Op. 22, to become aware that the composer is repeating in 1835 an old idea of 1830. And he was to do the same thing

[1] *A Hundred Years of Music* (Duckworth, 1938).
[2] I. Valetta solemnly points out how the finale of Chopin's Variations, Op. 2, resembles the 'Vergin vezzosa' of Bellini's *The Puritans*. If it is so, Bellini must have travelled to Warsaw to take an idea from Chopin: the Variations were written in 1827, the opera was produced in 1835! See p. 58.
[3] Ten if we count, as we may, the slow movements of the two concertos.

again in 1844, in the B minor Sonata. Zdzislas Jachimecki has called attention to these significant resemblances:

This particular melodic curve is one of Chopin's 'fingerprints'; it occurs again and again in his music—see also the F♯ major Nocturne, Op. 15.

So far nothing has been said of the other influence which was for ever at work, colouring Chopin's musical thought and determining the direction of his development—the melodies and rhythms of his native Poland. To show how the main currents of influence—on the one hand the piano music of the school of Hummel and Field together with Italian opera, on the other the Polish folk idiom—are intermingled in Chopin's work, is beyond the scope of this volume. From the outset attentive listeners were struck by the unfamiliar Slav element, even in works like the concertos, whose outward aspect is so Hummelian. As one would expect, it is in the mazurkas and polonaises that this influence is most obvious—the mazurkas, indeed, might be regarded as a 'laboratory' where Chopin performed his most interesting experiments in fusing into one substance folk music and 'art music'; but the trace of it is never lost, not even in the nocturnes or waltzes.

Thanks to the investigations of modern Polish musicologists (notably Helena Windakiewiczowa) the relationship of Chopin to the folk music of his country has been clearly established. It should be realized that in consciously using primitive material for the creation of works of art, Chopin was doing something

which no serious Polish musician before him had dreamt of.
Composers like Kamieński, Stefani, Kurpiński and Elsner himself had no particular affection for folk music. Elsner, indeed,
warned Chopin against clinging too long to 'one method, one
manner, one national idiom' as the '*non plus ultra* of an artistic
model.' The young composer answered modestly but confi-
dently that he had 'the perhaps audacious, but noble, desire to
create a new world' for himself.

What that new world was we now know. From our point of
vantage in the twentieth century we can see what Elsner could
not in 1831—that for Chopin there could be no looking back
to 1800; that with him, though he did not realize it, music began
to look forward to 1900 and beyond. Others, like Schumann
and Berlioz, might raise a louder uproar, but it was Chopin
who, for all his reserve and indifference, was the real revolutionary: it was he who placed the first explosive charge against
that long-revered edifice of classical diatonic harmony which now
lies in utter ruin and disintegration. Strange that a poet's reverie
should forebode the end of an epoch!

CHAPTER XII

CONCERTOS, STUDIES, PRELUDES

IT will scarcely be profitable to devote space to Chopin's earliest works, for the reason that they present little interest to the general musical public, which practically never has the chance of becoming acquainted with them. Indeed one might ask: How many musicians have ever heard a complete performance (with orchestra) of the 'Là ci darem' Variations, Op. 2, the *Fantasia on Polish Airs* or the *Krakowiak*, Op. 14? These, with the Rondo, Op. 1, the *Rondo à la Mazur*, the Sonata, Op. 4, and the Trio in G minor, must remain the province of the musicologist who is interested in the sources of Chopin's maturer style.[1]

Two works, however, have maintained themselves in the concert repertory, in spite of the hard things which the scholars have said against them. These are the Concertos in F minor and E minor, written by the lad of twenty, a fact that should be borne in mind by those who hold them up to scornful comparison with Beethoven's mature works. At the time when Chopin was a student in Warsaw Beethoven's piano concertos were practically unknown there.[2] His only models were the fashionable concertos of Kalkbrenner, Ries, Hummel and Field, in which the orchestra is relegated to the inferior position of providing an accompaniment to the 'expressivities' and virtuosic display of the soloist. This situation, it must be admitted, was agreeable to Chopin, who was entirely absorbed by the piano and had neither the gift for creating music in any other setting nor the inclination to master

[1] For the only serious study (in English) of Chopin's evolution the reader may be referred to Gerald Abraham's *Chopin's Musical Style*, a work of great interest and value, but slightly marred by the author's acceptance of the 'standard' chronology of Chopin's works.

[2] Elsner himself says that 'Beethoven's piano works have had to give way to the taste of a more modern fashion' (1831).

the art of writing for the orchestra. He had had the privilege of meeting Hummel in 1828, and when he came to write his concertos the inexperienced youth naturally followed the older man more or less closely, so far as the scaffolding of the works was concerned. Once he had got rid of the indispensable but irksome orchestral sections, Chopin was like a schoolboy released from the drudgery of the class-room. He could write for the piano part original and beautiful music, leaving the orchestra to plod on, for the most part, as the tedious companion of a blissfully oblivious soloist.

Not thus are masterpieces of concerted music created. It is the juvenile charm of the two concertos, the poetry of their slow movements and the brilliance of the piano writing that has kept them alive in spite of glaring weaknesses of construction. (One ought not imagine, however, that Chopin was utterly incapable of writing for the orchestra. The accompaniment to the declamatory middle section of the *Larghetto* of Op. 21 is quite a model of its kind.)[1]

All that remains of the third piano Concerto which Chopin planned to write is preserved in the *Allegro de Concert*, Op. 46, a work patched up in 1841 from materials nearly ten years old. We do not know why Chopin did not complete this Concerto: perhaps the thought of another struggle with the orchestra caused him to drop the project. 'You don't tell us whether you have finished your third Concerto,' his father writes to him in Paris. The *Allegro de Concert* is clearly the first movement of a piano concerto arranged as a solo, with little attempt to disguise the fact. It is quite easy to see where the orchestral *tutti* end and the solo begins. The themes do not represent the Chopin of 1841, although certain portions of the work belong to his later style. Taken as a whole it is unconvincing, though brilliant and exceedingly difficult.

By the time he was eighteen Chopin had become aware that

[1] The reader is reminded that when the concertos are played to-day it is generally with Klindworth's (F minor), Tausig's (E minor) or someone else's 'improved' orchestration.

for the purposes of the new piano style towards which he was feeling his way the old stereotyped keyboard exercises were insufficient. While engaged in writing his first Concerto and other concert pieces, he began to compose studies which would enable himself and others to overcome the technical difficulties these works present to the pianist. Thus came into existence the first set of twelve Studies, Op. 10, a remarkable contribution to the literature of the piano, and one whose merit is enhanced if the composer's age is taken into account. These pieces are extraordinarily mature: no trace of stumbling. The lad of eighteen set out to write technical exercises and ended by creating a new *genre*, the *étude* as we know it, wherein material for technical study is made the vehicle for the expression of a deeper musical conception. With few exceptions, each study is concerned with a single motive, whose musical and pianistic possibilities the composer exhausts. Chopin, freed from the obligation to develop his ideas along prescribed lines—always a bugbear to him—could work at ease within the framework which best suited him, and nowhere does he show himself more of a master in handling the smaller musical forms than in these twenty-seven short pieces.

These first studies form a series the members of which are connected by key-relationship. Thus Nos. 1 and 2 (C major and A minor), 3 and 4 (E major and C♯ minor), 5 and 6, etc., are associated by being in relative major and minor keys. This was intentional, not accidental—in later years Chopin carried out this intention completely, in the Preludes. The connection between Nos. 3 and 4 is emphasized by the fact that at the end of the the E major Study Chopin wrote in his manuscript: *Attacca il presto*, i.e. No. 4. No. 7 is a stranger in their midst, having been written later than the others: at first the present Nos. 8, 9, 10 and 11 were numbered 7, 8, 9 and 10. The twelve Studies, Op. 25, were written after Chopin arrived in Paris, while the *Trois Nouvelles Études* (1839) belong to a separate category, having been 'made to measure' at Moscheles's request. In spite of their prosaic origin they are as characteristic of the composer as any of the others. Although the studies were composed relatively early in Chopin's career they thoroughly cover the ground which he was to explore at leisure in later years. Wherever a pianistic difficulty makes its appearance in his works, you may be sure that somewhere in the studies a suitable preparation for it will be found.

It has often been pointed out how Chopin frequently took an idea from men like Clementi or Cramer and turned it to a fresh use. Thus where Cramer confines himself to broken chords within an octave:

Chopin, in the first Study of Op. 10, obtains vastly greater brilliance and sonority by spreading his arpeggio over the tenth:

Here, at the outset, is Chopin's immediate recognition of one of the richest of the pianoforte's latent resources: the infinite variety of resonances created by what one might call 'widespreadness plus pedal.' In 1829 Chopin was first in this field and the dissonances produced by these richly coloured arpeggios surging over a steady bass were a hint of things to come.

For beauty of melody the third Study, in E major, is unsurpassed by anything else in Chopin. It has been left to our generation to turn it into a vulgar jazz ballad. Even when played in its original form it is nearly always taken far too slowly. Those who linger sentimentally over its phrases should know that Chopin did not intend it to be dragged thus: he originally marked it *Vivace ma non troppo,* the subsequent *poco più animato* being omitted. Afterwards he changed it to *Lento ma non troppo*. In both cases, however, the emphasis is on the *non troppo*. The structure of the melody is irregular: 5 plus 3 and 5 plus 7 bars— not to be explained away as shortened or lengthened four⁄ or eight⁄bar periods. H. Windakiewiczowa shows that Polish folk tunes are built up, not of four⁄bar periods, but of one⁄bar 'cells,' and Chopin is here seen unconsciously falling in with the line of thought of his beloved folk music. In the middle section the music attains a previously unknown fullness and brilliance. Diminished sevenths were common currency, but they had not been used to produce effects like this. Note the skill with which Chopin returns to his first theme after the outburst of bravura— a passage of memorable beauty.

The famous 'Black Key' Study, No. 5, is a good example of 'inspiration' derived from improvisation at the keyboard. Who could extract more sparkle and glitter from the simple pentatonic scale? This is the Chopin of the *salon*, showing what he can do with one hand tied down to five notes—with a little help from outside!

Already in the sixth Study, in E flat minor, comes a foretaste of Wagner's *Tristan* chromaticism. The plaintive melody, accom⁄ panied by a middle part crawling within a narrow space, rises to an intense lament. Harmonically, this was one of Chopin's most notable achievements to date. Among an abundance of subtleties one may call attention to the A major which makes an unexpected appearance in the E♭ minor cadence just before the end.

No. 10, in A♭ major, shows the young composer evolving a tone⁄picture of captivating elegance from a tiny motive engendered by a mere wrist⁄movement. How Chopinesque is the final section with its delicate flutterings and hesitations! When the German critic Rellstab first beheld these studies he did not know what to make of them and sarcastically advised his readers to have a surgeon at hand when practising. In the case of the E♭ major Study, No. 11, one can understand his misgivings, for nowhere in piano literature before 1830 is there to be found any⁄ thing resembling the series of immense arpeggioed chords for both hands which this study presents. Bound up with this original 'lay-out' is a new tonal scheme, the result being a 'serenade' full of colour and beautiful 'instrumentation,' if one may apply such a word to the effects which a skilful player can obtain in this piece.

The circumstances in which the so-called 'Revolutionary' Study is said to have been composed have already been mentioned. If the first challenging chord and downward rush of semiquavers were indeed evoked by the news of the fall of Warsaw [1] it is nevertheless to be assumed that the Study in its final form was the fruit of much careful thought. The ebb and flow of the left-hand passages is produced by no fewer than eight different pianistic figures which form a background for the declamation of the right hand. In the coda, as Leichtentritt remarks, Chopin finds an admirable solution to the problem of checking the music in its career and bringing it convincingly to a halt. He achieves his purpose by spreading his eight-bar theme over sixteen bars, thereby creating an impression of exhaustion and collapse, which heightens the effect of the outburst with which the Study ends.

The second set of studies, Op. 25, published in 1837, completes the exposition of piano technique begun in the first, and with undiminished interest and musical value, the high-water mark being reached in No. 11 (the so-called 'Winter Wind') and No. 12, in C minor. Chopin constantly played Nos. 1 and 2, and Schumann's account of his performance has already been quoted. The construction of No. 3 is unusual and ingenious. Beginning in F major the music makes its way by a series of modulations to the key of B major. Why B major for the middle section of a piece in F? Since the octave F–F' is exactly halved by the augmented fourth F–B, it follows that any series of modulations proceeding from F to B will, if continued from B in the same manner, cover the same amount of ground and arrive back at F. Realizing this, Chopin constructs his Study on the plan F–B–F, in which the section F–B is exactly paralleled

---

[1] Or was it not, perhaps, the beginning of Weber's C major Sonata, Op. 24?

by section B–F. (Leichtentritt illustrates this with a geometrical diagram!)

In Nos. 6 (thirds), 8 (sixths) and 9 (octaves) that which might have easily degenerated into empty virtuosity is transformed into sound-patterns whose grace compensates for the insignificance of the material from which they are made. No. 7, in C♯ minor, belongs to a different category. Far from being merely a study for the left hand, it is a duet, a dramatic scena, which rises to great heights of expression. Chopin's contemporaries listened in wonder to the new poetic utterance of this meditation. Many writers have provided romantic commentaries on it, mostly with a literary flavour. All are superfluous. The work justifies its existence simply as the expression of a poetic mood.

Most impressive in its range and power is No. 11, in A minor. It originally began with a headlong plunge into the main theme, but Chopin afterwards changed his mind and added those first four bars which prepare the way quietly and ominously for what is to follow. From the start the torrent of sound carries all before it. No trace here of effeminacy or hysteria. The work is virile, energetic and boisterous, and reveals a composer who is fully master of his craft. This spirited mood is carried over into the last Study, in C minor, a sombre and stately *cantus firmus* over which flow great waves of arpeggios—a derivative, in fact, of the first Study in C major.

The twenty-four Preludes, Op. 28, although not written with any didactic purpose, have this in common with the Studies that each of them, with few exceptions, is concerned with the exposition of a single musical idea. Indeed there is nothing in Nos. 8, 12, 16 or 19 to distinguish them from the works contained in Opp. 10 and 25. The title *Preludes* is not a particularly happy one. These pieces have obviously nothing of the character of introductions to more substantial works; they are not preludes in the sense in which Bach's 'Preludes' are understood. They are rather a collection of tone-poems, whose dimensions correspond perfectly to the nature of their contents. Every mood is represented; the whole gamut of the emotions is run before we reach the end of these twenty-four pieces in all the major and minor keys. One passes, for example, from No. 7, a slightly sentimental mazurka reminiscence which ends almost before it has begun, to the fully worked-out and tempestuous No. 8, and thence to the pompous, slow-moving No. 9 (one of the darkest pieces ever written in the bright key of E major). Chopin surpassed himself in these miniatures wherein his gifts for fine detail could have full scope. Whether the pieces owe their existence to improvisatory play with pianistic figures, e.g. Nos. 1, 3, 5, 8, 10, 23, or whether the melodic and harmonic substance is more weighty (Nos. 13, 15, 17, 21, 24), in each case subject-matter and treatment are most happily matched. They cannot all be discussed here but some noteworthy features may be pointed out.

In No. 2, in A minor (1838), Leichtentritt sees oriental characteristics: a fragmentary melodic outline repeated at different levels with strange dissonances in the monotonous accompaniment, the effect of the whole being sinister and depressing. In No. 4 the pathos of the melody is intensified by the slow, chromatic descent of the bass, which creates an impression of movement out of the key although there is no real modulation. No. 8, in F♯ minor, is remarkable for its rich figuration forming a swirl of sound around the principal motive. There are many anticipations of Wagner here:

No. 13 has the character of a nocturne. The *più lento* section with its expressive inner parts holds the essence of a genuine poetic sentiment, far removed from sentimentality. We have travelled far in the last hundred years, and our skins have become thick. Yet one hard-bitten music critic has confessed that, as he listened to Rosenthal playing this Prelude, he felt with emotion that it was the music of a vanished age, heard as in a shell that that has been cast up on the shore of time.

No. 15 (the 'Raindrop' Prelude of George Sand's account) is dominated by a single note: A♭ (=G♯) incessantly repeated in two different settings, first in a quiet idyllic passage and then as the clanging accompaniment to a solemn, processional theme. Having accepted what would normally be an irksome restriction, Chopin turns it to wonderful account. In No. 16 he sports with the keyboard, making the listener hold his breath until the mad stampede is over, while a moment later, in No. 17, an impassioned melody soars over a full and rich accompaniment. The end of this Prelude is a poem in itself: the song is heard through the haze which rises from softly booming A♭s deep in the bass. At such moments the piano became for Chopin something more than an instrument on which his music *could* be played: its sound was the *only* medium in which the phantom he was pursuing could be materialized.

No. 19, in E♭ major, gives a brief glimpse of a light-hearted mood. Let it be observed how, in the last bars, the rhythmic change and lengthened melody notes put a brake on the music and bring the swiftly turning wheel to a stop. The last prelude, in D minor, is a worthy companion piece to the 'Revolutionary' Study. The resemblance between Chopin's theme and the opening of the 'Appassionata' Sonata need not be stressed. The tremendous sonority of this Prelude can be attributed to the way in which the left-hand figure is disposed on the keyboard. Great expanses have to be covered, and from the physical difficulty of execution emerges a special tone-colour and accentuation. How far we are from the old conventional Alberti bass prattling away within the space of a fifth or so! Wild, heroic and pathetic, this rhapsody invites 'interpretation' in terms of a programme, but let us allow those final Ds to slam and bolt the door on the twenty-four Preludes without degrading them to mere cannon-shots or blows of fate!

The solitary Prelude, Op. 45, may be classed with the Nocturnes. It wanders through many keys—not aimlessly, however, for with each new key the melodic phrases take on a fresh colour. Finally all the tints of the rainbow are flashed before us in a kaleidoscopic cadenza made up of rapidly changing chords. Once again Chopin stretches out his hand to the future.

CHAPTER XIII

WALTZES, NOCTURNES, IMPROMPTUS, SONATAS

OF all Chopin's compositions those which first brought him undoubted success in Paris were the Nocturnes and Waltzes. Some of them enjoyed immense popularity, and no *soirée musicale* was complete without the strains of the *Grande Valse Brillante*, Op. 18, or the E♭ major Nocturne, Op. 9. Chopin must have been aware that (as Liszt complains)

Art, true art, catches a chill in splendid apartments hung with red damask, and swoons away completely in *salons* of pale yellow or shimmering blue. . . . When at court, keep it short: what you actually say matters little, provided that the rhythm gets into their toes and makes them think of yesterday's or to-morrow's waltz!

To speak thus is not to disparage the Nocturnes and Waltzes as music; but by comparison with those other works whose merits and significance were beyond the grasp of the fashionable world, they must relinquish the foremost place they once held. They represent only one side of Chopin, although they are, of course, eminently characteristic. It would be idle to deny that he enjoyed and valued the elegance, refinement, good manners and remoteness from vulgarity which reigned in the best *salons*. He was intelligent enough to see through the artificiality and insincerity which flourish in this atmosphere; but then one cannot have everything in an imperfect world, and he was not at all prepared to withdraw austerely into his shell. And so he would courteously play the 'pretty waltz' or 'divine nocturne' in response to the mute appeal of Mme la Comtesse's eyes. At their best these compositions can hold their own with his other works: even at their weakest they are not without a certain 'period' charm.

In 1830 Chopin wrote home from Vienna:

During supper Strauss or Lanner play waltzes. After each waltz they receive terrific applause; and if they play a *Quodlibet*, i.e. a potpourri

149

of opera tunes, songs and dances, the public is so pleased that it goes off its head—it just shows you how corrupt the taste of the Viennese is.

These old waltzes were mere primitive dance tunes with no higher pretensions. With Chopin the waltz forsook the noisy ballroom or beer-garden and became a *salon* piece, assuming the fine manners and ardours of the *jeunesse dorée*. (In our time these dance poems have found something approaching their true *milieu* in the rarefied atmosphere of the ballet. They were never meant to be danced by ordinary mundane creatures of flesh and blood.) Chopin carried the waltz far beyond the point where Schubert and Weber had left it. (He seems, by the way, to have only made the acquaintance of the latter's *Invitation to the Dance* long after he arrived in Paris.)

Nine waltzes were published by the composer himself; the others (drastically edited) appeared after his death and should not be taken into account when one considers Chopin's method of putting together a complete waltz. Op. 18, in E♭ major, though not the best of the nine, illustrates the plan generally adhered to—a suite of sixteen-bar waltz movements in contrasting character, purely rhythmic, coquettish or ardently sentimental, leading to a coda in which the excitement of the dance comes to a head. The A♭ major Waltz of Op. 34 shows this form at its highest point: it is the Chopin waltz *par excellence*, full of gallantry and *noblesse*. At the end it is as though a door suddenly closes, and the listener begins to move away from the bustling scene; only fragments of the dance are heard and finally nothing but the tapping of the waltz rhythm. The A minor Waltz (Vienna, 1831) bears the stamp of the introspective Slav temperament. For a while Chopin ceases to be the man of the world and lets his thoughts turn sadly to the Polish scene. Op. 42 has the additional caprice of a melody in duple time imposed upon the 3–4 bass. This waltz turns out to be in the nature of a rondo, wherein, oddly enough, it is not the main theme that constantly returns but a serpentine connecting passage! For *éclat* and virtuosity this piece has few equals. The three works of Op. 64 do not take us beyond the point already reached. The little Db major Waltz, with which Chopin charmed London society in 1848, has had the life beaten out of it, and the same must be said of the one in C♯ minor, although the beautiful *più lento* section, with its syncopations and passionate yearning, still retains its freshness. The last Waltz, in Ab major, has been spared. It possesses a discreet, suave elegance and much more harmonic interest than its companions—note the unexpected swerve into E major in the final section. The dance element disappears altogether in the C major trio with its broad cello melody.

Two other dances call for mention, both of them single essays, not particularly successful and never repeated. They are the *Bolero*, Op. 19, and the *Tarantella*, Op. 43. The former is often quite wrongly taken to be a 'Bolero à la Polonaise'—a most unhappy description for a work which has a good deal of reasonably genuine Spanish colour. Chopin was very familiar with Auber's *Masaniello*, which contains a bolero, and was probably led by the poverty of his model to try his hand at producing something better. (It was only much later, when he became acquainted with Pauline Viardot-Garcia, that he could have any first-hand information about Spanish music.) On the other hand, the fact that (deplorable confession!) he had to refer to Rossini's songs to make sure of the correct notation for his *Tarantella* does not prove that he merely copied Rossini. By 1841 Chopin was not obliged to copy any one. Tarantellas must all be very much alike, and it can at least be said on behalf of Chopin's that it catches the spirit of the frenzied dance. There is no Italian gaiety in the work: the composer is bent on killing or curing the poor victim of the tarantula's bite!

It is well known that Chopin took the title and general aspect of the Nocturne from John Field. (This small-scale lyrical form appears also in Schubert's *Impromptus* and *Moments musicaux*.) Here and there we find echoes, reminiscences, of Field, e.g. in the middle section of Op. 32, No. 2, but in distinction of melody, wealth of harmony and originality of piano style Chopin's Nocturnes leave Field's far behind. There is nothing remarkable in the form of these pieces: generally speaking they employ the simple formula 'A–B–A' (shortened), the middle section 'B' being quick in tempo and dramatic in character. The melody is 'sung' by the right hand against the background of a waving arpeggio accompaniment. Chopin's instinct led him to provide the ideal accompaniment for each different melody. There is usually a coda, and for this moment the composer reserves some of his most enchanting touches. The music sighs itself into silence and the listener is left to ask: 'Do I wake or sleep?'

The early Nocturnes, in C minor (published in 1938) and E minor, Op. 72, have little to recommend them, nor do the accents of the celebrated Op. 9, No. 2, carry beyond the *salon*. Nos. 1 and 3 of Op. 9 are of greater interest, the first for its carefully balanced proportions, the second for its delicate ornamentation.

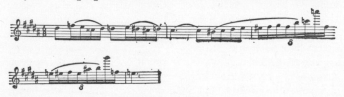

In Op. 15 Chopin's independence of his models is more clearly marked. By an imaginative lay-out of melody and accompaniment he creates, in the first Nocturne, a feeling of unearthly remoteness, which is heightened by contrast with the abrupt violence of the middle section. No. 2, in F♯ major, takes its character from its key, which lends itself to lusciousness. The piece rises to a certain degree of superficial passion—but we are still in the *salon*. However the detail is very beautiful, the *fioriture* and 'vocal' effects being especially noteworthy. With Op. 27 we arrive at two perfect specimens of the *genre*, sufficient in themselves to establish Chopin's title in this domain. In the first, in C♯ minor, the uneasy, hesitant melody, floating over an accompaniment of extraordinary depth, evokes a unique picture of night and mystery. Into this obscurity Chopin introduces a dramatic episode and builds it up skilfully to an irresistible climax. Brains

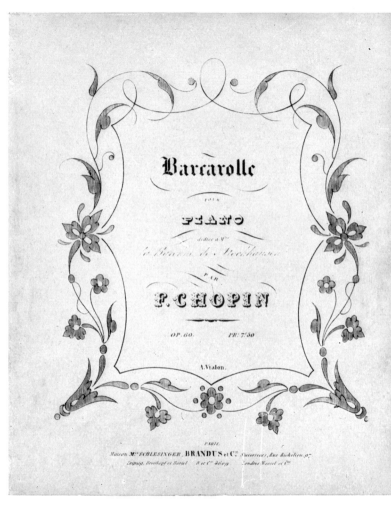

TITLE-PAGE OF THE 'BARCAROLLE' (1846)

and imagination worked together here to good purpose. The Nocturne is rounded off by a coda (in the major) of ideally poetic effect. The second Nocturne of this opus is in complete contrast: no brooding air of mystery in this music. It is serenely lyrical, not without a touch of sentimentality—the temptation of thirds and sixths is hard to resist—but not languishing . . . the performer is to blame if it becomes that. The coda provides a further example of Chopin's gift for producing new-sounding effects by essentially simple means. In this case straightforward chromatic movement over the fundamental D♭ is turned into something 'rich and strange' by the way in which the parts are laid out on the keyboard.

Op. 32 contains only one thing to detain us—the unexpected and melodramatic coda of the Nocturne in B major. At this point Chopin undoubtedly had some piece of story-telling in mind. The romance is interrupted and the troubadour silenced. As one commentator chooses to put it: 'The love-song found its end in Blood and Death'—after which it only remains to be said that this Nocturne ends on the *minor* chord—not the major found in so many editions. For richness of modulation the G major Nocturne of Op. 37 is outstanding. Chopin's principal means of expression here consists in presenting his themes in a great variety of keys. One colour follows another in a rapid but orderly succession—of the 140 bars of this piece only about twenty are in G major! (Compare the Prelude, Op. 45.) To find Op. 48, No. 1, described as a Nocturne is somewhat surprising: the conception seems too big for the framework of a composition bearing that title. There is grandeur, pathos and direct simplicity about this work. The solemn march-like opening leads to a broad, massive tune which is helped towards its climax by thunderous octave passages. To return to a plain restatement of the first theme, after the exaltation and vehemence of the chorale, would be out of the question. Chopin therefore allows the agitation to communicate itself to the remainder of the work, the pathetic character of the first theme being entirely transformed by this different treatment.

Of the two Nocturnes, Op. 55, the second, in E♭ major, is
superior to the first, in which one detects a languid insipidity.
[Paul Egert claims that this languor is due to the incorrect
tying of the Cs at the beginning of the principal phrase. He
states that Chopin's autograph corrections prove that he intended
the theme to be

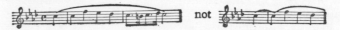

Even so, this correction does little to remove the impression that
Chopin's imagination was not particularly stirred when he wrote
this piece.] The E♭ major Nocturne (sadly neglected) breaks
away from the all-too-prevalent ternary form. 'A duet for two
solo instruments with *basso continuo*' is how it has been described.
The middle voice adds an increasingly passionate commentary to
the 'endless melody' of the upper part, and the flowing accompaniment itself rises now and then above its normal function to join
in the song. Few, surely, will agree with Niecks that the last
two Nocturnes, Op. 62, show a falling-off. The one in B major
is remarkable for the profusion of Chopinesque ornamentation in
the final section—the *non plus ultra* of pianistic filigree work.
And there are harmonic touches of a kind which one would seek
in vain in the earlier nocturnes. Consider how Chopin finds
a new way of returning to the tonic after a digression:

The finest nocturne of all bears a different name: *Barcarolle*, Op. 60. It represents the climax of Chopin's lyricism, his final outpouring of melody, a synthesis of his piano style and a summary of his achievement as a harmonist. Superficially (thanks to the thirds and sixths) it might appear to be a mere glorification of 'Italianism,' but apart from the fact that Chopin's inspiration was independent of any naïve Venetian *canzone*, the work is rich in 'impressionistic' effects which transport the listener away from Italy to the poet's nameless dream-world. One has but to think of the modulatory passage leading to the *dolce sfogato* improvisa-tion, and the elaborate coda, a web of richest harmony woven above the F♯ pedal-note.

Two other works have so much in common with the Nocturnes that it will not be out of place to mention them here—the *Andante spianato* of Op. 22 (which has no connection with the Polonaise that follows) and the *Berceuse*. The *Andante* is not exactly a night-piece: it has rather the character of an idyll, in a landscape bathed in soft, bright sunlight. The trio, marked *semplice,* brings no darker contrast before the return of the rippling G major stream. One cannot understand why Chopin should have patched up a trivial, noisy passage in order to harness this fragile pastorale to his Polonaise. The *Berceuse* is one of those happy inspirations which can never be repeated. A rocking *ostinato* bass, a short melodic phrase dissolving into sixteen variations—and there we have *the* cradle-song to discourage any one from attempting to write another. Chopin conducts the sequence of the variations with such finesse that the listener is blissfully unaware of the lack of harmonic interest. But this poetry defies analysis. Who will cut open the nightingale's throat to discover where the song comes from?

Early in 1834 Chopin sent his sister an album containing the Nocturnes, Op. 15, which Schlesinger had just published. In it was also a copy of Moscheles's *Impromptu* in E♭, Op. 89, which had appeared simultaneously with the Nocturnes.[1] A glance at

[1] The album also contains a number of fantasias and variations by Pixis, Hünten and Herz on the identical 'favorite motif' from Hérold's

Moscheles's piece shows whence Chopin derived the idea for the
work issued after his death as a *Fantaisie-Impromptu*, and explains
why the composer did not publish it, in spite of its superiority
over Moscheles's commonplace work: the plagiarism would have
been too obvious. Here is Moscheles:

His first *Impromptu* being, as it were, still-born, Chopin did not
return to this form (borrowed, together with the title, from
Schubert) until 1837. The three *Impromptus*, Opp. 29, 36 and 51,
do not belie their name. The first especially has all the air of a
carefree improvisation. Closer inspection of the first section
reveals a skilful hand at work. From the fullness of tone one
would hardly credit that not more than two notes were being
struck together. Thanks to the pedal and keyboard lay-out, the
ear is made to hear harmony in several parts.

The *Impromptu* in F♯ major is on a larger scale, and the contrast
between its parts is more striking—a pompous march in D major
follows the pastoral notes of the first section. Various opinions
are held concerning the unusual modulation by which Chopin
turns into F major after the march. Some writers find it awkward
and amateurish; others see in it a stroke of genius. One cannot
deny that when the passage is played as Chopin indicated,
i.e. *diminuendo—rallentando—piano*, down to *pianissimo* for the mur-
muring entry of F major, the effect is completely artistic. The
last pages of the work are an example of Chopin's exquisite
ieu perlé. The third *Impromptu*, in G♭ major, has never found
much favour: the composer himself dismisses it as a piece written
to oblige a friend. Yet although not strikingly original, it is

opera *Ludovic* which Chopin used in his Variations, Op. 12. There
was evidently a great demand for such things for *salon* consumption.
Chopin's Variations are no better than the rest.

certainly typical of its period (1842). There is a studied elegance in its lines and harmonies, even if the element of spontaneity is lacking.

Chopin's sonatas met with no more approval than his concertos from the academic minds of the nineteenth century. This is understandable in the case of the early C minor Sonata (1827), a work scarcely recognizable as Chopin's; but an exaggerated respect for the letter of the law governing the mythical 'true sonata form' (an invention of the lecture-room rather than of the composer's workshop) has been the cause of much injustice to the two Sonatas, in B♭ minor and B minor, of whose 'wrongness' quasi-mathematical proof is to be found in some text-books. This is not to argue that Chopin's Op. 35 and Op. 58 are above the law. They are not; but we owe it to the composer to discover *what* law he was attempting to conform with, before we decide that his work cannot be good, since it does not agree with the principles laid down by Herr Professor X in 1825. It does not settle the question to accuse Chopin of ignorance and incompetence. What he did in 1839 in the first movement of Op. 35, he chose to do again in 1844 in the B minor Sonata. We may take it, therefore, that he intended to write the sonatas in the way that he realized best suited him, as a composer whose gifts lay in the direction of long lyrical or dramatic periods rather than the closely reasoned development of short, pregnant themes. It will be answered that such a composer had better leave the sonata form alone; to which the retort is: 'Yes, if you rule that a sonata cannot exist except in the form fixed for all eternity by certain older masters, whose achievements in that form we all devoutly admire.' Schumann was one whose respect for 'the rules' led him to make a strangely absurd pronouncement on the B♭ minor Sonata. He said it was a pity Chopin did not substitute an *Adagio* in D♭ major for the repulsive Funeral March! Thus the whole point of the Sonata was lost on him, for this very Funeral March is the central core of the whole work. It was the march (written long before the other movements) which furnished Chopin with the seed from which the first movement and scherzo sprang and stimulated him to embody within the framework of a sonata the emotions which the vision of death aroused in him. This is not the place to analyse the Sonata in detail. Judged even by its own 'laws' it is not faultless—far from it—but one may surely claim that the *total artistic impression* which the work makes on an un-biased listener is one of unity, a unity transcending the technical question of form. To say that the four movements 'have little thematic or other affinity' is to deny the evidence of one's eyes and ears. From the first solemn question:

to the last whisper of the finale, the work is driven forward by one *dramatic* impulse. The wild frenzy of the development (?) section of the first movement, the chromatic gusts of the scherzo and the strange finale—each of these has its place in Chopin's musical-dramatic scheme. The finale, indeed, so far from being one of four independent pieces, wilfully bound together to form a sonata (thus Schumann), has no existence apart from the preceding movements. As music it defies ordinary analysis. The eye may see on paper how logically it is constructed, but the ear receives only an 'impression,' impossible to convey in words but none the less intense.

The B minor Sonata has not the conciseness of Op. 35. Not-withstanding its great beauties, the first movement is overloaded with thematic material, some of it of an indigestible kind. The superb flow of melody in the lyrical passages does not entirely compensate for the feeling of strain elsewhere, even though we admit the composer's right to adapt the sonata form to suit his purposes. Leaving aside the questions of fitness and unity, how-ever, one must agree that in this sonata Chopin surpassed himself in wealth of *ideas* of the first order. Its four movements contain some of the finest music ever written for the piano. Colour,

Sonata for Cello and Piano

grace, passion, reverie—all are here at the command of a composer who had reached the height of his powers.

The Sonata for cello and piano, Op. 65, Chopin's last published work, was brought into the world with great effort due not so much to lack of 'inspiration' as to the composer's search for new means of expression, such as are also foreshadowed in the *Polonaise-Fantaisie*. Zdzislas Jachimecki considers that the first and last movements represent an absolutely modern type of chamber music. Without going so far, one may agree that Chopin was clearly moving away from the accepted 'romantic' style, which explains why Niecks found in these two parts nothing but 'immense wildernesses, with only here and there a small flower,' and why Chopin did not venture to inflict the whole work on the fashionable audience at his last Paris concert. It is interesting to speculate on what Chopin's development would have been had he lived another twenty years. As it is, this sonata should be regarded not as an example of his sad decline, but as an experiment which might have led him to rich new fields.

CHAPTER XIV

POLONAISES, MAZURKAS, SCHERZOS, BALLADES

'THE story of Chopin's music begins with a Polonaise and ends with a Mazurka.' Therein is symbolized a lifetime's devotion to that patriotic idealism the cult of which has ever been an outstanding trait in the Polish character. Chopin had a French father and bore a French name ('We never cease to regret that you are not called Chopiński,' wrote Maria Wodzińska): all the more, therefore, did he insist that he himself was a Pole. The fire of patriotism within him seemed to receive added fuel from the circumstances of his origin, and when he left his native country for good, he took with him memories and aspirations which lost nothing of their intensity as the years passed. In one of his last letters to his old school friend Fontana (April 1848) we see him full of passionate hope that the day of freedom is soon to dawn:

It will not come to pass without frightful happenings, but at the end of it all is a Poland splendid, great—in a word, Poland ! . . . Everybody here is convinced that before the autumn we shall see our affairs taking shape.

Such is the spirit that breathes in his Polonaises. A threefold motif runs through them: pride in the past, lamentation for the present, hope for the future.

The Chopin polonaise (we speak of the mature works published by the composer himself) owes next to nothing to the undistinguished example of Ogiński, Kurpiński and Elsner, though the characteristic rhythm of the polonaise is, of course, common to all. Ogiński's tunes were, however, extremely popular, and in his first attempts young Chopin kept pretty close to them.[1]

[1] It is extremely doubtful whether Chopin knew Weber's polaccas when he composed his first polonaises.

His very first Polonaise (1817), in G minor—twenty-two bars with a sixteen-bar trio—is merely an imitation of Ogiński; one could expect little else from a child of seven. A recently discovered manuscript of the D minor Polonaise, Op. 71, No. 1 by Nicholas Chopin, with scribblings by the boy Frederick, shows that this work is much earlier than supposed. Already the 'Chopinesque' colour and glitter and command of the keyboard are in full evidence. The progress towards virtuosity is maintained in the Polonaise in A♭ major dedicated to Zywny (1821), and further originality appears in the G sharp minor Polonaise of 1822. This progress is kept up in the attractive Polonaise in B♭ major (1828) and the more sentimental F minor (1829). In the G♭ major Polonaise of 1829 occur ideas which were put to better use many years later in Op. 53, in A♭ major. It is difficult to speak with certainty of the form of all these works, since we do not always know how the editors have manipulated the manuscripts for publication. For the most part they keep to the simple ternary form of the Ogiński-Kurpiński model. The Polonaise in E♭ major for piano and orchestra, Op. 22, is a show-piece of the utmost brilliance, which never fails to produce its effect in the hands of a virtuoso. The part of the orchestra is insignificant and the work is usually performed as a solo. Yet one cannot dismiss it as worthless on account of its superficiality. The originality of the piano writing alone entitles it to kinder consideration.

In none of the foregoing Polonaises is the heroic note struck. Only when he had left Poland did Chopin begin to see the polonaise in another light—as an epic form in which he might enshrine his country's glory, as Mickiewicz had enshrined it in the pages of *Pan Tadeusz*. We, in our prosaic age, can scarcely imagine the fantastic splendour with which the polonaise was danced by the Polish nobility, in full national costume, in the seventeenth and eighteenth centuries. It had lost most of its character by Chopin's time, but his vivid imagination was able to conjure up the visions of the past. Considered not as a 'tone-poem,' but as a straightforward polonaise, the famous A major work of Op. 40 must be given the palm.[1] Superbly direct and uncomplicated, stripped of all superfluity—there is neither introduction nor coda—its vigorous measures symbolize the departed glories of the old aristocracy. The polonaise, be it remembered, was the processional dance of the nobility, not the people. To use the word 'vulgar' (as some have done) in referring to this much-played work is nonsense.

The remaining Polonaises come within the category of 'tone-poems.' They reveal the varied aspects of the Polish character, as well as Chopin's reactions to the sufferings of the nation. Thus the first Polonaise of Op. 26 is by turns defiant, chivalric and sentimental; while the second is threatening and gloomy. In the first there is a wealth of chromatic harmony employed with poetical effect, e.g. the enharmonic 'aside' in the trio (quoted by Jachimecki):

In the E♭ minor work it is the characteristic *rhythm*, together with dynamic variations, which provides Chopin with his chief means of expression. Consider the opening: *Maestoso (pp)—poco ritenuto —accelerando—poco rit. (cresc.)—accelerando (p)—ritenuto (cresc.)— a tempo (f)—cresc. to fff—agitato (p)*. The resulting tonal picture is extraordinarily vivid.

The opening theme of the C minor Polonaise, Op. 40, No. 2, is believed by Polish writers to be an unconscious reminiscence (in the minor key) of Kurpiński's *Coronation Polonaise*, which was sung to the words 'Welcome, O King!' The two themes certainly resemble each other, and it is quite probable that, as Chopin brooded over the past, Kurpiński's theme arose from his sub-conscious mind and assumed the dark colour of his mood. This

[1] There is no truth in the stories of the composition of this Polonaise at Majorca, accompanied by hallucinations and visions of knights and ladies. It was written before Chopin set foot on Majorca.

Polonaise has certain features in common with Op. 26, No. 1, notably in the A♭ major trio, which contains another example of Chopin's use of chromatic digressions.

With Op. 44 we arrive at that type of fantasia based on the polonaise which Chopin evolved as he felt the need to put into the normal polonaise framework more than it could comfortably hold. He did not use the title *Polonaise-Fantaisie* until he was forced to do so by the altogether unusual form of Op. 61, but the idea was already in his mind in 1840 (see also his letter of 24th August 1841). The F♯ minor work, besides containing a polonaise proper, of tremendous sweep and energy, is remarkable for the presence of a mazurka that serves as the trio. Nothing in Chopin is more original and audacious than the thunderous passage beginning:

The transition from this warlike picture to the idyllic mazurka is realized with great art, and even more so the return to the main polonaise. The introduction and coda are entirely in keeping with the character of a fantasia. The former rises like a whirl-wind from a tiny motive; the coda carries the violence of the music to a climax and then allows it to fall away, until only a distant murmur is left.

The mention of this coda leads one to speak (out of strict chronological order) of the *Polonaise-Fantaisie*, Op. 61, itself. What was hinted at in Op. 44 is carried out here with all the art at Chopin's command. The work is not absolutely successful: it fails to attain that splendid concentration of purpose which sets a crown on the great A♭ major Polonaise, Op. 53. But it works on the hearer's imagination with a power of suggestion equalled only by the F minor Fantasy or the fourth Ballade. It grows on one. The 'symphonic' introduction might well be found in one of Wagner's later works—indeed the names of Wagner (*Tristan, Siegfried, Götterdämmerung*) and Richard Strauss constantly occur when modern writers discuss the *Polonaise-Fantaisie*. The harmonic web (the richest in Chopin) is closely woven but not thick or heavy: the piano speaks in a language that had not been heard before. One single example must suffice to illustrate Chopin's gift for alighting upon new tonal effects—the long, ever-increasing trill in one, two, three, four parts over a pedal-note just after the 'intermezzo'—an unforgettable moment if the pianist is master of his craft. In the last pages of this epic Chopin bids farewell to his country's heroic past. The cavalcade which he has conjured up seems to vanish across the plain, leaving him alone, until a final loud chord breaks the spell.

Between Op. 44 and the *Polonaise-Fantaisie* comes the A♭ major Polonaise, Op. 53, a work whose praises it is unnecessary to recite. All are agreed that the possibilities of the polonaise as a *genre* are exhausted in this grandiose tone-poem. It unites the directness and strength of the 'military' Polonaise with the imagination and poetry of the Ballades. It never descends to facile realism, yet succeeds in bringing before our eyes a picture of unique splendour. Well might the exiles in Paris rise to their feet when Chopin had finished and strike up the old song: 'Poland has not perished yet, since her sons are living!'

The evolution of the polonaise from a simple dance-form to a tone-poem has a counterpart in Chopin's mazurkas, where may be traced the progress of a primitive folk dance towards a new art-form—a dance-fantasy to whose style the word 'symphonic' (in its primary meaning) has not inaptly been applied, e.g. in the case of Op. 50, No. 3, in C♯ minor. Strangely enough, this development of Chopin's style was for a long time taken as a sign of his decline; the very mazurkas which interest us most to-day were dismissed as 'less happy inspirations.' The nineteenth century saw in the Mazurkas as a whole little more than harmonic and rhythmic aberrations which, like a spice, added a 'delightful piquancy' (Niecks's phrase in 1888) to an otherwise familiar dish. The moment Chopin crossed the line of the piquantly familiar he found himself alone; the Polish note in his music, which had been one of the elements of his success in Vienna in 1829, was accept/able only up to a point. Thus the B♭ major Mazurka, Op. 7, No. 1, quickly made its way in France, Germany and England, while the A minor, Op. 17, No. 4, uncompromisingly 'primi/tive' in character, called forth only comments like 'bleak and cheerless,' 'jarring notes,' 'weird character.'

This reaction is quite understandable. The Slavonic element which colours practically all Chopin's thought, whether in ballade, scherzo or sonata, and which neither 'Italianism' nor anything else could totally obliterate, did not prevent him from speaking first as a poet and only secondly as a patriot. The whole world has understood the poet's super/national message, addressed to the heart and imagination of mankind at large. Any attempt to make Chopin's works appear an exclusively Polish possession is childish and diminishes the composer's stature (it usually takes the form of suggesting that only Poles can play Chopin). How/ever, in the later mazurkas Chopin speaks in a language which the non/Polish world cannot fully grasp—hence the neglect and misunderstanding of works like Op. 50, No. 3, or the C minor Mazurka, Op. 56, No. 3. It is to be hoped that few modern musicians will speak of these later mazurkas as being 'less spontaneous,' 'composed with the head, not the heart, nor yet the heels' (James Huneker) or 'lacking in the *beautés sauvages* which charmed us in the earlier ones.' [1] None of Chopin's music is charged with such intense emotion as these 'scholarly' and 'reflective' works. The C♯ minor Mazurka just mentioned holds in its six pages the whole story of Chopin's obsession with the Polish theme; yet W. von Lenz says airily: 'It begins as though written for the organ and ends in an exclusive *salon.*'

[1] The Mazurka in A minor, dedicated to Émile Gaillard, has been dismissed as insignificant, 'a poor thing,' by those who imagined they were dealing with an unknown posthumous work. One feels the opinions might have been different had it been known that it belongs to Chopin's best period—1841. It was published in the first instance as Op. 43.

The suggestion has been made (by Béla Bartók) that Chopin had really no contact with the true folk music of the Polish peasants and that his mazurkas represent something artificial and exotic, without roots in the national soil. The composer's own modest words contradict this: 'You know how and with what success I have tried to get to the heart of our national music. . . .' Or again, a passage in his *Szafarnia Journal* (see page 12) shows an actual example of his curiosity to learn the folk tunes at their source:

> At last giving way to his curiosity, he [Master Chopin] took some coppers out of his pocket and promised them to the singer if she would repeat her song. . . . She began to sing a mazurka, a verse of which the editor of this paper [Chopin] begs to quote.

Indeed Chopin became a connoisseur of Polish national music and would not tolerate his less sensitive compatriots' tinkering with it—witness his furious outburst against Sowiński, who had published a collection of folksongs furbished up with wretched accompaniments. Nor did he choose to make *direct* use of folk themes in his own works. Among his sixty Mazurkas very few contain an identifiable folk tune (the *poco più vivo* of Op. 68, No. 3 [1829], is an exception). The mazurs, obereks and kujawiaks (the three main forms of the mazurka) which Chopin heard constantly in his early days were no more than a stimulus to his imagination, a point of departure from which he carried the basic materials to a new level, where they became embodied in a highly civilized art-music without losing anything of their native authenticity.

The following examples (from H. Windakiewiczowa's study of *The Basic Forms of Polish Folk Music in Chopin's Mazurkas*) illustrate how his mazurka themes are built up from one-bar 'cells'—not consciously, of course: Chopin's mind worked along these lines as naturally as the Polish language came to his lips:

(1) Type AABB: Mazurka in Db major, Op. 30, No. 3:

(2) Type AABC: Mazurka in C major, Op. 7, No. 5:

(3) Type AAAB: Mazurka in F♯ minor, Op. 6:

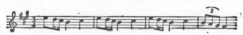

(4) Type ABBB: Mazurka in G major, Op. 67, No. 1:

The characteristic 'wave-motion' of the oberek frequently appears in the Mazurkas, e.g. Op. 50, No. 3:

Mixtures of rhythm (duple time with triple), as in Op. 33, No. 4:

Melodies based on the Lydian mode with its sharpened fourth (F♯ instead of F, in C major)—such are a few of the features of Polish national tunes which come to light in the Mazurkas. One need scarcely point out that the harmonies in which Chopin clothed his 'native wood-notes wild' are not to be traced back to folk music. The village fiddler, endlessly repeating the same fragment of melody over the droning of the bagpipe,[1] knew

---

[1] The peasant's bagpipe is heard dozens of times in the Mazurkas. See Op. 6, No. 2, as a first example. The earliest version of the A minor Mazurka, Op. 7, No. 2, has an introduction in A major which is actually marked *Duda* (bagpipe).

nothing of harmony. Chopin's multicoloured progressions, which fascinate the modern listener, would have made the Polish peasants stare. They are his personal commentary on the national theme. The striking contrast between the extremes of, on the one hand, the untouched folk tunes and, on the other, Chopin's refined treatment of the idealized mazurka, will be clearly brought out by the comparison of a passage in the F major Mazurka, Op. 68, No. 3 (1829) with one from Op. 59, No. 2, in A♭ major (1845)—a beautiful sequence in the composer's later manner:

We cannot discuss the Mazurkas in detail here. The music-lover who explores the treasure-house will be richly rewarded, for the Mazurkas contain beauties which Chopin reserved for these intimate tone-poems alone. Every kind of light and shade, of gaiety, gloom, eloquence and passion is to be found in them. Among the finest may be mentioned the famous Op. 7, No. 1, in B♭ major—a real dance, full of verve and fire; Op. 7, No. 3, the first of the tone-poems; Op. 24, No. 4—chivalric and romantic; Op. 30, No. 4—in the last bars a chain of parallel fifths and sevenths which shocked the pedants, but which are perfectly in

CHOPIN ON HIS DEATHBED
Drawn by T. Kwiatkowski

keeping with the *calando—diminuendo—smorzando* of the passage; Op. 33, Nos. 3 and 4; Op. 41 in C♯ minor—a dance-fantasy with 'symphonic' elements; Op. 50, No. 3; Op. 56, Nos. 1 and 3, the latter rich in 'prophetic' harmony; the whole of Op. 59—three splendid examples; Op. 63, No. 3—the final bars adorned by a strict canon in the octave, which Chopin seems to shake out of his sleeve with nonchalant grace.

[Chopin's nineteen Polish songs (sixteen published in 1859) are bound up with the poems they illustrate and with Polish romantic literature in general. A knowledge of their period and of the original language is necessary for a proper appreciation of them. They will not be discussed here.]

Lastly we come to Chopin's major contribution to the literature of the piano, nine works which belong to the European rather than the exclusively Polish heritage. These are the Scherzos, the F minor Fantasy and the Ballades—all on a considerable scale, and in forms which Chopin has made peculiarly his own. The title 'Scherzo' he borrowed from Beethoven to give, in the first instance, to a piece in 3–4 time and very quick tempo, possessing a kinship with the sonata form. Apart from this, Chopin's Scherzos have nothing in common with Beethoven's. They are void of 'humour' and, being self-contained works, they have dimensions which no sonata scherzo could possibly have: the B♭ minor Scherzo, for example, is cast in the form of a sonata movement with a trio intermezzo inserted before the 'working-out' section. It suited Chopin very well not to be tied down to any strict form, to be free to shape his course according to the dictates of inspiration and dramatic impulse. If, in music, the end justifies the means, then Chopin must be allowed to have achieved remarkable things within the framework chosen by himself; the listener is swept along by a flow of music that sounds like a fiery improvisation or rhapsody.

The B minor Scherzo, Op. 20 (1831), opens with an epoch-making challenge, a cry followed by a zigzag theme which surges upwards like a flame. After the agitation has exhausted itself there comes a trio, in the major, for which Chopin adapts the

Christmas folksong 'Sleep, little Jesus, sleep, my little pearl,' giving it a bell-like accompaniment (the *con anima* section has no connection with the folk tune). This intermezzo is linked up with the first period by the simple but effective device of over-lapping. The work ends with a coda wherein the dramatic tension reaches breaking-point. (Certain figures from this section were used again by Chopin in the codas of Opp. 31 and 39.)

The second Scherzo, in Bb minor, Op. 31, has an ecstatic lyricism which is lacking in the first, and is more ably constructed. It is a work that has everything to strike the imagination and charm the ear—suggestions of an impending drama: a whispered motive, an expectant pause, the answer in ringing chords; and then one of those soaring melodies of which Chopin had the secret. Particularly admirable is the way in which a quiet, expressive motive from the intermezzo:

is used in the development section to whip the music up to the highest pitch of excitement, and then to calm it down to silence. On its last appearance the lyrical melody achieves a completeness which the composer denied us at the first hearing, and at the end all the dramatic motives are brought together in a triumphant finish. Excessive performance may have dimmed the brightness of this work, but should not blind us to its merits as thrilling and convincing music.

In the C♯ minor Scherzo (begun at Majorca) Chopin uses a slightly different adaptation of the sonata form to accommodate his themes which are, in this case, a vigorous subject in octaves (not unlike Beethoven's scherzo themes) and a solemn chorale. The entry of the octaves subject is skilfully prepared. (Chopin was a master of this kind of preparation—see also the beginning of the Ab major Polonaise, Op. 53.) The *meno mosso* section in Db major brings a unique piece of piano writing: upon the deep last chord of each phrase there descends from the heights a delicately spun veil of sound. When the chorale goes into the minor key these arabesques impart a strange poignancy to the solemn theme. It is a great moment when the chorale rises again over the long G♯ pedal and the wave breaks into the surge of the last pages. Nowhere in these three Scherzos is there any trace of 'effeminacy,' 'hysteria' or 'morbidity.' They are the product of a sane and virile imagination working along purely musical lines.

The *Sturm und Drang* of the earlier Scherzos gives place in the fourth, in E major (1842), to the serene and joyous atmosphere of a 'forest murmurs' scene, painted in Chopin's own colours. If not ruined by being taken *prestissimo*, the first half of the coda, with its soft trill and sunny E major melody, suggests, for a moment, the woodland glade where Siegfried's forest-bird might have made its home. This is a longish work, more remarkable for subtle touches, both in harmony and construction, than for those broad effects which make an instantaneous appeal in the other Scherzos. It is consequently less often heard; yet a first-rate performance brings out beauties which should not remain unknown.

The F minor Fantasy, Op. 49 (1840–1), stands by itself. In general character it belongs to the ballade class, but in view of the number of themes employed and other differences (4–4 time instead of 6–8, for example) Chopin refrained from giving it that name. However, the title *Fantasie* does not mean that the work is without a plan. On the contrary, the various sections are harmoniously related to each other and to the whole scheme. We have been asked to believe that Frederick Chopin told Franz Liszt, who told Vladimir de Pachmann, who told James Huneker (the comedian who forms the last precious link in this chain), that this noble and thoughtful work was composed 'at the close of one desperate, immemorial day' by the pianist who was 'crooning at the piano,' and illustrates a scene of reconciliation between Chopin and George Sand in the presence of Liszt, 'Madame Camille Pleyel *née* Mock and others.' One ventures to suggest that such rubbish goes back no farther than to Messrs. Pachmann and

Chopin

Huneker.[1] The reason for mentioning it is that Chopin's reputation as a serious composer has been damaged by these tales,
which are the daily bread of the writers of programme notes, and
musicians have been repelled by the idea of his music's having
come into existence in this fashion. The F minor Fantasy needs
no accessories of this kind. The programme (if any) is a purely
ideal one. The march-like theme with which the work opens,
the dramatic and lyrical episodes, the B major oasis of the *lento
sostenuto*, the final chromatic avalanche—these spring from a
musical, not a pictorial source.

How much trouble has been caused by Schumann's remark
that, in writing his Ballades, Chopin had been 'angeregt durch
Dichtungen von Mickiewicz'! From this casual statement, that the
composer had been 'stimulated,' 'encouraged,' 'given the idea' by
Mickiewicz's poems, far-fetched conclusions have been drawn.
By ingenious and tortuous methods a complete programme has
been attached to each Ballade. With the best will in the world
it is impossible to see how logically organized works like Opp.
23, 47 and 52 can be forced into the strait jacket of the poems
which the programme-hunters have selected for the purpose. All
we can say is that, at a time when the national consciousness of
the Poles was being worked upon by Romantic influences in
literature, and exasperated by political events, Chopin could not
remain indifferent while the poets (especially the exiles) assumed
the task of strengthening the nation's morale and keeping alive
their own faith in her destiny. He was no conscious propagandist;
yet observe how a Frenchman like Mallefille [2] was made aware
of the spirit behind the G minor Ballade:

MY DEAR FRIEND!—Some time ago, in one of those soirées where,
surrounded by select and sympathetic hearers, you give full rein to your
inspiration, you let us hear that Polish Ballade which we love so much.
When you had finished we remained silent and pensive, still hearing

---

[1] It may be remembered that from the same source we learn that
Liszt one day, after dinner it is true, modestly declared that Pachmann
was the greatest pianist in the world!

[2] Cf. p. 74.

the sublime song whose last note had long vanished into space. . . .
What thoughts had the melodious voice of your piano awakened in us?
I cannot say; for each one sees in music, as in clouds, different things.
. . . The old Believer [Mickiewicz], to whose evangelic voice we
hearken with respectful admiration, seemed, with closed eyes and
clasped hands, to question Dante, his ancestor, on the secrets of heaven
and the fate of the world. . . . Accept these lines as a proof of my
affection for you and of my sympathy for your heroic country.

Why should Mickiewicz react thus if Chopin were simply
illustrating one of *his* poems? Why did Mallefille not learn the
story if there was one?

The instrumental ballade came into being when Chopin took
from the existing forms of song, rondo, sonata first movement
and variations those elements which he required for the creation
of a new and plastic form adapted to the expression of epic,
heroic or lyrical ideas. The new name absolved him from the
necessity of conforming in any way to the 'laws' governing
the original forms. Provided that his 'Ballade' had in itself that
final artistic unity which is the only criterion of success or failure,
then the composer could do as he pleased. We should no more
decide from a Ballade that Chopin did not understand sonata
form than we should say that a man who builds a concert hall
instead of a house does not understand the use of bricks.

The first Ballade having been written in 6–4 time, Chopin
kept to this measure (in its 6–8 equivalent) in the succeeding ones.[1]
The G minor Ballade (sketched in 1831) is concerned with two
complementary rather than strongly contrasted themes in G minor
and E♭ major, both of which are transformed, in the course of
the work, from quiet beginnings to outbursts of passionate declamation and triumphant song. The legendary atmosphere is created
in the first bars: it is as though the bard were collecting his thoughts
and hesitating before beginning his tale. At its second appearance
the tranquil E♮ theme is completely changed. Now in brilliant
A major it storms upward towards its climax, and collapses on

[1] The F minor Ballade was originally written in 6–4 time, altered
later to 6–8 so as to be in keeping with the *con moto* indication.

reaching it, in a way that vividly recalls the Prelude to *Tristan and Isolde*. From this point the excitement increases, but the agitated passage-work leads back, not to the first subject in G minor, as one would expect, but the E♭ theme (still presented in its heroic aspect). Thus when the 'story-telling' G minor theme does return it can lead nowhere except to the furious coda —a *presto con fuoco* full of dramatic happenings, which brings the Ballade to a tumultuous close.

In thus playing fast and loose with the sonata form Chopin was not necessarily betraying his ignorance and inability to appreciate the significance of that form. Any one can be taught to obey rules, to modulate in this way and recapitulate in that—that is what musical academies are for: legions of music students are every day turning out blameless specimens of the 'classic' forms. But Chopin was clearly not attempting to develop his music along the accepted lines: the very nature of that music would not permit it. It is idle therefore to reproach the composer with neglecting to do something which, as he announces at the outset in the words 'Ballade for Piano,' he has no intention of doing.

The above observations apply equally to the other Ballades. The F major Ballade, Op. 38, is marked by the most violent contrast between the tender, dreamy opening and the hurricane that is suddenly let loose. Schumann did not remember having heard (in 1836) the 'impassioned episodes' which he later found in the published text. That proves little, however, for Chopin was practically never known to play this Ballade in its entirety. He (and Princess Marcelline Czartoryska after him) used to play an extended version of the first section only, in F major. (A. J. Hipkins heard the princess play this in the fifties.) Not content with insisting that this work illustrates the story of how the inhabitants of Switez were engulfed in the enchanted lake, Jachimecki goes so far as to make the last bars a setting of the actual text of Mickiewicz's poem: 'And who is the maiden? I—know—not'—*finis*. The listener who has never heard of Mickiewicz or his poem need not worry. The Ballade exists for the whole world as beautiful and convincing music in its own right.

The 'climate' of the A♭ major Ballade, Op. 47, is very different. Here all is brightness, gallantry and rhythmical movement. Darker episodes there are, but they soon pass. The whole Ballade is built up from the two motives contained in the first two bars—a fragment of ascending scale and a lilting figure of two notes.[1] How promising is that opening! These first pages are of incomparable elegance and charm. Chopin's craftsmanship never forces itself upon one's notice. The music flows with an ease which conceals the art whereby the artistic result is achieved. With the change to C♯ minor a dramatic note appears. The tension rises until the whole instrument is resounding with a wealth of sound such as no one had hitherto drawn from it. In the development which follows Chopin prepares for the climax of the work—the grandiose return of the opening theme—by a long sequence of powerful effect in which the two principal motives are brought together. Like an incoming tide the waves of sound seem to retreat, only to return each time a semitone higher until finally they carry all before them.

The last Ballade, in F minor (1842),[2] is cast in a shape which cannot be positively defined in terms of the classical forms. One can but say that an analysis of the work reveals details of structure which *remind* one of a rondo, a sonata or a set of variations. Yet it is easy to see that the Ballade is not lacking in a logic of its own. A brief prelude serves to create the poetic atmosphere and prepare the scene for the entry of the main theme, a strangely haunting refrain whose origin is to be found in the F minor Study of the *Trois Nouvelles Études* (1839). This theme undergoes remarkable transformations before the end of the Ballade is reached. A second, idyllic melody which appears in the key of B♭ major forms a perfect contrast to the first theme. We may observe now with what a sure instinct Chopin allows the character

[1] See p. 134.
[2] The peak of absurdity is reached in associating this Ballade with Mickiewicz's *The Three Budrys*—a *humorous*, lively tale!

of his themes to decide what course the work shall follow. It is this secondary theme which is destined by its very nature to be transfigured into the stream of impassioned melody which carries the Ballade to its highest point. This function could not have fallen to the lot of the first theme. Its task is to provide the sub-stance of the formidable coda which holds the listener breathless until the final chord.

With the Ballade in F minor Chopin reaches his full stature as the unapproachable genius of the pianoforte, a master of rich and subtle harmony and, above all, a poet—one of those whose vision transcends the confines of nation and epoch, and whose mission it is to share with the world some of the beauty that is revealed to them alone.

APPENDICES

APPENDIX A

CALENDAR

(Figures in brackets denote the age reached by the person mentioned durin the year in question.)

Year	Age	Life	Contemporary Musicians
1810		Fryderyk Franciszek Chopin born, Mar. 1, at Zelazowa Wola, Poland, son of Nicholas Chopin (39), a tutor. At the end of the year the family moves to Warsaw.	Nicolai born, June 9; Schumann born, June 8. Adam aged 7; Auber 28; Balfe 2; Beethoven 40; Bellini 9; Berlioz 7; Bishop 24; Boïeldieu 35; Catel 37; Cherubini 50; Clementi 58; Czerny 19; Donizetti 13; Dussek 49; Field 28; Glinka 7; Gossec 76; Grétry 69; Gyrowetz 47; Halévy 11; Hérold 19; Hummel 32; Kalkbrenner 22; Lesueur 50; Loewe 14; Marschner 15; Méhul 47; Mendelssohn 1; Mercadante 15; Meyerbeer 19; Onslow 26; Paer 39; Paisiello 69; Pleyel 53; Rossini 18; Salieri 60; Schubert 13; Spontini 36; Spohr 26; Steibelt 45; Vogler 61; Weber 26; Zelter 52.
1811	1	Second sister, Isabella, born July 9	Hiller born, Oct. 24; Liszt born, Oct. 22; Thomas (A.) born, Aug. 5.

Year	Age	Life	Contemporary Musicians
1812	2	Nicholas Chopin (41) becomes professor of French at the Military Cadet School and at the elementary School of Artillery and Military Engineering. Third sister, Emilia, born.	Dussek (51) dies, March 20; Flotow born, April 27; Thalberg born, Jan. 7.
1813	3		Alkan born, Nov. 30; Dargomizhsky born, Feb. 14; Grétry (72) dies, Sept. 24; Macfarren born, March 2; Verdi born, Oct. 10; Wagner born, May 22.
1814	4	Grand Duchy of Warsaw comes again under Russian rule.	Henselt born, May 12; Vogler (65) dies, May 6.
1815	5		Franz born, June 28; Heller born, May 15; Kjerulf born, Sept. 15.
1816	6		Bennett (Sterndale) born, April 13; Paisiello (75) dies, June 5.
1817	7	Begins to take piano lessons from Adalbert Zywny (61). First Polonaise, in G minor, published. March dedicated to Grand Duke Constantine and scored for military band by another hand.	Gade born, Feb. 22; Méhul (54) dies, Oct. 18; Monsigny (88) dies, Jan. 14.
1818	8	Plays at a charity concert in Warsaw, Feb. 24, performing a concerto by Gyrowetz (55). Invitations to aristocratic houses follow. In Sept. presents two Polonaises to the empress.	Gounod born, June 17; Isouard (43) dies, March 23.
1819	9		Offenbach born, June 21.
1820	10	Angelica Catalani (40)	Moniuszko born, May 5;

Year	Age	Life	Contemporary Musicians
		sings in Warsaw and is so impressed with C. that she presents him with a watch.	Serov born, Jan. 23; Vieuxtemps born, Feb. 20.
1821	11	Dedicates a Polonaise to Zywny (65) on his birthday, April 23.	
1822	12	Begins to receive some instruction from Elsner (53), who has founded the Warsaw Conservatory in 1821. Composes Polonaise in G♯ minor.	Franck born, Dec. 10; Raff born, May 27.
1823	13	Enrolled as a pupil at the Warsaw Lyceum. Studies Carl Anton Simon's book on harmony.	Kirchner born, Dec. 10; Lalo born, Jan. 27; Reyer born, Dec. 1; Steibelt (58) dies, Sept. 20.
1825	14	Wins first-year prize at the Lyceum. Edits the *Szafarnia Journal*, a holiday diary, with his sister.	Bruckner born, Sept. 4; Cornelius born, Dec. 24; Reinecke born, June 23; Smetana born, March 2; Viotti (71) dies, March 3.
1825	15	Plays before Tsar Alexander I (48) who gives him a diamond ring. Rondo, C minor (Op. 1) published.	Salieri (75) dies, May 7; Strauss (J. ii) born, Oct. 25; Winter (70) dies, Oct. 17.
1826	16	Composes B♭ minor Polonaise for Wilhelm Kolberg. Holiday at Reinerz, with mother and sister Emilia (13). Gives two concerts at the Kurhaus for the benefit of orphans. Enters the Conservatory as a full-time music student.	Weber (40) dies, June 4–5.
1827	17	His sister Emilia (14) dies, April 10. Variations on 'Là ci darem,' Sonata in	Beethoven (57) dies, March 26.

Year	Age	Life	Contemporary Musicians
		C minor (Op. 4) and smaller pieces (e.g. Mazurka, Op. 68, No. 2) composed.	
1828	18	*Rondo à la Mazur* (Op. 5) published, Feb. Trio in G minor begun. Visit to Berlin, Sept. Fantasy on Polish Airs (Op. 13). *Krakowiak* Rondo (Op. 14). Makes the acquaintance of Hummel (50).	Bargiel born, Oct. 10; Schubert (31) dies, Nov. 19.
1829	19	Paganini (45) in Warsaw. C. finishes course at the Conservatory, July. Concerto in F minor (Op. 21). Visit to Vienna, where he gives two concerts, Aug. 11 and 18. Visits to Prague, Teplitz and Dresden. Returns to Warsaw in Sept. Reveals love for Constantia Gladkowska (19). Begins composing piano studies. Second visit to Prince Radziwill (54) at Antonin, where he writes Polonaise for piano and cello. His father's request for a State grant turned down.	Gossec (95) dies, Feb. 16.
1830	20	First public concert at Warsaw, March 17, at which he plays the Concerto in F minor. (Repeated on March 22.) Third concert, Oct. 11, at which E minor Concerto is first performed. C. leaves home on Nov. 2, *en route* for France and Italy.	Catel (57) dies, Nov. 29; Goldmark born, May 18; Rubinstein born, Nov. 28.

Year	Age	Life	Contemporary Musicians
		At Wola, on outskirts of Warsaw, a Cantata especially composed by Elsner (61) is sung. C. travels with Titus Woyciechowski to Vienna, via Breslau, Dresden and Prague.	
1831	21	Profitless sojourn in Vienna. Is on friendly terms with Hummel (53), Thalberg (19) and Czerny (40). Plays E minor Concerto at Mme Garcia ⁄ Vestris's concert, April 4. Leaves for Munich in July and gives concert there, Aug. 28. At Stuttgart, Sept., hears of capture of Warsaw by the Russians. ('Revolutionary' Study, Op. 10, No. 12, composed [?]). Arrives in Paris, mid⁄Sept. Considers taking lessons from Kalkbrenner (47) but abandons the idea. Makes acquaintance of Liszt (21), Hiller (21), etc.	Pleyel (74) dies, Nov. 14.
1832	22	Gives first Paris concert, Feb. 26, after several postponements. Friendship with Mendelssohn (23) and Berlioz (29). Presented to the Rothschilds and begins career as piano teacher to the aristocracy. Begins publication of works composed in Warsaw (Opp. 6 and 7).	Clementi (80) dies, March 10; Zelter (74) dies, May 15.
1833	23	Plays with Liszt (22) at a	Brahms born, May 7;

Year	Age	Life	Contemporary Musicians
		dramatic performance for the benefit of Harriet Smithson (33), April. Several other appearances at semiprivate concerts. Friendship with Bellini (32). Opp. 8–12 published.	Hérold (42) dies, Jan. 19.
1834	24	Visit to Aachen for the Musical Festival. Excursion to Düsseldorf with Mendelssohn (24). Unfavourable criticism from Rellstab (35). Plays at Berlioz's (31) concert at the Paris Conservatoire in Dec. Opp. 13–19 published. *Fantaisie-Impromptu*, Op. 66, composed.	Boïeldieu (59) dies, Oct. 8; Borodin born, Nov. 12; Ponchielli born, Sept. 1.
1835	25	Unsuccessful appearance at the charity concert for Polish refugees, April 5. On April 26 C. triumphs with the *Andante spianato and Polonaise*, Op. 22. Visit to Carlsbad to meet his parents, July. Visit to Dresden, Sept., where he meets Maria Wodzińska (16) and falls in love. Visit to Leipzig, where he meets Schumann (25) and Clara Wieck (16). Opp. 20 and 24 published. Seriously ill at Heidelberg. Reports of his death circulated.	Bellini (34) dies, Sept. 24; Cui born, Jan. 18; Saint-Saëns born, Oct. 9; Wieniawski born, July 10.
1836	26	Visit to Marienbad, July, to meet the Wodzińskis. The whole party returns to	Delibes born, Feb. 21.

Year	Age	Life	Contemporary Musicians
		Dresden, where C. proposes to Maria Wodzińska (17) and is accepted, on pledge of secrecy. Visit to Leipzig, where he meets Schumann (26) again. Opp. 21–3, 26 and 27 published. First meeting with George Sand (32), autumn.	
1837	27	In view of C.'s state of health, the Wodzińskis gradually allow the engagement to Maria (18) to be put aside. Visit to London, July. Growing friendship with George Sand (33). Opp. 25 and 29 32 published.	Balakirev born, Jan. 12; Field (55) dies, Jan. 11.
1838	28	Plays at court, Feb., and at Alkan's (25) concert, March. Visit to Rouen, where he plays his E minor Concerto. C. and George Sand (34) resolve to spend the coming winter at Majorca and go there in Nov. The party move to the monastery of Vallemosa. Dec. Opp. 33 and 34 published. Schumann (28) dedicates his *Kreisleriana* to C.	Bizet born, Oct. 25; Bruch born, Jan. 6.
1839	29	A miserable winter spent at Vallemosa. Preludes (Op. 28) completed. Scherzo (Op. 39) begun. Return to France in Feb. Spring spent at Marseilles, with excursion to Genoa in May. Summer	Mussorgsky born, March 21; Paer (68) dies, May 3; Rheinberger born, March 27.

Year	Age	*Life*	*Contemporary Musicians*
		at Nohant. C.'s health restored. Sonata (Op. 35) completed. Return to Paris, Oct. Meeting with Moscheles (41), with whom he appears at court, at Saint-Cloud. Op. 28 published.	
1840	30	Whole year spent in Paris with George Sand (36). Opp. 35–42 published.	Götz born, Dec. 17; Stainer born, June 6; Svendsen born, Sept. 3; Tchaikovsky born, May 7.
1841	31	Brilliant concert given, April 26. Summer at Nohant. Music-making at Nohant with Pauline Viardot-García (20). On return to Paris C. joins George Sand (37) at Rue Pigalle. Opp. 43–9 published.	Chabrier born, Jan. 18; Dvořák born, Sept. 8; Pedrell born, Feb. 19.
1842	32	Another semi-private concert given, Feb. 21. Summer at Nohant. Delacroix (33) is among the guests. Op. 50 published.	Boito born, Feb. 24; Cherubini (82) dies, March 15; Massenet born, May 12; Sullivan born, May 13.
1843	33	No further public appearances until 1848. Summer at Nohant. Opp. 51–4 published.	Grieg born, June 15; Sgambati born, May 28.
1844	34	Death of C.'s father, Nicholas Chopin (73), in Poland. Summer again spent at Nohant, where his sister Louise visits him. Opp. 55 and 56 published.	Rimsky-Korsakov born, March 18.
45	35	C.'s health declining. Summer at Nohant, where dissensions are arising between C., George Sand (41) and	Fauré born, May 13.

Year	Age	Life	Contemporary Musicians
		her son and daughter. Opp. 57 and 58 published.	
1846	36	After a very severe winter, summer spent at Nohant. Family quarrels. George Sand (42) begins publication of her novel *Lucrezia Floriani*. C. leaves Nohant for ever in Nov. Opp. 59–62 published.	
1847	37	Marriage of George Sand's (43) daughter, Solange, to the sculptor Clésinger, May, while C. is ill in Paris. In a family quarrel C. sides with Solange, thus completing the break with George Sand. Opp. 63–5 published.	Mackenzie born, Aug. 22; Mendelssohn (38) dies, Nov. 4.
1848	38	C.'s last concert in Paris, Feb. 16. Departure for London at end of April. Plays before the queen, May 15. Two successful matinées in June and July. His health is gravely undermined. Summer spent in Scotland at various private houses. Concerts at Manchester, Glasgow and Edinburgh, Aug.–Oct. Return to London, beginning of Nov. Plays at Guildhall, Nov. 16. Returns to Paris, Nov. 23.	Donizetti (51) dies, April 8; Duparc born, Jan. 21; Parry born, Feb. 27.
1849	39	Obliged to give up lessons. The Stirling family assist him with a gift of 15,000 francs. Summer spent at	Nicolai (39) dies, May 11. Adam aged 46; Alkan 36; Auber 67; Balakirev 13; Balfe 41; Bargiel 21;

Year	Age	Life	Contemporary Musicians
		Chaillot, where his sister Louise comes to nurse him. Removes to 12 Place Vendôme in the autumn. Chopin dies there, Oct. 17.	Bennett (Sterndale) 33; Berlioz 46; Bishop 63; Bizet 11; Boito 7; Borodin 15; Brahms 16; Bruch 11; Bruckner 25; Chabrier 8; Cornelius 25; Cui 14; Czerny 58; Dargomizhsky 36; Delibes 13; Duparc 1; Dvořák 8; Fauré 4; Flotow 37; Franck 27; Franz 34; Gade 32; Glinka 46; Goldmark 19; Gounod 31; Götz 8; Grieg 6; Gyrowetz 86; Halévy 50; Heller 34; Henselt 35; Hiller 38; Kirchner 26; Kjerulf 34; Lalo 26; Liszt 38; Loewe 53; Macfarren 36; Mackenzie 2; Marschner 54; Massenet 7; Mercadante 54; Meyerbeer 58; Moniuszko 29; Mussorgsky 10; Offenbach 30; Onslow 65; Parry 1; Pedrell 8; Ponchielli 15; Raff 27; Reinecke 25; Reyer 26; Rimsky-Korsakov 5; Rheinberger 10; Rossini 57; Rubinstein 19; Saint-Saëns 14; Schumann 39; Serov 29; Sgambati 6; Smetana 25; Spohr 65; Spontini 75; Stainer 9; Strauss (J. ii) 24; Sullivan 7; Svendsen 9; Tchaikovsky 9; Vieuxtemps 29; Wagner 36; Wieniawski 14.

APPENDIX B

IN ORDER OF COMPOSITION

THIS list represents the *main* sequence of composition as far as it can be ascertained from contemporary evidence—manuscripts, letters, diaries, etc. Where composition was spread over several years, e.g. the Preludes, the first available date is given. The list does not claim to give the precise order within each year.

Date	Op. No.	Title	Published
1817	—	Polonaise in G minor	1817
		'To Mme la Comtesse Victoire Skarbek' (1927)	
1817	—	Military March	—
1817	—	Polonaise in B♭ major	(1934)
1820	71, No. 1	Polonaise in D minor	1855
1820	—	Mazurka in D major	1910
1821	—	Polonaise in A♭ major	1902
		For A. Zywny (23rd April 1821)	
1822	—	Polonaise in G♯ minor	1864
		For Mme Dupont	
1824	—	Variations for flute and piano on	
		Rossini's *La Cenerentola*	(1955)
(1825	17, No. 4	Mazurka in A minor [first sketch])	(1834)
1825	1	Rondo in C minor	1825
1826	—	Polonaise in B♭ minor ('Adieu')	1879
		For Wilhelm Kolberg	
1826	—	Variations on 'The Swiss Boy'	1851
1826	72	Several Écossaises (3 published)	1855
1826	—	Variations in F major (piano duet)	—
		For T. Woyciechowski	
1826	—	Waltz in C major	
1826	—	Variations (for piano duet) on an	
		Irish air.	—

Chopin

Date	Op. No.	Title	Published
1826	—	Mazurka in G major	1826 (1851)
1826	—	Mazurka in B♮ major	1826 (1851)
1826	5	Rondo à la Mazur	1828
1827	—	*Andante dolente* in B♭ minor	—
1827	68, No. 2	Mazurka in A minor	1855
1827	4	Sonata in C minor	1851
1827	72, No. 2	Funeral March in C minor	1855
1827	72, No. 1	Nocturne in E minor	1855
1827	—	Waltzes in A♭ major and E♭ major	1902
		For Mlle Elsner	
1827	2	Variations on 'Là ci darem' from Mozart's	
		Don Giovanni for piano and orchestra	1830
1828	73	Rondo in C major for two pianos	1855
		(Originally written for piano solo)	
1828	71, No. 2	Polonaise in B♭ major	1855
1828	13	Fantasia on Polish Airs, for piano and	
		orchestra	1834
1828	14	Krakowiak. Concert Rondo for piano	
		and orchestra	1834
1828–9	8	Trio in G minor for piano, violin and cello	1833
1829	—	*Souvenir de Paganini* in A major	1881
1829	—	Polonaise in G♮ major	1872
		(The authenticity of this, queried by	
		Niecks, is now established)	
1829	74	Songs: 'The Maiden's Wish'	1857
		'What she likes'	
1829	71, No. 3	Polonaise in F minor	1855
1829	21	Concerto in F minor for piano and orchestra	1836
1829	70, No. 3	Waltz in D♭ major	1855
1829	3	Polonaise for cello and piano	1831
1829–32	10	Twelve Grand Studies	1833
1829	—	Mazurka in D major	1875
		(Revised in 1832)	
1829	—	Polonaise in G♮ major	1870

Appendix B—Catalogue of Works

Date	Op. No.	Title	Published
1829	—	Mazurka in G major	1879
1829	—	Waltz in E major	1871
1829	69, No. 2	Waltz in B minor	1852
1829	68, No. 3	Mazurka in F major	1855
1829	68, No. 1	Mazurka in C major	1855
1830	—	Waltz in E minor	1868
1830	11	Concerto in E minor for piano and orchestra	1833
1830	3	Introduction to Polonaise for cello and piano	1833
1830	—	*Lento con gran espressione* in C♯ minor	1875
1830–1	6	Four Mazurkas	1832
1830–1	7	Five Mazurkas	1832
		(In the first French edition [1833] the Mazurka in C major is included in Op. 6)	
1830	74	Songs: 'The Messenger' 'Out of my sight' 'The Warrior' 'Drinking Song'	1859
1830	—	Song: 'Enchantments'	1910
1830–1	9	Three Nocturnes	1832
1830–1	15, Nos. 1 and 2	Nocturnes in F major and F♯ major	1833
1830–1	22	Grand Polonaise in E♭ major for piano and orchestra	1836
1831	18	Waltz in E♭ major	1834
1831	74	Songs: 'Sad River' 'The Bridegroom' 'Lithuanian Song'	1859
1831	34, No. 2	Waltz in A minor	1838
1831–2	20	Scherzo in B minor	1835
1831–5	23	Ballade in G minor	1836
1832–6	25	Twelve Studies	1837
		(Nos. 1 and 2: 1836; No. 11: 1834; No. 7: 1836)	
1832–3	17	Four Mazurkas	1834

Chopin

Date	Op. No.	Title	Published
1832	16	Rondo in E♭ major	1834
1832	—	Grand Duo for piano and cello on themes from Meyerbeer's *Robert le Diable*. Composed with Franchomme. Also published as a piano duet (with Chopin's fingering) and described as 'Op. 15'	1833
1832	—	Mazurka in B♭ major (24 June 1832) For Alexandra Wolowska	1909
1833	15, No. 3	Nocturne in G minor	1834
1833	12	Variations Brillantes on the Rondo from Hérold's *Ludovic* (first performance of the opera: 16th May 1833)	1833
1833	19	Bolero in A minor	1834
1833	—	Mazurka in C major	1870
1834–5	24	Four Mazurkas	1836
1834	—	*Cantabile* in B♭ major	1931
1834	—	Mazurka in A♭ major For Celina Szymanowska	1930
1834–5	27	Two Nocturnes in C♯ minor and D♭ major	1836
1834–5	26	Two Polonaises in C♯ minor and E♭ minor	1836
1834	—	Prelude in A♭ major For Pierre Wolff (18th July 1834)	1918
1834	—	Fantaisie-Impromptu ('Fantaisie for Mme d'Este')	1855
1834	22	*Andante spianato*	1836
1835	70, No. 1	Waltz in G♭ major	1855
1835	67, No. 1	Mazurka in G major For Mlle Mlokosiewicz	1855
1835	67, No. 3	Mazurka in C major For Mme Hoffman	1855
1835	34, No. 1	Waltz in A♭ major	1838
1835	69, No. 1	Waltz in A♭ major For Maria Wodzińska	1855
1836–9	28	Twenty-four Preludes	1839

Appendix B—Catalogue of Works

Date	Op. No.	Title	Published
1836	74	Song: 'The Leaves are falling'(3 May 1836)	1855
1836–9	38	Ballade in F major	1840
1836–7	30	Four Mazurkas	1837
1836	74	Song: 'The Ring' (8th September 1836)	1859
1836–7	32	Two Nocturnes in B major and A♭ major	1837
1837	—	Nocturne in C minor	1938
1837	29	Impromptu in A♭ major	1837
1837	31	Scherzo in B♭ minor	1837
1837	74	Song: 'My darling'	1859
1837	—	*Hexameron*, Variation in E major (contributed to a collection by various composers)	1839
1837–8	33	Four Mazurkas	1838
(1837	35	Funeral March of the B♭ minor Sonata)	(1840)
1838	34, No. 3	Waltz in F major	1838
1838	37, No. 1	Nocturne in G minor	1840
1838	74	Song: 'Spring'	1859
1838	40, No. 1	Polonaise in A major	1840
		Originally dedicated to T. Woyciechowski	
1838	41, No. 1	Mazurka in E minor (28th November 1838)	1840
1838–9	40, No. 2	Polonaise in C minor	1840
1839	39	Scherzo in C♯ minor	1840
1839	35	First movement, Scherzo and Finale of B♭ minor Sonata	1840
1839	41, Nos. 2, 3 and 4	Mazurkas in B major, A♭ major and C♯ minor	1840
1839	37, No. 2	Nocturne in G major	1840
1839	36	Impromptu in F♯ major	1840
1839	—	Trois Nouvelles Études	1840
1840	—	Song: 'Dumka: Mist in my eyes' (25th March 1840)	1910
1840	42	Waltz in A♭ major	1840
1840	—	Mazurka in A minor. (Published in the album *Notre Temps*. Also in 1845 as *Mazurka élégante*)	1842

Chopin

Date	Op. No.	Title	Published
1840	—	*Sostenuto* in E♭ major (20th July 1840)	1955
1840–1	44	Polonaise in F♯ minor	1841
1840–1	46	Allegro de Concert (Originally intended as first movement of a piano Concerto—1832)	1841
1840–1	49	Fantasia in F minor	1841
1840–1	47	Ballade in A♭ major	1841
1841	—	Fugue in A minor	1877
1841	—	Mazurka in A minor For E. Gaillard	1841
1841	43	Tarantella in A♭ major	1841
1841	48	Two Nocturnes in C minor and F♯ minor	1841
1841	45	Prelude in C♯ minor	1841
1841	74	Song: 'Handsome Lad'	1859
1841	50	Three Mazurkas in G major, A♭ major and C♯ minor	1842
1842	51	Impromptu in G♭ major	1843
1842	52	Ballade in F minor	1843
1842	53	Polonaise in A♭ major	1843
1842	54	Scherzo in E major	1843
1842	70, No. 2	Waltz in F minor For Mme Belleville-Oury	1855
1843	—	Albumblatt in E major For Anna Szeremetieff	1910
1843	—	Waltz in A minor	1955
1843	55	Two Nocturnes in F minor and E♭ major	1844
1843	56	Three Mazurkas in B major, C major and C minor	1844
1843	57	Berceuse in D♭ major (Played by Chopin on 2nd February 1844)	1845
1844	58	Sonata in B minor	1845
1845	74	Song: 'Twofold End' 'Mist in my Eyes'	1859

Appendix B—Catalogue of Works

Date	Op. No.	Title	Published
1845	59	Three Mazurkas in A minor, A♭ major and F♯ minor	1845
1845–6	60	Barcarolle in F♯ major	1846
1845–6	61	Polonaise-Fantaisie	1846
1845–6	65	Sonata for piano and cello	1847
1845–6	62	Two Nocturnes in B major and E major	1846
1846	63	Three Mazurkas in B major, F minor and C♯ minor	1847
1846–7	64	Three Waltzes in D♭ major, C♯ minor and A♭ major	1847
1846	67, No. 4	Mazurka in A minor	1855
1847	74	Song: 'Melody (*The Promised Land*)'	1859
1848	—	Waltz in B major For Mrs. Erskine (12th October 1848)	—
1849	67, No. 2	Mazurka in G minor	1855
1849	68, No. 4	Mazurka in F minor	1855

(There are a few posthumous pieces whose date it is impossible to fix, e.g. the *Largo* in E♭ major, published in 1938, and others like the *Contredanse* in G♭ whose authenticity is doubtful.)

WORKS IN ORDER OF OPUS NUMBERS

Op. No.	Title	Dedication
1	Rondo in C minor	Mme Linde
2	Variations for piano and orchestra on 'Là ci darem'	Titus Woyciechowski
3	Introduction and Polonaise for piano and cello	Joseph Merk
4	Sonata in C minor	Joseph Elsner
5	Rondo à la Mazur	Alexandrine de Moriolles
6	Four Mazurkas (F♯ minor, C♯ minor, E major, E♭ minor)	Pauline Plater
7	Five Mazurkas (B♭ major, A minor, F minor, A♭ major, C major)	M. Johns

Chopin

Op. No.	Title	Dedication
8	Trio for piano, violin and cello	Prince Radziwill
9	Three Nocturnes (B♭ minor, E♭ major, B major)	Mme Camille Pleyel
10	Twelve Grand Studies	Franz Liszt
11	Concerto for piano and orchestra (E minor)	F. Kalkbrenner
12	Variations on a theme from Hérold's *Ludovic*	Emma Horsford
13	Fantasia on Polish Airs for piano and orchestra	J. P. Pixis
14	Krakowiak. Concert Rondo for piano and orchestra	Princess Adam Czartoryska
15	Three Nocturnes (F major, F♯ major, G minor)	F. Hiller
16	Rondo in E♭ major	Caroline Hartmann
17	Four Mazurkas (B♭ major, E minor, A♭ major, A minor)	Lina Freppa
18	Grand Waltz in E♭ major	Laura Horsford
19	Bolero in A minor	Comtesse de Flahault
20	Scherzo in B minor	T. Albrecht
21	Concerto for piano and orchestra (F minor)	Delphine Potocka
22	*Andante spianato* and Polonaise (E♭ major)	Baronne d'Est
23	Ballade in G minor	Baron de Stockhausen
24	Four Mazurkas (G minor, C major, A♭ major, B minor)	Comte de Perthuis
25	Twelve Studies	Comtesse d'Agoult
26	Two Polonaises (C♯ minor, E♭ minor)	J. Dessauer
27	Two Nocturnes (C♯ minor, D♭ major)	Comtesse d'Apponyi
28	Twenty-four Preludes	Camille Pleyel (French edition) J. C. Kessler (German edition)
29	Impromptu in A♭ major	Comtesse de Lobau

Appendix B—Catalogue of Works

Op. No.	Title	Dedication
30	Four Mazurkas (C minor, B minor, Db major, C# minor)	Princesse de Württemburg
31	Scherzo in Bb minor	Adèle de Fürstenstein
32	Two Nocturnes (B major, Ab major)	Baronne de Billing
33	Four Mazurkas (G# minor, D major, C major, B minor)	Comtesse Mostowska
34	Three Waltzes (Ab major, A minor, F major)	1. Mlle de Thun-Hohenstein 2. Mme G. d'Ivri 3. Mlle A. d'Eichtal
35	Sonata in Bb minor	—
36	Impromptu in F# major	—
37	Two Nocturnes (G minor, G major)	—
38	Ballade in F major	Robert Schumann
39	Scherzo in C# minor	A. Gutmann
40	Two Polonaises (A major, C minor)	J. Fontana
41	Four Mazurkas (E minor, B major, Ab major, C# major	E. Witwicki
42	Waltz in Ab major	—
43	Tarantella in Ab major	—
44	Polonaise in F# minor	Princesse de Beauvais
45	Prelude in C# minor	Princesse Czernicheff
46	*Allegro de Concert* in A major	Friederike Müller
47	Ballade in Ab major	Pauline de Noailles
48	Two Nocturnes (C minor, F# minor)	Laure Duperré
49	Fantasia in F minor	Princesse de Souzzo
50	Three Mazurkas (G major, Ab major, C# minor)	Léon Szmitkowski
51	Impromptu in Gb major	Comtesse Esterházy
52	Ballade in F minor	Baronne N. de Rothschild
53	Polonaise in Ab major	Auguste Léo
54	Scherzo in E major	Clotilde de Caraman[1]

---

[1] *Not* Jeanne de Caraman (Chopin's correction).

Chopin

Op. No.	Title	Dedication
55	Two Nocturnes (F minor, E♭ major)	Jane Stirling
56	Three Mazurkas (B major, C major, C minor)	Mlle C. Maberly
57	Berceuse in D♭ major	Élise Gavard
58	Sonata in B minor	Comtesse de Perthuis
59	Three Mazurkas (A minor, A♭ major, F♯ minor)	—
60	Barcarolle in F♯ major	Baronne de Stock-hausen
61	Polonaise-Fantaisie in A♭ major	Mme A. Veyret
62	Two Nocturnes (B major, E major)	Mlle de Könneritz
63	Three Mazurkas (B major, F minor, C♯ minor)	Comtesse Czosnowska
64	Three Waltzes (D♭ major, C♯ minor, A♭ major)	1. Delphine Potocka 2. Baronne de Roth-schild 3. Comtesse Branicka[1]
65	Sonata for piano and cello in G minor	A. Franchomme

Published Posthumously with Opus Numbers

Op. No.

66	Fantaisie-Impromptu in C♯ minor
67	Four Mazurkas (G major, G minor, C major, A minor)
68	Four Mazurkas (C major, A minor, F major, F minor)
69	Two Waltzes (A♭ major, B minor)
70	Three Waltzes (G♭ major, F minor, D♭ major)
71	Three Polonaises (D minor, B♭ major, F minor)
72	Nocturne in E minor, Funeral March in C minor, Three Écossaises (D major, G major, D♭ major)
73	Rondo for two pianos in C major
74	Seventeen Polish songs.

Works published without opus number will be found in the chrono-ogical list.

---

[1] *Not* Baronne Bronicka.

APPENDIX C

PERSONALIA

Alard, Delphin (1815–88), French violinist and composer for his instrument, student at the Paris Conservatoire, where he succeeded Baillot (q.v.) as professor.

Alboni, Marietta (1823–94), Italian contralto singer, pupil of Rossini, made her first appearance in 1843, at the Scala in Milan. Sang with much success in Paris and London.

Alkan, Charles Henri Valentin (1813–88), French pianist and composer, chiefly of *études* and caprices for his instrument. Finally settled in Paris as a teacher in 1833.

Baillot, Pierre Marie François de Sales (1771–1842), French violinist, studied in Rome and later under Catel, Cherubini and Reicha in Paris; joined Napoleon's private band in 1802 and began to give chamber concerts in 1814. He was professor at the Conservatoire and composed works for his instrument and chamber music.

Boïeldieu, François Adrien (1775–1834), French composer of operas. Spent eight years in Russia, returning to France in 1811. His best-known work, *La Dame blanche* (1825), owed much of its success to French nationalistic reaction from the Rossini worship of previous years.

Castellan, Jeanne Anaïs (born 1819), French operatic soprano, pupil of Bordogni and Nourrit (q.v.) at the Paris Conservatoire. Sang regularly at Covent Garden 1848–52. In 1849 she was the original Bertha in Meyerbeer's *Le Prophète*.

Catalani, Angelica (1780–1849), Italian soprano singer, made her first appearance at the Fenice Theatre, Venice, in 1795. Went to Portugal in 1804, to London in 1806 and became manager of the Italian Opera in Paris in 1813.

Cherubini, Maria Luigi (1760–1842), Italian composer, a complete master of the contrapuntal style. Settled in Paris in 1788. His best-known opera is *The Water-Carrier* (1808). In 1822 he became director of the Paris Conservatoire, in which commanding position he was able to exercise great influence over French musical life. His *Treatise on Counterpoint and Fugue* (1835) was closely studied by Chopin.

Cinti-Damoreau, Laure (1801–63), French opera singer, student at the Paris Conservatoire. Made her first appearance at the Théâtre Italien at the age of eighteen and at the Opéra in 1826. She remained there until 1835 and the following year joined the Opéra-Comique. Rossini and Auber wrote parts for her.

Clementi, Muzio (1752–1832), Italian composer and pianist, the creator of a true piano style as distinguished from that of the harpsichord. Trained Cramer (q.v.) and Field. His system of piano-playing is summed up in the celebrated collection of studies, *Gradus ad Parnassum* (1817).

Cramer, Johann Baptist (1771–1858), German pianist, pupil of Clementi (q.v.). Composed valuable piano studies—*Grand Practical Piano School* (c. 1810).

Czerny, Karl (1791–1857), pianist and composer in Vienna, pupil of Beethoven, Hummel and Clementi, teacher of Liszt. Wrote vast quantities of music, mainly instructive works for his instrument.

Davison, James William (1813–85), English writer on music, critic of *The Times*, 1846–79, editor of the *Musical World*, husband of the pianist Arabella Goddard.

Elsner, Joseph Xaver (1769–1854), Polish composer, first director of the Warsaw Conservatory, founded in 1821. Wrote twenty-two Polish operas and numerous other works.

Ernst, Heinrich Wilhelm (1814–65), Moravian violinist and composer for his instrument, pupil of Böhm in Vienna. Lived in Paris for six years and afterwards travelled much.

Fétis, François Joseph (1784–1871), French musicologist, appointed professor at the Paris Conservatoire in 1821 and librarian in 1827. Author of a *Biographie universelle des musiciens*, a *Histoire générale de la musique* and many theoretical works.

Franchomme, Auguste Joseph (1808–84), French violoncellist, in the orchestra first of the Paris Opéra, then of the Théâtre Italien. Member of Alard's (q.v.) quartet.

Grisi, Giulia (1811–69), Italian opera singer, made her first appearance at the age of seventeen. Bellini wrote the part of Adalgisa in *Norma* for her. She first went to Paris in 1832 and to London in 1834. She married Mario (q.v.).

Gutman, Adolf (1819–82), German pianist and composer for his instrument, pupil of Chopin in Paris.

Appendix C—Personalia

Gyrowetz, Adalbert (1763–1850), Bohemian composer, prolific writer of orchestral, operatic and chamber music.

Habeneck, François Antoine (1781–1849), French violinist, conductor and composer, pupil of Baillot at the Paris Conservatoire, where he was afterwards professor and conductor of the orchestra.

Hérold, Louis Joseph Ferdinand (1791–1833), French composer. Of his many operas the most successful were *Zampa* (1831) and *Le Pré aux Clercs* (1832).

Herz, Henri (Heinrich) (1806?–88), Austrian pianist and composer for his instrument, settled in Paris.

Herz, Jacob Simon (1794–1880), brother of the preceding, teacher of the piano and minor composer.

Hiller, Ferdinand (1811–85), German pianist and composer, pupil of Hummel, settled in Paris 1828–35, later at Frankfort, Leipzig and Dresden.

Hummel, Johann Nepomuk (1778–1837), German-Hungarian pianist and composer, a master of the light Viennese style. Himself a pupil of Mozart and Clementi (q.v.), he trained Czerny (q.v.) and Thalberg (q.v.).

Kalkbrenner, Friedrich Wilhelm Michael (1788–1849), German pianist and composer for his instrument, settled in Paris.

Klengel, August Alexander (1783–1852), German organist and composer, pupil of Clementi, appointed court organist at Dresden in 1816.

Kurpiński, Karol Kasimir (1785–1857), Polish composer, conductor and violinist. Pupil of his father, a village organist, later violinist at Warsaw and a colleague of Elsner.

Lablache, Luigi (1794–1858), Italian bass singer, made his first stage appearance at the Teatro San Carlo in Naples and later became famous all over Europe.

Lanner, Joseph Franz Karl (1801–43), Viennese composer of dance music, second only to Johann Strauss, jun.

Lefébure-Wély, Louis James Alfred (1817–70), French organist and composer, student at the Paris Conservatoire and organist at the Madeleine 1847–58.

Lesueur, Jean François (1760–1837), French composer and theorist, professor of composition at the Paris Conservatoire from 1818.

Lind, Jenny (1820–87), Swedish soprano—the 'Swedish nightingale.' Her European fame dates from about 1844 and was at its height during the London seasons 1847–8. She retired from the operatic stage in 1849, devoting herself thereafter to oratorio and concert work.

Lipiński, Karl Joseph (1790–1861), Polish violinist, travelled much and became leader of the Court orchestra at Dresden in 1839.

Malibran, Maria Felicità (1808–36), Spanish soprano singer, daughter of Manuel Garcia, whose pupil she was. She made her stage appearance in London in 1825. Married Malibran in 1826 but, the match being unhappy, lived with Bériot from 1830, marrying him, after a protracted divorce, six months before her death.

Mario, Giovanni Matteo, Cavaliere di Candia (1810–83), Italian tenor singer, made his first appearance, in Paris, 1838. The following year he paid his first visit to London. He married Grisi (q.v.).

Merk, Joseph (1795–1852), Austrian violoncellist, leader of the Opera orchestra in Vienna from 1818 and professor at the Conservatorium from 1823. He composed much for his instrument.

Moscheles, Ignaz (1794–1870), Bohemian pianist and composer, studied in Prague and Vienna, later travelled a great deal and lived much in Paris and London.

Nourrit, Adolphe (1802–39), French tenor singer, made his first appearance, at the Paris Opéra, in 1821, remaining attached to that theatre for sixteen years.

Osborne, George Alexander (1806–93), Irish pianist and composer for his instrument, pupil of Pixis (q.v.) and Kalkbrenner (q.v.) in Paris, settled in London in 1843.

Paer, Ferdinando (1771–1839), Italian opera composer, appointed *maestro di cappella* at Venice in 1791, afterwards settled successively in Vienna, Dresden and Paris.

Pasta, Giuditta (1798–1865), Italian opera singer, studied in Paris, made her first appearance in 1815 and went to London in 1816. In Paris she was first heard at the Théâtre Italien in 1821.

Pixis, Johann Peter (1788–1874), German pianist and composer for his instrument, settled in Paris and at Baden-Baden in 1845.

Pleyel, Camille (1788–1855), piano maker, music publisher and pianist in Paris, son of Ignaz Pleyel (1757–1831).

Prudent, Émile Racine Gauthier (1817–63), pianist and composer in Paris.

Radziwill, Anton, Prince (1775–1833), Polish amateur musician, composer and violoncellist. His chief work is incidental music to Goethe's *Faust.*

Appendix C—Personalia

Réber, Napoléon Henri (1807–80), French composer, pupil of Lesueur (q.v.), appointed professor of harmony at the Paris Conservatoire in 1851 and of composition in 1862.

Rellstab, Heinrich Friedrich Ludwig (1799–1860), writer on music in Berlin, appointed critic to the *Vossische Zeitung* in 1826.

Ries, Ferdinand (1784–1838), German pianist and composer, pupil of Beethoven.

Rubini, Giovanni Battista (1795–1854), Italian tenor singer, first appeared at Pavia, went to Paris for the first time in 1825 and to London in 1831.

Sontag, Henriette (1806–54), German soprano singer, student at the Conservatoire of Prague, where she appeared at short notice at the Opera at the age of fifteen. Afterwards appeared and studied in Vienna, first went to Paris in 1826 and to London in 1828.

Sowiński, Wojciech (1803–80), Polish composer and musicologist, pupil of Czerny. After travels in Italy he finally settled in Paris. In 1856 published *Les musiciens polonais et slaves*.

Spontini, Gasparo Luigi Pacifico (1774–1851), Italian composer who settled in Paris in 1803. His principal operas are *La Vestale* (1807) and *Fernand Cortez* (1809).

Stamaty, Camille Marie (1811–70), composer and teacher of Greek extraction, born in Rome but settled in Paris from childhood.

Tellefsen, Thomas Dyke Acland (1823–74), Norwegian pianist, pupil of Chopin, with whom he came to England in 1848.

Thalberg, Sigismund (1812–71), German pianist and composer for his instrument, studied under Hummel and Sechter in Vienna and made his first public appearance there in 1826.

Viardot-García, Pauline (1821–1910), Spanish operatic singer, daughter of Manuel Garcia and sister of Malibran (q.v.), studied piano as well as singing and made her first appearance as a vocalist in 1837, in Brussels. In 1839 she paid her first visit to London.

Wieck, Clara (1819–96), German pianist, one of the outstanding performers of the nineteenth century. She first introduced Chopin's compositions to German audiences. Married Robert Schumann in 1840.

APPENDIX D

BIBLIOGRAPHY

(a) WORKS OF BIOGRAPHICAL IMPORTANCE

Binental, Leopold, 'Chopin (Documents and Souvenirs)' (Polish). (Warsaw, 1930.)
—— 'Chopin.' (Paris, 1934.)
—— 'Chopin: Life and Art' (Polish). (Warsaw, 1937.)
Bory, Robert, 'La Vie de Chopin par l'image.' (Geneva, 1949.)
Bronarski, Ludwik, 'Chopin et l'Italie.' (Lausanne, 1944.)
Brookshaw, Susanna, 'Chopin in Manchester.' (1938.)
Ganche, Édouard, 'Frédéric Chopin: sa vie et ses œuvres.' (Paris, 1921.)
—— 'Dans le souvenir de Frédéric Chopin.' (Paris, 1925.)
—— 'Voyages avec Frédéric Chopin.' (Paris, 1934.)
—— 'Souffrances de Frédéric Chopin.' (Paris, 1935.)
Hedley, Arthur, 'Selected Correspondence of Chopin.' (London, 1962.)
—— 'Chopin' (in Grove's *Dictionary of Music,* London, 1954).
Hoesick, Ferdynand, 'Chopin: his Life and Work' (Polish). (Warsaw, 1904–11.)
—— 'Chopiniana' (Chopin's correspondence, etc.) (Polish). (Warsaw, 1912.)
Karasowski, Moritz, 'Life and Letters of Chopin.' (German, 1877; English, 1879.)
'*Karénine, Wladimir,*' 'George Sand: sa vie et ses œuvres.' (Paris, 1899–1926.)
Karlowicz, M., 'Souvenirs inédits de Chopin.' (Paris, 1904.)
Kobylanska, Krystyna, 'Chopin in his Own Land.' (Cracow, 1955.)
Lenz, Wilhelm v., 'The Great Piano Virtuosos of our Time.' (German, 1872.)
Liszt, Franz, 'Frederick Chopin.' English translation by J. Broadhouse. (London, 1879.)
Mirska, Maria, 'In Chopin's Footsteps.' (Polish. Warsaw, 1945.)
Niecks, Frederick, 'Frederick Chopin as a Man and Musician.' (London, 1888.)
Opiehski, Henryk, 'Collected Letters of Chopin.' (Polish, Warsaw, 1937; English, London, 1932.)
Rocheblave, Samuel, 'George Sand et sa fille.' (Paris, 1905.)

Appendix D—Bibliography

Sand, George, 'Histoire de ma vie.' (Vol. x, 1856.)
—— 'Correspondance.' (Paris, 1882–4.)
—— 'Un hiver à Majorque.'
—— 'Lucrezia Floriani.'
Sikorski, R., 'Souvenirs of Chopin.' (Polish, 1849.)
Sydow, Bronislaw E., 'Bibliografia Chopina.' (Polish. Warsaw, 1949.)
—— 'Correspondance de Chopin.' (French. Paris, 1956–60.)
Volkmann, H., 'Chopin in Dresden.' (Dresden, 1933; Supplement, 1936.)
Zagiba, Franz, 'Chopin und Wien.' (German. Vienna, 1951.)

(*b*) PRINCIPAL WORKS RELATING TO CHOPIN AS A COMPOSER

Abraham, Gerald, 'Chopin's Musical Style.' (London, 1939.)
Barbag, S., 'Study of Chopin's Songs' (Polish.) (Léopol, 1927.)
Bronarski, Ludwik, 'Chopin's Harmony' (Polish.) (Warsaw, 1935.)
—— 'Chopin Studies,' 2 vols. (Lausanne, 1946.)
Brown, Maurice J. E., 'Chopin: an Index of his Works.' (London, 1960.)
Egert, Paul, 'Friedrich Chopin' (German). (Potsdam, 1936.)
Hadow, W. H., 'Studies in Modern Music,' vol. ii. (London, 1926.)
Jachimecki, Z., 'Frédéric Chopin et son œuvre.' (Paris, 1930.)
Kelley, E. S., 'Chopin the Composer.' (New York, 1913.)
Kleczyński, J., 'Chopin's Greater Works.' (Leipzig, 1898. English translation by N. Janotha.)
Leichtentritt, H., 'Analyse von Chopins Klavierwerken.' (Berlin, 1921.)
Meister, E., 'Style-elements and the Historical Basis of Chopin's Piano Works' (in German). (Hamburg, 1936.)
Thugutt, Wanda, 'Analysis of Chopin's Mazurkas' (Polish). (Warsaw, 1927.)
Windakiewiczowa, H., 'Basic Forms of Polish Popular Music in Chopin's Mazurkas' (Polish). (Cracow, 1926.)
Wójcik-Keuprulian, B., 'Chopin's Melody' (Polish). (Lwów, 1930.)

(*c*) OTHER WORKS

Audley, Mme A., 'Frédéric Chopin: sa vie et ses œuvres.' (Paris, 1880.)
Bidou, Henri, 'Chopin.' (Paris, 1925.) English translation by Catherine Alison Philips (London, 1927).
Delacroix, Eugène, 'Journal.' (Paris, 1893–5.)

Chopin

Dunn, J. P., 'Ornamentation in the Works of Frederick Chopin.' (London, 1921.)

Finck, Henry T., 'Chopin and other Musical Essays.' (New York, 1899.)

Hadden, J. C., 'Chopin.' (London, 1903.)

Heine, H., 'Lutèce.' (Paris, 1855.)

Hipkins, E. J., 'How Chopin Played.' (London, 1937.)

Huneker, J., 'Chopin: the Man and his Music.' (London, 1901.)

Jonson, E. Ashton, 'Handbook to Chopin's Works.' (London, 1905.)

Koczalski, R., 'F. Chopin: Betrachtungen,' etc. (Cologne, 1935.)

Leichtentritt, H., 'Friedrich Chopin.' (Berlin, 1905.)

Maine, Basil, 'Chopin.' (London, 1933.)

Mariotti, G., 'Chopin' (in Italian). (Florence, 1933.)

Maurois, André, 'Frédéric Chopin.' (New York, 1942.)

Murdoch, William, 'Chopin: his Life.' (London, 1934.)

Opieński, H., 'Chopin' (Polish). (Lwów, 1909).

Ottlich, M., 'Chopins Klavierornamentik.' (Berlin, ? 1938.)

Paderewski, I., 'Chopin—a Discourse.' (London, 1911.)

Poirée, E., 'Chopin.' (Paris, 1907.)

Porte, J. F., 'Chopin: the Composer and his Music.' (London, 1935.)

Pourtalès, Guy de, 'Chopin ou le Poète.' (Paris, 1927.) Translated as 'Frederick Chopin: a Man of Solitude' (London, 1930.)

Revue musicale, La, special number devoted to Chopin. (Paris, 1931.)

Scharlitt, B., 'Chopin.' (Leipzig, 1919.)

—— 'Friedrich Chopins gesammelte Briefe.' (Leipzig, 1930.)

Schumann, Robert, 'Music and Musicians.' (London, 1880.)

Seguel, M., 'Chopins Tempo Rubato.' (1928.)

Szulc, A., 'Fryderyk Chopin.' (Poznan, 1873.)

Tarnowski, Count, 'Chopin' (extracts from his diary). (London, 1899.)

Umińska and Kennedy, 'Chopin, the Child and Lad.' (London, 1925.)

Valetta, I., 'Chopin: la vita, le opere.' (Turin, 1910.)

Vuillermoz, É., 'La Vie amoureuse de Chopin.' (Paris, 1927.)

Weinstock, Herbert, 'Chopin.' (New York, 1949.)

Weissmann, A., 'Chopin' (in German). (Berlin, 1912.)

Willeby, C., 'Frédéric François Chopin.' (London, 1892.)

Wodziński, Count, 'Les Trois Romans de Frédéric Chopin.' (Paris, 1886.)

Zukowski, O., 'Chopin in the Light of Polish Poetry' (Polish). (Lwów, 1910.)

INDEX

INDEX

A

ABRAHAM, Gerald, 136, 139
d'Agoult, Marie, Countess, 71, 73
Alard, Delphin, 103
Albert, Prince Consort, 105, 108
Alboni, Mme, 109
Alexander I, 12, 19
Alexis, clairvoyant, 113
Alkan, C. V., 55
Allegro de Concert (Op. 46), 59, 140
Andante spianato (from Op. 22), 54, 106, 124, 155
Anderson, Mrs., 57
Auber, 41, 44, 151

B

Bach, 10, 24, 54, 75, 79, 84, 125, 128, 132, 145
Baden, Grand Duke of, 127
Baillot, Pierre, 44, 47
Ballades (*as a whole*), 134, 172-6
    G minor (Op. 23), 40, 57, 120
    F major (Op. 38), 79
    A♭ major (Op. 47), 89, 106, 109
    F minor (Op. 52), 88, 125
Balzac, 43
Barcarolle (Op. 60), 59, 102, 103, 123, 133, 155
Barciński, Anton, 7

Bartók, Béla, 166
Beethoven, 10, 22, 44, 54, 124-6, 139, 169, 170
Belleville, Mlle de, 31
Bellhaven, Lady, 112
Bellini, 58, 59, 67, 136
Berceuse (Op. 57), 103, 106, 107, 122, 124, 133, 155
Berlioz, 44, 50, 51, 125, 133, 138
Bimental, Léopold, v, 2
Blanc, Louis, 86
Boïeldieu, 23, 44
Bolero (Op. 19), 151
Borie, Victor, 99
Brault, Augustine, 93, 95, 99
Broadwood, James, 67, 129
Bronarski, Ludwik, v
Brookshaw, Miss S., vi, 81
Brunner, J., 13
Brzowski, Joseph, 72
Bülow, Hans von, 121
Byron, Lord, 82, 88

C

Carlyle, 104
Carlyle, Jane Welsh, 73, 112
Castellan, Mme, 116, 117
Catalani, Mme, 4, 11, 12
Cauvières, Dr., 81
Charles X, 43
Châtiron, Hippolyte, 87

Index

209